WEIGHT WATCHERS

MANAGING STRESS

WEIGHT WATCHERS®

MANAGING STRESS

365 Meditations for Serenity and Strength

Macmillan • USA

MACMILLAN

A Simon & Schuster Macmillan Company
1633 Broadway
New York, NY 10019-6785

Library of Congress Cataloging-in-Publication Data
Weight Watchers managing stress: 365 meditations for serenity and
strength/ Weight Watchers International.
p. cm.
Includes index.
ISBN 0-02-861000-8
1. Weight loss—Psychological aspects.   2. Stress management.
I. Weight Watchers International.
RM222.2M3212 1997
613.2'5'019—dc21   96-54718
    CIP

Interior design by Scott Meola

INTRODUCTION

Weight Watchers has written a book of meditations to help you fulfill the promise in every day and to offer support and encouragement on your weight loss journey.

In these pages you can explore some of the many challenges that you may encounter along the way and share the experiences of others who are traveling this road with you. These are reflections on how stress can reinforce negative habits and emotions as well as deter positive actions in your life. You will find reflections on how optimism, courage, physical activity and laughter can boost your confidence and enhance your self-esteem, reinforcing your commitment to go on. There are practical hints for dealing with real-life situations and remaining focused on your goals.

It is our hope that this little book will help make your trip a little smoother.

For best weight-loss help, we recommend that you attend Weight Watchers meetings, follow the Weight Watchers Food Plan and participate in a plan of regular physical activity. For the Weight Watchers meeting nearest you, call 1-800-651-6500.

Every man naturally persuades himself that he can keep his resolutions, nor is he convinced of his imbecility but by length of time and frequency of experiment.

SAMUEL JOHNSON

Many people start each new year with a set of resolutions, a list that is often long and unrealistic. *I will not eat chocolate. I will always speak in a soft tone. I will run 6 miles every day.* But on the first day of exercise, it's too cold to go outside. When you venture forth a week later, you discover that walking around the block is about all you can handle. And by the end of January, you have gotten into a loud and angry argument and secretly eaten a whole box of chocolates. You feel like a failure. You are stressed.

This year, simplify your resolutions. Resolve to practice rather than master new skills. When you focus on the act of practicing, you don't have to judge the results. Rosa decided she would practice meditating. She says that as long as she practices, she is succeeding. It doesn't make any difference how successful her meditation session is. Melanie decided to practice exercising. It doesn't make any difference what she does or how long she does it. "If I move my body at all, it counts."

Whenever you practice, you succeed. Knowing what to do is a start, but the real results come when you make these skills part of your daily lives. It takes time and patience—practice—to turn what you know into habits. Remember that every day is a new beginning. Take a few minutes today to take care of yourself and practice something that will benefit you.

∾ THOUGHT FOR THE DAY ∾

You can begin anything at any time. Rather than wait for the first of the month or Monday morning, begin whenever you're ready. Midmorning, late afternoon and right this minute are good times too.

JANUARY 2

Every city is a living body.

SAINT AUGUSTINE

Although cities can be stressful, they also offer wonderful opportunities. If you live in or near a city, take advantage of the cultural activities that your metropolitan area has to offer. Instead of waiting for out-of-town visitors to arrive, be a tour guide for yourself. Get a map, then take the scenic route around the area, stopping to see places of historical interest. Spend a day at a museum or art gallery, or take a walking tour. Ask a friend to join you for dinner and discover why your city is known for its local cuisine.

Spend the day at the zoo with a child and see it through his or her eyes. Bring a sketch pad, tape recorder or camera to record your impressions. Take advantage of any tours offered so you can meet the zookeepers and animal trainers.

Attend free lectures at the various cultural arts centers. They are bound to be interesting, entertaining and informative. Dust off that old camera and take pictures of one subject, such as children or buildings. You might spend a few days photographing only architectural details—doors, windows, cornices, elaborate overhangs. Or, document one day in your neighborhood.

Be a volunteer. Serve food at a shelter, stuff envelopes for a political candidate, make phone calls for a charity. The more resources you acquaint yourself with, the better you'll understand what your city has to offer. It reflects the visions of many people and can give you renewed appreciation for your regional history.

THOUGHT FOR THE DAY

Take a class. Learn to sing, dance, ice skate. Learn a new craft. Decorate a flower pot, plant some ivy, then take it to an elderly person.

I never travel without my diary.

OSCAR WILDE

Sometimes hunger comes from emotional needs rather than physical needs. For example, you may find that you reach for an ice cream bar rather than confront a difficult person or reach for a bag of chips when bored. Food often works to quell anxiety, to comfort and calm feelings. But the risk is that you add another problem to your emotions — the problem of extra pounds.

One of the most effective ways to regain control is to keep a journal. Start by writing down the events that ended with a giant bowl of ice cream. Include what was said, who called, who came over, how you felt, the time of day and any other details. Sometimes you need to see things in writing to realize fully what you're doing — putting things on paper in black and white makes it obvious. Your journal gives you a chance to try out new responses to stressful situations. You can write down what you're going to do the next time your boss yells at you or a friend snubs you.

Use your journal to move forward as well as stay on track. Set a reasonable goal that can be met in three months or less. For example, you might decide to have a certain amount of money or lose a specified number of pounds. As you succeed in meeting your goals, you'll become more confident, more willing to take on new challenges.

∞ THOUGHT FOR THE DAY ∞

Learn to nurture yourself instead of the rest of the world. Use your journal to get clear on what's important to you, what you believe your life's purpose is, what you want it to be.

JANUARY 4

Have no friends not equal to yourself.

CONFUCIUS

If you have been significantly overweight for a period of time, your social life may have suffered. Losing weight means you are ready to reenter the world but it also means that you may have to learn dating skills. When you were overweight, you may have felt pressured to make the most of every dating opportunity. Whether the person was good for you or not, you were willing to devote yourself to the other's interests and personality. Your sense of urgency was probably obvious but you were disappointed when the second or third evening out didn't materialize.

The most important thing you need to cultivate is dignity and respect. If your date isn't treating you well, then he or she doesn't deserve your company. You should trust your instincts when you begin going out again, be ready to stand up for yourself, yet be understanding and forgive your insecurities. You need to allow yourself to talk up more and start saying what you think. You need to work on not being so self-conscious.

Losing weight renews your sense of well-being. You feel better physically and mentally. You have a renewed zest for living. You're more optimistic about the people that you meet and the people that you want to share your life with.

When you do start dating again, you should stop worrying about whether the person will like you. Instead, you should pay attention to the date. What are his or her interests? Is that person fun to be with? The ideal date is someone whose company you enjoy as much as you enjoy your own.

THOUGHT FOR THE DAY

There are other ways to develop relationships besides dating. Turn off that television, then make plans to go out with friends. Start pursuing the hobbies that you have put aside. Do more physical activities like dancing, biking and hiking. Join a health club and exercise regularly.

To get the best results, you must talk to your vegetables.

CHARLES, PRINCE OF WALES

If you are trying to lose weight, you should be eating plenty of fruits and vegetables, at least five servings every day. Although most people barely manage two servings, in fact you can eat all the fresh fruits and vegetables you want without sabotaging your food plan. Yet many people think produce is not available or too expensive or too time-consuming to prepare.

Enough of these excuses. Most produce is available year round. You can always get broccoli, bananas, oranges, carrots, apples and more. Produce is usually the best buy in the supermarket, too. It typically has the lowest profit margin of all foodstuffs. And for convenience, it's hard to beat peeling a banana or biting into an apple. If you don't want to peel fruit, you can always open a can. Canned fruits packed in juice, not syrup, are the best choices. Frozen fruits are good too.

Start with small changes, such as using fruits for snacks. Freeze grapes, banana slices and juice pops for delicious hot weather treats. Set reasonable goals like eating one more produce serving a day. Chopped vegetables can be added to practically any dish. Most vegetables can be washed, cut and eaten raw. Frozen vegetables will save cooking time but be sure to buy packages with no added sauces or butter seasonings. For those who dislike the taste of veggies, remember that tastes are mostly learned. If you get out your cookbooks and experiment, if you try them often enough, you'll learn to like them.

∾ **THOUGHT FOR THE DAY** ∾

Summer is a good time to eat more fruits and vegetables. Everything is available and at its lowest cost. And summer is when most everyone is in the mood to diet.

*In everything the middle course is best; all things in
excess bring trouble.*

PLAUTUS

For many people, the holidays are a whirl of spending, socializing, seeing your relatives and probably eating more than usual. The new year is suddenly upon you. You find yourself back in those old sweats, let down after the holiday highs and depressed because you feel you've lost control.

It's time to take a deep breath, forgive yourself and put the holidays behind you. Today is today and you deserve a pat on the back for being willing to get back on track. You can assess the damage by getting on that scale and weighing yourself—it may not be as bad as you feared. You can list why you want to lose weight. For example, you deserve to be healthy, you want to look better, you want to improve your self-confidence.

You may need to remind yourself to start with small steps. You may have lots of behaviors that you want to change but concentrate on only one at a time. Set a goal of drinking six to eight glasses of water every day or starting an exercise program or stopping those between-meal snacks rather than attempting all three at once. Once your first goal has become a habit, start on a new goal.

∞ THOUGHT FOR THE DAY ∞

*The next time you pass a mirror, you can give yourself a big smile of
appreciation. You're taking responsibility for your own behavior.
You're heading back to healthy habits again.*

JANUARY 7

Fake food—I mean those patented substances chemically flavored and mechanically bulked out to kill the appetite and deceive the gut—is unnatural, almost immoral, a bane to good eating and good cooking.

JULIA CHILD

Many people spend a lot of time, money and effort on diets and diet products. The latest trend is counterfeit calories—fake fat and mock meat. The implicit promises are that you can have all you want without paying a penalty in calories and weight gain, and that they taste as good as the real thing. But if replacement foods sound too good to be true, they are.

The reason we like fat is that it makes food taste better—it adds flavor. Fat substitutes are made from whey or egg whites and are lower in calories than real fats. Most can be heated or baked but are unsuitable for frying. Other fat substitutes are non-digestible because their fat molecules are too big to be broken down in the digestive tract. Since they are not digested, they pass through our bodies with essentially no calories but at the same time they deplete certain vitamins from our systems. There is a digestible modified corn starch fat that is used in some foods, and there is a converted oat starch that is available to the food industry but is not as yet on the supermarket shelves.

Mock meats were developed to accommodate vegetarians and others who want to reduce the amount of meat in their diets. These are made from vegetables, tofu, soy protein, nuts, seeds, brown rice and other grains. Most meat analogues are low in calories but read the label to be sure.

∞ THOUGHT FOR THE DAY ∞

*Fake foods discourage you from making behavioral changes.
The promise that you can eat all the fake foods you want is untrue.
You still have to learn self-restraint.*

JANUARY 8

The wise, for cure, on exercise depend.

JOHN DRYDEN

Aerobics classes are good places both to work off stress and exercise your body. Simple dance steps get your heart rate up. The music in aerobics classes is rhythmic and fun with a strong beat to keep you energized and in motion. Some people like to do aerobics after work to release the stresses of the job.

Depending on how much jumping there is, aerobics classes are usually taught as high, medium or low impact. Low impact means you'll always have one foot on the floor. A low impact workout is just as beneficial and you are less likely to harm your knees and ankles. A good aerobics instructor will demonstrate the low impact version of all moves during the class. The steps are simple, requiring little skill and no prior dance experience. You'll feel like a pro by the end of your first class.

Take a few minutes before the music starts and choose a stress to "work out" during the class. Remind yourself that every drop of sweat is cleansing your mind and eliminating tension from your body. As you do the cool-down at the end of the class, congratulate yourself for having released your tension in a healthful way.

∾ THOUGHT FOR THE DAY ∾

Since incorporating a variety of activities into your fitness plan increases long-term compliance, three to four days of aerobics is enough for most people. Use the in-between days for strength training or long walks.

The aim of argument, or of discussion, should not be victory, but progress.
JOSEPH JOUBERT

When you live with others, occasional disagreements and conflicts are inevitable. How you fight can make a difference in the relationship. If your fights seem endless and nothing gets resolved, you need to learn better ways of arguing.

To begin with, no one is perfect, including you, so you should have realistic expectations. No one can read your mind and anticipate your every need or desire. Plus, you might not meet those expectations for the other person either. So you have to decide whether the issue is important enough to warrant an argument. Ask yourself if you can live with the fact that your spouse is never going to put the toothpaste cap on the tube or the dishes on the right shelf. It might be better to save your arguments for the big things like money or kids or in-laws.

Once you decide to confront your partner and you know that the discussion is going to get heated, you should be prepared to fight fair. That means no name calling, no derogatory statements, no sarcastic remarks, no comparisons with other despised persons. (Unless the fight is about your in-laws, they shouldn't be mentioned.) Stick to the issue at hand. This is not the time to dredge up old hurts or old fights. Be careful not to exaggerate—"most of the time" might be appropriate but "always" and "never" are overstatements.

Remember that when you argue, you want to do it in a way that resolves the conflict satisfactorily without demeaning the other person or yourself. You want to be able to feel you handled the situation well.

∽ THOUGHT FOR THE DAY ∽

If you are going to relive the fight in your mind, try to relive it without shame and judgment. Insert a new script, then practice it so that the next discussion will be better.

Some values are. . . like sugar on the doughnut, legitimate, desirable, but insufficient, apart from the doughnut itself. We need substance as well as frosting.

RALPH T. FLEWELLING

Ways of handling stress vary from person to person, even from one crisis to another. But because stress often interferes with a daily routine, many people turn to food. They start eating from the vending machines, they have pizza delivered, they drink too much beer, they plop in front of the television with a bag of chips. They ignore their own needs, abandon their goals, lose their motivation and soon find themselves exhausted and overweight.

Other people, however, go out of their way to take care of themselves during stressful periods. They have learned that watching their diet and exercising regularly makes it easier to get through the crisis. They can think more clearly and have more energy.

Remember that even if a situation seems out of control today, *you* don't have to be. You can still take care of yourself. You can choose healthy foods like salads and baked potatoes, even if you're pressed for time and eating on the run. You can take a brisk, 20-minute walk wherever you are—make two or three circuits around the block, building or parking lot; or walk up and down several flights of stairs. If you stay nourished and fit, you'll be more effective in dealing with the stress around you.

∾ THOUGHT FOR THE DAY ∾

Decide how a stressful situation can become a catalyst for positive change. Use it to rethink what is important to you, what should have priority in your life.

*My mother bids me bind my hair
with bands of rosy hue.*

ANNIE HUNTER

If you're feeling a little drab, even out of style, maybe you need to do something about your hair. First find a good salon. Ask friends for recommendations or look for people on the street with hair like your own and ask them where they get their hair cut. Before making an appointment, sit outside and watch the people leaving the shop.

Before you get your hair cut, you should talk to the stylist and be clear about what you want. If you're not sure, pick two things you like, either about your hair or your features, and ask how a new style can play them up. If your hair is uneven and growing out from a shorter hair style, an up-to-date bob is a good choice. It's a crisp clean look that enhances any shape face.

You may need a perm to tame unruly hair or add gentle soft waves. New products available in the better salons make bad perms a thing of the past. Even the new perms, however, use chemicals that weaken hair so your hair will require extra conditioning and care afterwards. Ask the stylist to recommend products that are formulated to moisturize and protect your hair.

Remember that the best hair style is one that makes you feel self-assured, confident and comfortably in fashion.

∞ THOUGHT FOR THE DAY ∞

*Buy shampoos that prevent the build-up of styling gels and sprays;
oil and dirt make the color look dull and lifeless. Regular trims
keep split ends under control.*

JANUARY 12

*I am a camera with its shutter open, quite passive,
recording, not thinking. Recording the man shaving
at the window opposite and the woman in the kimono
washing her hair. Some day, all this will have to be
developed, carefully printed, fixed.*

CHRISTOPHER ISHERWOOD

If you're one of those people who is uncomfortable when a
camera is pointed your way, learn a few tricks so you'll always
look great. To start with, if you feel beautiful, you'll look beautiful. When you're going to have your picture taken, get a good
night's sleep so you look healthy and rested. Stay away from
the camera if you're sleep deprived, suffering from a cold or
the flu or just feeling down in the dumps. Your bad mood and
poor health will show.

Practice some poses. Use a full-length mirror and turn your
body at different angles until you find a few poses that are best
for you. If you face the camera straight on, you'll look wider
and broader, so turn your hips away from the camera at a 45-
degree angle. If you're sitting, cross your feet at the ankles or
cross one leg over the other at the knee to create a slim leg line.
If you're standing, bend your arms at the elbow or hold them
behind you. Rather than stare at the camera, look to one side
or look over the shoulder of the person taking the picture.
Move a little bit too. Models often are pictured in the middle
of a turn or stride.

Finally, use a facial expression that is quiet but friendly.
You can take a lovely picture without a big toothy grin. While
the camera person is making last-minute adjustments, try to
think of something pleasant so that nice thoughts will be
reflected on your face.

THOUGHT FOR THE DAY

*Ask a friend to help you practice by using a
Polaroid camera to capture different poses.*

JANUARY 13

A healthy body is a guest chamber for the soul.
FRANCIS BACON

One of the best things you can do for yourself when you are under stress is to take care of your body. That means that in addition to exercise, you need to eat a diet high in nutrients and fiber and low in fat. To make sure you're making good food choices, an occasional review of what you are eating is helpful.

In general, it's fat, not sugar, that makes you fat. The occasional piece of hard candy is better for you than a high-fat chocolate bar. Although a daily vitamin is a good insurance policy, a pill is not a substitute for a healthy diet. Nutrients are absorbed better by your body when they are in their natural form in foods instead of supplements. Mono-unsaturated oils like olive oil and canola oil are better for you than other oils. But oils are still fats and you should use a minimal amount.

Many people are big meat-eaters, getting twice as much protein as they really need. Too much protein leaches calcium from your bones. Also meat, especially red meat, contains a lot of fat. The average female needs only 45 grams of protein a day; the rest of the food intake should be complex carbohydrates like whole grains that provide fiber, yet contain fewer calories than fats or proteins and a small amount of fat. Your body works harder to turn carbohydrates into body fat. Carbohydrates themselves are not fattening; it's the butter, gravy, cream cheese and sour cream that you dollop on top. Better toppings are tomato sauces, fresh herbs, nonfat yogurt or steamed vegetables.

∽ THOUGHT FOR THE DAY ∽

If the food package says light *or* low fat, *that only means there's less fat in this version than in the regular version. There still may be plenty of calories. Check the label before you buy.*

JANUARY 14

I thank God for my handicaps, for through them, I have found myself, my work, and my God.

HELEN KELLER

As your body ages, you may have to deal with arthritis. Although there are many kinds of arthritis, you are probably most familiar with osteoarthritis—the inflammation and wear and tear on your joints that you experience as you get older. You may have put repeated stress on a particular joint, you may be dealing with an old injury or you may simply have a genetic predisposition toward this condition. In any case, your joints become inflamed and the cartilage begins to break down. Typically affected areas are weight-bearing joints, such as hips and knees.

Arthritis can be frustrating, and at times painful, but it can be managed. The goal in arthritis is to preserve the function of your joints and keep your daily activities going. Medication is available to reduce the pain and swelling of arthritis attacks but in the long term, physiotherapy and exercise are vital. Exercise keeps your body mobile. If you're not using a particular joint, the muscles around it will get stiff, making movement even more difficult. Extra weight can be an issue because every extra pound adds stress on the affected joints.

Arthritis tends to be a chronic condition and even though you may feel fearful and uncertain about its progress, it helps simply to admit you have a problem. Accepting your limitations helps you clarify for yourself and others what you can and can not do. Friends, family and coworkers will be more willing to help you if they understand what's going on.

∞ THOUGHT FOR THE DAY ∞

Talk to an occupational therapist to learn how to protect your joints using special tools and better posture.

Our feelings are our most genuine paths to knowledge.

AUDRE LORDE

When emotional situations become a trigger for you to eat, it's time to learn to separate your feelings from your need to eat. This means you have to be willing to experience your feelings. If you feel sad, you need to cry. If you're angry, you need to let the anger out by shouting or pounding on a pillow. If you feel silly, you have to be willing to laugh out loud for as long as you want.

Learning to recognize, then *feel* your emotions may take effort. One technique for learning how to recognize feelings is to watch a movie and try to identify the feelings that the characters in the movie are expressing. If you can label the many different feelings that an actor is portraying, you will soon learn to recognize those feelings in yourself. As you watch the movie, ask yourself if you ever felt that way and when. After you've learned to identify your feelings, you can then identify the cues that your body gives you at the same time

Start by trying not to eat if you think food and feelings may be linked; a food diary is a useful tool for making yourself aware of these links. In one column write down everything you eat; in the second column make note of what is happening around you; in the last column write down how you feel while eating.

∞ THOUGHT FOR THE DAY ∞

Be aware that positive as well as negative feelings can trigger an urge to eat. Learn to celebrate or reward yourself with something besides a piece of candy or a special dinner.

✓ *Anger is a brief madness.*

HORACE

"It was one of those days," Keisha explained. "My car wasn't working, I missed a deadline, the children were fussing, my husband and I were quarreling and the phone was ringing."

We all have difficult days when nothing seems to go right, and frustration grows moment by moment. These are times when a good solution is to work out, sweat a lot, exercise away the anger and stress.

Exercise helps calm you because it works the tension out of your body. Exercise hard enough and long enough and you will release all the negative energy you are carrying in your muscles and mind. A good workout session will cleanse your body of the poison of the day; each exhale will clear your mind of anger and frustration.

Decide what is the best exercise for you to do the next time you work yourself into an emotional lather. May turns on an aerobics tape when she need to work off a lot of stress. "I turn up the volume, push my body hard and let the music and instructor take over. By the time the tape is finished, I'm hot and sweaty and in a good frame of mind again." Try an aerobics class if you prefer the company of others.

∞ THOUGHT FOR THE DAY ∞

Hop on your bicycle and pedal steadily for twenty minutes or more before you turn around. By the time you get back home, you'll be feeling great.

JANUARY 17

If it is well with your belly, chest and feet, the wealth of kings can give you nothing more.

HORACE

If your feet are killing you by the end of the day, the solution might be less complicated than you think. You just need to buy shoes that fit. To find out whether your shoes are the right size, you can stand on a piece of paper and trace around a bare foot. Now put a favorite shoe on top of the foot outline. If the outline is bigger than the shoe, the shoe is too small.

Improperly fitting shoes can cause a host of problems. When the front of the shoe, the toe box, is too narrow, it squeezes the big toe and causes bunions. When the toe box is too short, toes have nowhere to go and begin to curl under or develop a hammer toe. Pressure, crowding and irritation also cause corns and calluses to form.

Remember that your feet hold you up and get you from one place to the next, so they deserve extra special care. Starting today, protect them by slipping on a pair of shoes that are comfortable, roomy and suitable for today's activities. Fashionable and sensible shoes come in attractive styles for all occasions.

◈ THOUGHT FOR THE DAY ◈

Make sure you're wearing the proper shoes when you exercise. Sneakers may look alike, but many are designed to be sport-specific.

JANUARY 18

There are no such things as applied sciences, only applications of science.

LOUIS PASTEUR

Additives and preservatives are in many of the foods you eat. They make it possible to have more foods available and to keep food longer before it starts to spoil. Although the additives and preservatives make up less then one percent of the food you eat, you should be familiar with some food additives that the Food and Drug Administration (FDA) feels are safe.

To make foods more appealing, color dyes are used. Caramel, for example, is a food coloring which is added to many of the soft drinks, baked goods and beer that you consume. Some dyes are under scrutiny because of doubtful safety, especially red dye # 3 and yellow dye #5. Yellow dye #5 in particular has been known to cause allergic reactions in highly sensitive people.

If possible, avoid sodium nitrite. It is used in cured meats such as bacon, bologna, ham, hot dogs, salami and luncheon meats. It prevents spoilage and gives cured meats a pinkish color. However, foods high in sodium nitrite are also high in sodium. Furthermore, sodium nitrite can react with other substances to turn into carcinogenic compounds in your body. Because of this the Department of Agriculture has reduced the amount of sodium nitrite that can be used in foods.

Most of the questionable additives are designed to enhance eye appeal but looks are no guarantee of nutrition. If you want to avoid additives and preservatives as much as possible, then you need to buy fresh foods and do your own cooking.

THOUGHT FOR THE DAY

If you suspect you are sensitive to a certain additive, eliminate it completely from your diet for four days, then eat food that is high in that additive and see if you notice a physical reaction.

JANUARY 19

Between two evils, choose neither;
between two goods, choose both.

TYRON EDWARDS

Many of the circumstances in your life are beyond your control, especially the behavior of other people at home or at work. You can, however, control your response to those circumstances—and in so doing, you can empower yourself. Imagine that other peoples' problems are in suitcases and that they are putting their baggage at your front door. They may be ringing the doorbell, knocking loudly for your attention, begging you to pick it up and bring it in your house. But you don't have to. You can pick up their baggage—or you can leave it outside where it belongs.

You may know coworkers who are often unhappy and difficult to work with. You can choose to buy into their misery and be miserable yourself. Or you can choose to quietly do your job, knowing that when the work day is over, you can leave that unhappiness behind. You can choose to be honest when others around you are acting unethically. You can choose to be responsible when others around you are sloughing off. You can choose to be nice when others around you are mean-spirited. Rather than join in, you can walk away. Make sure that you are not picking up another person's baggage today. You probably have your hands full with your own.

∾ THOUGHT FOR THE DAY ∾

Remember that you always have choices. You can
say no or limit your participation. Or you can look for
another situation that is better than this one.

Writers live twice.

NATALIE GOLDBERG

Brenda began to keep a journal to record business expenses. "At first I only kept a log of mileage and miscellaneous expenses." As time went on, her journal evolved into a record of her personal life—daily events, who she saw, what she did, how she felt. "Writing every day helps me through the difficult times," Brenda said. "Sometimes I reread old journals and I can see how I've handled things in the past and how I've changed."

Although you take the minutiae of your life for granted, these daily doings are what your life is all about. Keeping a journal helps you validate your experiences. And your journals can be a priceless record for future generations.

Start a journal today and make a brief entry every day. If you're hesitant about writing about feelings or relationships, start with the weather. Who did you talk to today? Where did you go? What did you do? What was the highlight, or lowlight, of this day? Your journal is for you and you alone. You needn't show it to anyone ever. Reread your journal only occasionally—perhaps once a year. You may be pleasantly surprised by the positive changes you have made over the years. Remember that as long as you are learning, you're not aging—you're growing.

∽ THOUGHT FOR THE DAY ∽

If you enjoy entertaining, keep a journal of your parties. Along with menus, table decorations and favorite recipes, be sure to include a list of who was there.

JANUARY 21

Variety's the very spice of life, that gives it all its flavor.
WILLIAM COWPER

When you are trying to lose weight, you may find it surprisingly stressful. Learning how to change your eating habits and make better choices about food also means you probably have to confront some emotional issues. Some might think that an easy way around this problem is not to deal with food at all and turn to a magic liquid diet. Liquid diets do have a great deal of appeal. They are easy—add powder to a glass of milk or water and stir. They also let you avoid food completely, so you can hide from your fears that are related to food. But the day comes when you have to eat real food again.

Liquid meals have some significant dangers. You will lose body protein and lean muscle tissue. You can sustain heart damage, such as arrhythmia and other irregularities caused by not eating enough calories or potassium. Gastrointestinal problems are common and other side effects can include dizziness, lightheadedness, hair loss and reduced energy.

Remember that eventually you're going to have to learn how to make healthy choices from a wide variety of real foods. The sooner you learn new habits and new skills, the sooner you'll be in control of food. When you gain control, the real magic occurs. You look better, feel better and discover that you're strong and powerful.

∞ THOUGHT FOR THE DAY ∞

You have to eventually learn how to stop eating the foods that are harmful to you. Avoiding food temporarily sounds like a good idea but it solves nothing.

JANUARY 22

Wait for that wisest of all counselors, Time.

PERICLES

If you're about to embark on a major change in your lifestyle, take a moment to make sure the timing is right. Take a serious look at how you feel about your lifestyle. If you're ready to leave parts of it behind, good. You're ready if you know deep in your heart that you're willing to work hard to make positive changes.

You also need to think about what's going on in your life right now. If you're starting a new job or moving across the country or negotiating a divorce, it's probably not a good time to start a weight loss program. You need to be realistic about whether you have enough energy left over to meet the challenge of yet another change. Don't use minor events as an excuse because then there will never be a perfect time to start. If things are generally going along fairly smoothly, then the timing is right. The biggest obstacle in your path is often yourself.

You should also think about the reasons you want to make these changes. For example, if you're losing weight because your spouse or doctor insisted or because of a special event, then you're probably not going to follow a diet for long. The reasons for making lifestyle changes must come from within. If you're motivated, if you're doing these things for yourself, you're more likely to be successful.

∞ THOUGHT FOR THE DAY ∞

A good way to get started on any program of change is to exercise. Regular exercise gives you more energy and an improved sense of well-being.

The greatest success is successful self-acceptance.
BEN SWEET

Rewarding yourself for success helps keep you motivated. You need these rewards every now and again because making lifestyle changes can be a long process, even a difficult one at times. Regular rewards make it easier to remain enthusiastic about your goals. If you feel that rewards should come only from others, you need to think again. It's nice when others notice but it's not their job to reward you. It's your job to do the work and it's your job to give yourself a reward.

A good reward should fit these criteria: it should have personal meaning to you. It should be something you like, something that makes you feel good about your achievement (be sure to think of things that aren't food-related). It should be appropriate to the goal reached—in other words, small goal, small reward, large goal, large reward. If the reward is too large or too small, it becomes meaningless. A bubble bath by candlelight is a nice way to reward yourself for getting through a wedding reception without overeating but to buy a fur coat because you exercised every day this week is overdoing it.

Giving yourself a reward may mean that you're changing some old rules and taking back personal power. This is good because it is a sign that your sense of self-worth and entitlement is growing.

∽ THOUGHT FOR THE DAY ∽

Give yourself a reward as soon as you've earned it so that you can reinforce your good behavior. It's a pleasant way to remind yourself that hard work pays off.

JANUARY 24

Sport gives players an opportunity to know and test themselves.

RITA MAE BROWN

Martial arts are becoming an increasingly popular form of exercising. Although there are many approaches and styles, all require a good posture, flexibility, strength and the ability to learn specific movement patterns. For the most enjoyment, take time in the beginning to choose a style and technique that is well-suited to your body and psyche.

Before you sign up, observe a few classes. Watch classes where most of the students are your age and at your ability level. After class, talk to some of the students, getting their advice and opinions; find out how long they've been training. When you talk to the instructor, ask about his or her goals for the students as well as about the philosophy that underlies the various styles. Trust yourself to know whether you're going to be compatible with a certain class, teacher or style.

Decide what martial arts training can do for you. Certainly you'll improve your overall physical conditioning along with strength and balance. You will also learn some valuable discipline, self-control and self-defense skills that will heighten your confidence. You might also be interested in the tradition of a particular style. Some forms involve throwing, others feature kicking and punching and others are popular because of the mental benefits and use in stress reduction. But all will help tone your major muscle groups and improve your coordination. Every style has something to offer. With a little bit of research, you can find the best one for you.

THOUGHT FOR THE DAY

An important part of martial arts training is developing the connection between your mind and body. As your body masters physical skills, your awareness of your connection to the world around you will become stronger too.

It is easier to stay out than get out.

MARK TWAIN

When you crave food, it's usually a specific food or taste that you want. A vague urge to eat is something different. These urges can take you by surprise although they are more often triggered by the situation than by any physical hunger. When you go to a baseball game, for example, you have the urge for a hot dog and beer. At a reception or party, you have the urge for a piece of cake.

The first step to managing these urges is to become aware of them. Take note of the event or situation that has triggered this urge. You may need to remind yourself that urges can make you impulsive and before you know it, you're eating mindlessly. The idea is to slow down, be calm, take control of the situation.

One of the easiest things to do is to remove the temptation. At a restaurant, you can ask the server to remove the rolls and butter or you can push them to the opposite corner of the table. At home, you can take the serving dishes off the table. In your car, you can turn away from the bakery and park on another street. Another way to manage the situation is to eat something else. Sometimes a crunchy vegetable or a cup of tea will satisfy the urge. Remember what works, so you can use the technique again.

THOUGHT FOR THE DAY

Try to do something else when you have the urge to eat. Clean a closet, read a magazine, make a phone call or walk around the block. The urge to eat will usually pass in 10 or 15 minutes.

JANUARY 26

The ideal is in thyself, the impediment too is in thyself.

THOMAS CARLYLE

You may have a lot of assistance as you work on making lifestyle changes. You attend a support group regularly, your family offers advice and comfort and your friends are at your side. In the end, however, you still have to learn how to be your own best friend.

The real support that you need has to come from within yourself. Only you can give yourself the perfect support at the perfect time because you're the only one who really knows what you want from moment to moment. For example, perhaps you hope someone will compliment your appearance. But you can compliment yourself too. You can look in the mirror and say aloud that you look terrific.

You may like family and friends to express their pride in your accomplishments but that pride is more meaningful if it comes from yourself. Every time you pass up a piece of chocolate cake, every time you write down what you're eating, every time you reach for a glass of water instead of a glass of sugary soda, you can say "good job, well done." Although you might like to have an exercise partner, you can certainly make plans to exercise alone. You can go for a jog or go to the health club for an aerobics class by yourself and then be proud that you did it on your own. Reassure yourself today that you can succeed and reach your goals.

∾ THOUGHT FOR THE DAY ∾

Pay attention to the words and thoughts you say to yourself. Make sure this self-talk is positive.

*Kind words can be short and easy to speak,
but their echoes are truly endless.*

MOTHER TERESA

Making lifestyle changes can be difficult and challenging but it helps if you have understanding and supportive friends. An excellent place to find support is to go to regular meetings with other people who are dealing with the same issues. Some groups, for example, have you weigh in, track your progress, then enjoy a brief program presented by the meeting leader. That meeting's topic becomes the focus of the discussion.

At a support group, you can sit quietly and listen or you can share what you have learned, what works for you, how you handle special situations. Listening and sharing reminds you that lifestyle changes are sometimes easy, other times more difficult. It helps you keep problems in perspective. You're also likely to get extra encouragement and understanding because others at your support group have been in similar situations.

As you change the way you look and feel, you can also practice new behaviors. You can learn how to accept compliments gracefully, how to become comfortable with your new positive feelings or work at turning a negative self-image into a positive one. Consider becoming part of a support group this week.

∾ THOUGHT FOR THE DAY ∾

*Attending a support group keeps your commitment strong.
Each meeting is a reminder that your goals are worth pursuing.*

JANUARY 28

*Travel can be one of the most rewarding forms
of introspection.*

LAWRENCE DURRELL

Sometimes you need a break but don't have the resources for a lavish vacation. Perhaps all you really need is a weekend. There are probably lots of interesting places near where you live but odds are you take local sights for granted and rarely visit them.

Draw a circle of approximately 100 miles on a map of your area. This marks an area that you can easily visit and yet return home in one day. Mark the tourist attractions and other places that interest you. Chances are there are still a few sights that you haven't yet seen.

Make plans to be a tourist in your area. Treat yourself to some local travel and explore places that are new to you. Short side trips can be just as much fun and require less packing and planning too. After all, you already know how to get there. Consider using an alternate route. Travel along the back roads, avoiding the highways as much as possible. Stop at local places in small towns for a lemonade or iced tea. The best part is not where you end up, but what you discover along the way.

∽ THOUGHT FOR THE DAY ∽

Remember that teenagers can be terrific traveling companions. They generally have more patience and stamina than their elders and often tolerate mishaps with great good humor. And you may very well be delighted and surprised by their world view.

Progress in civilization has been accompanied by progress in cookery.

FANNIE FARMER

Everyone has eaten "invisible" calories. These are the unconscious bites, the little nibbles here and there that you barely notice. Unfortunately, these little extras add up. They become visible on your body and they slow down your progress of losing weight. Many people are most prone to nibbling when fixing meals but there are some ways you can help yourself.

Whenever practical, prepare several meals at once. A big pot of soup or a stew can be frozen into individual or family-size portions. If you make low-fat lasagna, try to make several at the same time. Lasagna freezes well and you'll have a few meals on hand for those emergency suppers or evenings when you have minimal time to spend in the kitchen.

A good time to cook is right after you've eaten. When you're full, you'll be less likely to do as much tasting as when you're hungry. Prepackaged frozen meals are great if you're in a hurry or arrive home too late to cook. Family members can also help by preparing meals occasionally as well as putting away the leftovers.

When you're serving food, you should put a portion of each food on everyone's plate, then bring it to the table like restaurants and hotels do. If there are platters of food on the table in front of you, you're likely to help yourself until every morsel is gone.

You'll nibble less if you remove opportunities for unplanned eating. A little structure in your environment will make it easier to stick with your weight loss goals.

∞ THOUGHT FOR THE DAY ∞

Be sure to keep track of what you munch on by writing down every bite. Then you can remember to readjust your calories for the rest of the day to account for what you just ate.

Anger is a signal, and one worth listening to.

HARRIET LERNER

One of the most difficult emotions to deal with is anger. You may have harbored anger and resentment for so long that you feel like a volcano about to explode. Facing anger takes courage and patience. Only by dealing with your anger can you free yourself from this destructive emotion.

Begin by simply acknowledging your anger. You may also need to recognize that anger is a normal emotion that everyone feels. Being angry has nothing to do with being nice. Nice people can get just as angry as anyone else.

Learning to express anger is important. You can write a letter—perhaps one that you don't plan to mail—to the person who has upset you. You can keep a journal or make a painting or see a counselor to talk about it. If you decide to confront the person you are angry with, you need to accept that the other person's behavior probably won't change. But confronting the situation means their behavior will have less power to anger you. When you express your anger in a healthy and appropriate way, you will feel better. Even if the situation stays the same, you will be different. You will know that your feelings count.

∽ THOUGHT FOR THE DAY ∽

When you express your anger, stick to the issue, then stop. Resist the temptation to bring up a laundry list of old hurts. Address just today's problem so you can end the discussion quickly and get on with your life.

*After a good dinner, one can forgive anybody,
even one's own relations.*

OSCAR WILDE

If you find that eating is a time when you lose control, it may be because you're not really savoring the experience. If you're going to develop appropriate eating behaviors, you need to do more than satisfy your physical cravings; You need to satisfy your mental cravings too. If you take time to taste the food, your meal or snack will be much more enjoyable.

Every meal should be presented nicely so that you can eat sitting down instead of standing up or leaning over the sink. The table should be set with placemat, utensils and napkin. The food should be served on a real plate, not a napkin or paper towel, your beverage in a glass. You should turn off the television, put down the newspaper and enjoy the food.

Remember to chew carefully while eating. Become aware of the aroma and flavor of the food. It also makes you eat more slowly and savor each bite. Before taking a second helping, wait for 5 or 10 minutes. Allow for the time lag of about 20 minutes for your brain to register that your stomach is full. While you eat, concentrate on the food in front of you. When you're conscious of what you're eating, you can enjoy your meal.

∾ THOUGHT FOR THE DAY ∾

Fill your plate from the pan on the stove instead of from a serving dish on the table. That way you won't have that second helping staring at you throughout the entire meal.

FEBRUARY 1

Worries go down better with soup than without.

JEWISH PROVERB

"Every time I get upset, my stomach gets upset too," says Sylvia. "I guess my stomach is my hot spot." Hot spots are the organs and systems that seem particularly vulnerable when you're under stress. You may have a physical predisposition to certain symptoms, such as digestive upsets or your symptoms might be related to an old injury.

Stress is often the trigger. Your body responds to stress by releasing adrenaline. Muscles contract and headaches and backaches begin. If your vulnerable area is your digestive system, you may feel cramps or suffer a bout of diarrhea. The key is to recognize these stress symptoms early and do what you can to minimize them. Watch your diet, do any recommended exercises regularly and get plenty of sleep.

Learn to be aware of what your body is telling you. Keep a diary and track your symptoms. Be sure to include any troublesome situation, what you ate, what your physical activity was (or wasn't) and how you felt. Your diary will help you discover patterns between what is going on in your life and your physical response to these events. Remember that awareness can be a powerful tool. Sometimes simply making the connection goes a long way in solving the problem.

∽ THOUGHT FOR THE DAY ∽

Take a few minutes in the middle of the day to relax your muscles. Close your eyes and lean back in your chair. Start by relaxing your feet, then work your way up your body to your head. Once you are completely relaxed, sit still for a few moments until you feel refreshed and ready to resume your day.

I will be the pattern of all patience.

WILLLIAM SHAKESPEARE

Each of us tends to eat at certain times of the day. It doesn't matter when as long as you know what your individual eating pattern is. Once you are aware of your pattern, you'll begin to see the relationship between how satisfied you feel and how often you eat. If you skip meals and snacks, for example, your hunger will build and you'll start to feel dissatisfied.

The most common eating pattern is a structured one. You eat three meals—breakfast, lunch and dinner at the same time every day. You snack at predictable times, such as late morning or midafternoon or before bed. The advantage to a structured eating pattern is that your body gets used to being fed at certain intervals, so it comes to expect food at those precise times. This kind of structure works best if you have a reliable schedule.

A second type of eating pattern is an unstructured one. You have no regular established eating times. If you have a changing work schedule or need a lot of flexibility in your life, then an unstructured plan is good. The disadvantage is that you are likely to go too long without eating. Then suddenly you're starving, so you may lose control and overeat.

There also are combination patterns because some days have predictable schedules, while others do not. What's important is not what your eating pattern is but simply that you recognize it and do your best to plan around it. Whatever works is fine. It only has to work for you.

∞ THOUGHT FOR THE DAY ∞

Think today about your most common eating patterns. Remember, to make any pattern effective, you first need to be aware of what it is.

*There is no place in a fanatic's head where
reason can enter.*

NAPOLEON

There are many things you can do to reduce the stress in your
life but obviously you can't eliminate it altogether. In dealing
with stress, you need to be careful that you don't turn ordinary
events into overwhelming events. Sometimes when under
stress, for example, you may start to assume the worst. "I bet
this headache is a brain tumor" or "My boss's door is closed; I
wonder if I'm going to be fired."

Stress can cause you to impose your perfectionist standards
on others. You expect your children to get straight As even
though you were a C student at the same age.

Stress can cause you to have unreasonable expectations.
When you come home from work, you expect that you shouldn't
be tired. You think you should be in a good mood, cheerful and
ready to plunge headlong into leisure time. Or, perhaps you are
on a weight loss program. Even though you may already have
lost quite a bit of weight, if the scale shows a mild fluctuation,
you feel that you're doomed to regain every pound.

You need to learn to recognize extreme thinking. This kind
of self-talk adds to your stress rather than reduces it. If you can
gain control over what you are saying to yourself, you will
reduce your stress levels. If you can change negative self-talk
into positive words, it will help you feel less anxious. And
when you quit exaggerating or assuming the worse, you'll be a
lot happier. The extra happiness by itself will help reduce your
stress.

∞ THOUGHT FOR THE DAY ∞

*Make an effort today to let go of perfectionism. Practice changing
negative words and thoughts to positive ones so that you can accept
your own and others' efforts without criticizing.*

Much unhappiness has come into the world because of bewilderment and things left unsaid.

FYODOR DOSTOYEVSKY

If you are trying to become more assertive, you might find it hard. Learning how to stand up for yourself, asking for what you want and need can be difficult, even frightening. But the best way to overcome your fear is simply to keep practicing.

Try these communication techniques. The first is a tip for ending a discussion or argument. Just say, "You may be right." You're not agreeing with the other person but merely ending the conversation. This is a good strategy when the discussion is about changes that you are making that may have been something of a surprise to the other person.

Another technique is called "straight talk," which is asking for what you need, want, prefer and telling why. When you use one of these sentences, fill in the blanks. "I need _____ because _____." Or, "I want ____ because _____." Or, "I prefer _____ because _____." For example, you might say to a family member, "I need you to keep the chips and crackers out of sight because they tempt me," or "I prefer to eat at restaurant A instead of B because their menu makes it easier for me to stay on my food plan." One of the important things about straight talk is that when you're talking straight to another person, you're also talking straight to yourself.

∞ THOUGHT FOR THE DAY ∞

If someone's behavior is bothering you, tell them. Otherwise they may have no idea that they are bothering you. Once they know, they may be happy to change but the only way to find out is to talk about it.

Pain—has a element of blank—
It cannot recollect
When it began—or if there were
A time when it was not.

EMILY DICKINSON

Ashley has suffered from migraines off and on for years. It wasn't until her daughter pointed it out that she realized there was a connection between her migraines and stress. You may suffer chronic aches and pains that seem to have no apparent cause and aren't severe enough for you to seek a doctor's opinion. But perhaps you should take another look.

People who have chronic respiratory problems may find they are more likely to suffer when under stress. At those times, their bronchial tubes may constrict, making it difficult to breathe or triggering an asthma attack. Your blood sugar rises when you're under stress, which can cause serious trouble for diabetics who may already have difficulty controlling their insulin levels. The amount of stomach acid you secrete will increase when you're under stress. This means more problems for those with chronic heartburn and ulcers.

Although you may not be able to control the stress, you should try to alleviate your symptoms. For one thing, you are liable to aggravate or worsen an already vulnerable area. For another, you are more easily distracted when stressed and thus more likely to hurt yourself by picking up a heavy carton incorrectly or burning your fingers on a hot skillet. But most important, when you address your symptoms, you're more likely to think about the cause and begin to make necessary changes in your life.

∞ THOUGHT FOR THE DAY ∞

Stress can also cause mental distraction. If you're driving a car and having trouble concentrating on the road, stop and have a cup of coffee. Taking a few minutes to calm down might save your life.

*What we must decide is perhaps how we are valuable,
rather than how valuable we are.*

F. SCOTT FITZGERALD

One of the stresses that may be in your life is that you feel you are not important. You feel bad about yourself, so you don't allow yourself to appreciate the changes that you are making. You find it difficult to accept compliments. "It's nothing," you say. "If I can do it, anyone can. It's not a big deal." You go along with the crowd and seldom speak out. Yet at the same time, you feel misunderstood, ignored, powerless.

It's time to practice believing in yourself; even if you don't, you can pretend that you do. You need to take every opportunity to feel important. You can offer your opinion in conversation. You can make your own decisions in spite of what everyone else is saying or doing. You can remember that your opinions matter. You can give yourself permission to speak out.

As you learn to feel better about yourself, your self-image improves and you start to feel that you are worthy. The more you share your experiences and thoughts with friends and trusted family members, the more you will have their support. You can start to accept compliments and hear the good things they are saying about your achievements. And their support will help you change your beliefs about yourself.

∾ THOUGHT FOR THE DAY ∾

*Write a life résumé. This personal résumé can
include hobbies and special interests, favorite books,
family recipes and your political opinions.*

Ultimately, love is self-approval.

SONDRA RAY

Dispelling negative behaviors and beliefs is important, as these attitudes can make it harder for you to achieve your goals. Start by identifying your negative beliefs. List all your unproductive beliefs in one column; next to each, write down how you translate it into negative self-talk. For example, one of your beliefs may be that you can't diet at Grandma's house because she offers you too many sweets. This becomes negative self-talk when you say that if you go to Grandma's house, you have to give up your diet.

After you identify them, you need to challenge those beliefs. When you challenge your ideas about what happens at Grandma's house, you have to see if these beliefs are really true. You need to ask yourself if an extra sweet at Grandma's means giving up on your diet altogether. Does this make any sense?

Next, you have to turn the negative beliefs and the messages into positive ones. "I can say no thank you when Grandma offers me ice cream," or "I will take my own snack to Grandma's," or "It's okay to have a few cookies at Grandma's because I will allow for it in today's food plan."

The last step is to repeat these positive messages and reinforce them. Write them down on a piece of paper and tape them on the refrigerator door. Read them aloud in front of a mirror. Purchase motivational tapes or make your own and listen to them. Like many skills, changing negative attitudes takes some practice and patience. The more aware you become of negative beliefs, the more able you will be able to act positively and appropriately in ways that support your goal.

∾ THOUGHT FOR THE DAY ∾

Whenever you hear yourself saying something negative, say "Stop that!" aloud. Then rephrase your thought as a positive one.

FEBRUARY 8

*Happy are they that hear their detractions
and can put them to mending.*

WILLIAM SHAKESPEARE

When you want to accomplish something, you often start with a goal. But sometimes you may set goals that are too vague. You want to "look better" or "lose weight" or "get in shape." These sound like good goals but they are so broad, there is no way to know whether you're making any progress, much less reaching your goals Take some time today to think about your goals for yourself. They need to be quite specific and clear so that you will have a way to see your own success.

If you want to lose weight, set some specific goals. "I will eat 1200 calories each day" or "I will write down everything I eat." If you want to shape up your body, think about specific ways that will be helpful to you. Then turn these suggestions into goals. "I will take a twenty-minute walk four times this week" or "I will sign up for an aerobics class before Thursday" or "Twice this week I will swim laps at the pool." Specific goals that relate to looking better might be "I will call the dentist this afternoon and make an appointment to have my teeth cleaned" or "I will get my hair cut before Saturday night" or "I will buy some hand lotion and use it at bedtime."

Remind yourself that goals don't have to be big. They just have to be specific — the more specific, the better. The idea is to set goals that you can reach.

∞ THOUGHT FOR THE DAY ∞

*You can set goals for many things: getting a raise or promotion
at work, improving your school grades, cleaning out a storage area
or writing notes to good friends.*

But [Lot's] wife looked back from behind him, and she became a pillar of salt.

GENESIS 19:26

Some people can clearly correlate salt intake with blood pressure—too much salt and blood pressure goes up. But this relationship isn't always there. It is estimated that only half of people who suffer from hypertension are sensitive to sodium. And out of the general population, it is estimated that 20 percent at most can show a rise in blood pressure when they take sodium.

Researchers are now beginning to suspect that sodium and stress work together to cause high blood pressure. Early studies show that chronic anxiety and stress may lead to chronic high blood pressure. The mechanism appears to be that stress hormones affect how your body regulates salt balance and an imbalance may lead to high blood pressure.

Although more research is being done, it can't hurt to watch your salt intake, particularly during stressful periods in your life. Even if you think salt doesn't bother you, it's a good idea to keep your total sodium intake to less than 3,000 milligrams of sodium a day. This is about one generous teaspoonful. To keep salt intake at a minimum, avoid fast food, canned goods, frozen dinners and salty snacks.

∾ THOUGHT FOR THE DAY ∾

If you are sodium sensitive, there are other spices available besides salt. Peruse your cookbooks for new recipes that will help you develop new tastes.

FEBRUARY 10

Only that which is deeply felt can change us.
MARILYN FERGUSON

When you're stressed, your feelings may be at a high level, intense and visible to everyone. But intense emotions are often quite uncomfortable. Growing up, you may have been told you shouldn't cry or you shouldn't complain or it isn't nice to get angry. In many situations you learn not to respond or show any reaction even though it may be painful for you at the time. But if you repress your feelings over a long period of time, you may ignore them to the point that you don't even know how you feel. Or you may disguise one feeling with another, such as covering a deep grief with words or actions of anger and hostility.

Take time today to experience and express the real feelings that you have. Talk to friends and loved ones who can respond positively and acknowledge their validity. If expressing any kind of emotion is difficult for you, you might want to ask a health care professional to help you learn how to handle and become comfortable with your feelings.

Be kind to yourself today and allow yourself to feel all your emotions. Your feelings are valid simply because they are there. Very often if you can learn to express them honestly and openly with someone you can trust, their intensity will diminish. As you become more comfortable with your feelings, you will also become more comfortable with the feelings of others.

∞ THOUGHT FOR THE DAY ∞

Decide who is a safe person in your life—perhaps a relative or childhood friend. Then get together for a cup of coffee and talk honestly about what is on your mind.

*Expectations are the most perilous form of dream, and
when dreams do realize themselves it is in the waking
world: the difference is subtly but often painfully felt.*

ELIZABETH BOWEN

Keep your expectations realistic. When you strive to make
changes in your life, you need to be realistic about what's going
to happen when and if you reach your goal or make a change.
If you harbor unrealistic expectations, you may set yourself up
to be greatly disappointed.

Make a list of the things you think will happen if you meet
your goals. Then review the list and decide if any of those
expectations are based on fantasy rather than reality. Look
deep inside yourself too. Are you harboring any illusions about
the impact of certain events in your life? For example, if you
lose a few pounds, you'll be thinner than before and will look
and feel much better. But much of your life will stay the same.
Even though you are making changes, others around you
probably won't. Your spouse may still nag and your children
will still be rambunctious.

When your expectations are realistic, you're more likely to
succeed. When you're living in a dream world, you may feel
frustrated most of the time. You're not going to enjoy the
process of change as much because when your fantasies don't
materialize, you'll feel disappointed, frustrated, even betrayed.
Let go of your fantasies and illusions. Stay grounded. Realistic
expectations create an ideal environment for change, success
and enjoyment of the process.

THOUGHT FOR THE DAY

*You may need to reassess how quickly you expect to reach your goal
and whether you expect to have any challenges or setbacks along the
way. On a weight loss plan, for example, it's realistic to expect to lose
an average of a pound or two a week. It's also realistic to expect a few
plateaus and fluctuations along the way.*

You don't get to choose how you're going to die. Or when.
You can decide how you're going to live now.

JOAN BAEZ

No matter how stressed you are, no matter how oppressive or unpleasant the circumstances, you still have choices. You may not like any of them but you still have choices. When you can't change the world around you, you can usually change your attitude and your reaction to these circumstances.

Don't make choices to win the love and approval of others. That won't work. Being more concerned with what someone else thinks about you rather than how you think about yourself is bound to backfire. In the end, you're only left with yourself. You may bend over backward to get someone's approval and find they still don't approve of what you're doing. That can be devastating.

Make sure you include what you want when you make your choice. When you allow someone else — such as your doctor, your spouse, a friend or your children — to choose for you, they may give you good reasons for changing your behavior, but you're the one who ultimately has to live with your choices. And no one can know your heart as well as you do.

Be true to your own motivations, your heart. Make the choices and changes you want to make, even when life throws you circumstances you don't like. No matter what others have told you, you can trust yourself.

∾ THOUGHT FOR THE DAY ∾

When you rely on yourself and the visions and values in your heart,
you rely on the best.

It's a recession when your neighbor loses his job; it's a depression when you lose yours.

HARRY S TRUMAN

If you're feeling anxious about your job, your worries may very well be real. According to a recent study at Harvard University, American men aged 35 to 54 are 25 percent more likely to be laid off or lose their jobs in the '90s than they were in the '80s. As corporations cut their work force drastically, you wonder if you'll be next.

Take action if you think a pink slip may land on your desk soon. Pay off your credit cards and any outstanding bills. If a cash flow crunch hits later, you may need your credit cards for an emergency. While you're still employed, pay cash or pass up the purchase. Before your insurance ends, catch up on any necessary medical or dental work, such as an annual physical or a filling that you've been putting off. Update your résumé so you'll be ready to start your job search immediately. Make a list of companies where your skills and background might be desirable and make some preliminary inquiries now. If you are laid off, be sure to take advantage of any unemployment counseling that your company offers.

If you find yourself looking for work, make your search a full-time job in itself. Be ready and willing to follow up on every lead. Opportunities will appear most quickly to those who are in a position to seize them.

∞ THOUGHT FOR THE DAY ∞

Talk to your lender if you have an outstanding loan. If a different repayment schedule is necessary, make sure to work one out before you are in arrears.

FEBRUARY 14

*There's no discouragement
Shall make him once relent.*

JOHN BUNYAN

Don't become discouraged if you step on the scale and find that your weight loss varies from week to week. If you're on a weight loss program and are tracking your weight regularly, you are bound to see an occasional jump in the numbers. Many factors contribute to the amount of weight you lose from week to week. Instead of becoming discouraged, consider these factors.

Most people lose more weight in the first few weeks of a weight loss program. At first, most are likely to lose water weight. And in the beginning of a weight loss program, participants tend to be more highly motivated, complying meticulously with every detail. As your body adjusts to getting fewer calories, your metabolism slows down, especially if you're not exercising. And as metabolism slows, so does weight loss.

Gender and age make a difference too. Women usually lose weight more slowly than men. Older people tend to lose weight more slowly than younger people. Weight loss also depends on the ratio of muscle tissue to fat tissue. And some people are simply genetically predisposed to burn fat more slowly than others.

Go easy on yourself when your weight loss fluctuates. If you're following your program goals and guidelines, you'll drop the pounds at the rate that's right for you.

∾ THOUGHT FOR THE DAY ∾

Remember that exercise burns calories. You're bound to lose more weight when you work out regularly each week.

Crises define life. In them you discover what you are.
ALLAN K. CHALMERS

When you're going through a difficult period, you often find that you have no energy to take care of yourself. The mental energy that you need if you are to stick to any discipline, such as a weight loss program, is hard to find. Stress can be an excuse, a pretext for comforting yourself with food. Yet you know that if you revert to some of your old ways, those behaviors merely add another layer to the stress that's already there.

During trying periods of your life, it is also important to have fun. You need enjoyment to balance the stress. You should exercise for pleasure not penance. You need to pursue hobbies that have nothing to do with food. Summer fairs, auto shows, electronics fairs, concerts, art exhibitions and community theater are only a few ways to get your mind off the ongoing stresses in your life.

When times are rough, it's especially important to take proper care of yourself. You should first decide that you're okay as you are today. Instead of saying, "I'll be proud of myself when I lose weight," you can say, "I'm proud of myself now." Keeping your weight stable is an important step, especially when the world around you is in chaos. Although losing weight may well be a future choice, you can give yourself permission to opt for stability right now.

THOUGHT FOR THE DAY

When working on lifestyle changes, get support from friends, a therapist or from a support group.

The first wealth is health.

RALPH WALDO EMERSON

You may have begun an exercise program because you are trying to lose weight and you have heard that exercise will help. It's true — exercise will help burn those extra calories. More important, the weight and inches you lose will be fat, not water or lean muscle tissue. Your body stores fat for excess fuel to do physical work. So when you exercise, you burn up the excess fat. If you're simply trying to maintain your weight, it will be easier if you're exercising regularly.

Exercise also helps build and strengthen muscles, but because muscle tissue replaces the fat tissue, you look firmer, not more muscle-bound. As your muscle mass increases, your metabolism speeds up and burns more calories at rest. That's why the person who exercises can eat more without gaining weight than the person who doesn't exercise.

One of the best reasons to exercise is that you feel better. Your health improves, you have more energy and you start to feel good about yourself and what you are doing for your body. As a result, you find it easier to stay committed to a weight loss program as well. Remember that a low-calorie regimen is a short-term solution to losing weight; the long-term key is exercise. The more you exercise, the more calories you burn, the more food choices you have.

∞ THOUGHT FOR THE DAY ∞

If you want to burn calories in the privacy of your home, push back your coffee table and work out with a video or exercise program on TV.

FEBRUARY 17

*A lot of fellows nowadays have a B.A., M.D., or Ph.D.
Unfortunately, they don't have a J.O.B.*

"FATS" DOMINO

Richard could see the layoff coming, but when it finally happened, he wasn't prepared for the emotional upheaval and depression that followed. Like most working men, Richard defined himself by what he did to earn a living. So when he lost his job, he felt as if he had lost his identity.

With counseling, Richard's outlook changed and he learned how to redefine himself. "Now I define myself as a father, friend and husband. I'm an expert horseback rider too. These identities are unique to me; I own them, not my company." Once again he has a good job, but Richard is fairly low key about it. "I love my work," he says, "but if I'm laid off again, it's going to be a cash-flow problem, not an identity crisis."

Take time today to define who you are apart from your work. List all the things that you do in your time away from work. Think about your hobbies and outside interests, then ask yourself if you use any of your free time for these. If you have children at home, give yourself the pleasure of being with them as they grow up. Remember today that when you spend time on yourself, friends and family, you are making an investment in your mental health.

∞ THOUGHT FOR THE DAY ∞

Even if you're in a secure job, take time to think about your retirement. Make plans now to have an "identity" once your working days have ended.

*When a man's stomach is full it makes no difference
whether he is rich or poor.*

EURIPIDES

Many people think that learning to eat healthfully or going on a weight loss program means that they're going to have to spend more money on food. In fact, the opposite is true. The most expensive foods are convenience and fast foods. Taking the time to prepare foods at home will save you plenty of money and calories. Here are some tips for eating healthfully and inexpensively.

Buy fruits and vegetables in season as that's when they are at their lowest price. Buy bagged produce—it's usually less expensive to buy a bag of apples than one or two at a time. Buy in bulk whenever it is practical but bear in mind that bulk purchases are cheaper only if you use everything you buy. Be careful about overbuying if your family is small or smaller than it used to be. In that case, buying in smaller quantities may be more cost effective, especially with perishables.

Use coupons wisely. They can save you money if you buy products that you need or use regularly. No matter how enticing the coupon, if you don't use that item or it is not on your food plan, it's a poor choice for you.

∾ THOUGHT FOR THE DAY ∾

*Remember that complex carbohydrates such as legumes and pasta are
often less costly than meat but are just as filling.*

FEBRUARY 19

A perpetual feast of nectared sweets.

JOHN MILTON

When you talk about your "sweet tooth," it's probably sweeter than you think. In fact, the average person in North America consumes about 43 pounds of refined sugar each year. It costs you too in empty calories and excess pounds. But perhaps the biggest problem that comes with eating too much sugar is tooth decay; sugar helps the bacteria that causes tooth decay to grow more rapidly.

Sugar is in more foods than you think. In some sodas, for example, there is as much as 10 teaspoons of sugar per can. Some fat-free foods and foods that use non-digestible fat are also very high in sugar.

It's important to understand that sugar doesn't do anything for you except add calories to your diet. Sugar offers no fiber, no nutrition. It may give a quick lift but this is soon followed by a big letdown as your blood sugar drops. When you are trying to eat right, it's important to make calories count. Get rid of the sugar in your eating plan today. To satisfy that sweet tooth, bite into a juicy peach or plum.

∞ THOUGHT FOR THE DAY ∞

Be sure to brush your teeth right away after eating sugary foods, especially sticky sweet foods like caramels and raisins. Although saliva washes away most of the sugar, some remains. And the longer sugar is in your mouth, the easier it is for decay to start.

Food is an important part of a balanced diet.

FRAN LEBOWITZ

If you have put on some extra pounds recently, it's time to do something about it. Gaining as little as 5 or 10 pounds is a signal that it's time to take a fresh look at what you are eating and assess how much physical exercise you're getting on a regular basis.

The world you live in makes it easy to gain weight. You're busy, you're stressed, you have little time to exercise, you're too tired to cook — after a while, you feel out of control. When this happens, it's time to take charge and start making some healthful choices. Unfortunately there are no miracle fixes or magic cures. The only way to lose weight is to eat healthful foods, eat smaller portions and exercise more.

But there are other things you can do. You can start with a realistic goal, you can make a commitment to achieving your goal and you can find as much support as you can. Join a group that is committed to the same goals as you are, where you can meet and talk to people who share the same goals and are following the same program of healthful eating. You can exchange tips and ideas and meet new friends. You can also talk to and learn from people who have been successful in their long-term goals and are there to encourage your success and applaud you along the way. Support and camaraderie nurture success.

∞ THOUGHT FOR THE DAY ∞

Borrow a cookbook from the library and try a few recipes. You might be inspired by the ease of preparation and the new taste ideas.

FEBRUARY 21

He that will not be counselled cannot be helped.

JOHN CLARKE

At one time or another you may have backed yourself into an emotional corner or found yourself boxed in by problems that seem to have no solutions. You're fearful and depressed, overwhelmed by feelings of constant tension and anxiety. You may try to escape by throwing yourself into a job or some other activity that will use up your time. Or you may try to ignore the problem altogether, hoping it will magically go away of its own accord.

Most people who have tried counseling find that they are helped in several ways. Simply by taking the initial step to seek help, they begin to feel more comfortable, relieved that they are doing something. They often discover that the source of their stress and anxiety is not what they thought. As Katherine sorted through the issues with her counselor, she began to see that her husband's excessive drinking was causing much of the family strife. As her counselor helped her evaluate what she could and could not change, she began to practice new ways of coping that helped her son as well as herself.

If your problems and fears color what you think and how you feel, perhaps you should consider counseling as a source of help. The rewards of counseling can be significant. You can learn new ways of forming meaningful and supportive relationships. You can learn to live more fully and with greater satisfaction. And most gratifying of all, you can put yourself on the road to inner peace and happiness.

∞ THOUGHT FOR THE DAY ∞

If you have tried counseling before, maybe it's time to pick up where you left off. Many people try counseling at different times for different needs. As you change and grow, you may also want to try a new therapist, one better suited to helping who you are today.

*Woman must not depend upon the protection of man,
but must be taught to protect herself.*

SUSAN B. ANTHONY

No one needs the stress of coming home to discover your house or apartment has been burglarized or your car has been stolen. Take steps now to make it more difficult for this to happen. Start by making sure that there are locks on all doors and windows—then make sure you use them.

Use lighting to your advantage. Keep a light on inside the house whether or not you're home. At night, keep the curtains drawn. Make sure that the outside of your house is well lit, too. Motion detector lights at the door and driveway are excellent deterrents. You may want to put in a fence around your property. Take another look at the trees and bushes around your home. Shrubs near windows should be pruned regularly so they can't be used as hiding places. Any tree branches that would make it easy to enter your home from an upper level should be removed by a professional.

Make sure that your car is always locked, even if it is in your driveway or garage. Never leave your car with the engine running, even if you're just jumping out to drop something in the mailbox. Park under a street light or other well-lit areas, close to a store or an office entrance. Take advantage of any escort service that the parking garage or office building may offer. If you use valet parking, lock valuables in your trunk and leave only the ignition key. Keep all other keys on your person.

∞ THOUGHT FOR THE DAY ∞

Connect a radio and lamps to an on-and-off timer, so that it appears as if you are there. Also consider installing an alarm system. It's a wise investment if you live alone or are often away.

*Nothing strengthens the judgment and quickens the
conscience like individual responsibility.*

ELIZABETH CADY STANTON

If you are going to reclaim time for yourself, you are going to
have to learn to say no effectively. Your family and friends may
be used to you always saying yes. They may be persistent when
you first start saying no simply because they're not used to
hearing you say it. You can start by being truthful. You can
say, "I wish I could but I can't. It's not possible right now."

Family members in particular may need to be reminded
that you can't always be there for them. You can suggest a time
later in the day or week when it will be more convenient for
everyone. To get control over your duties, make a list of everything and decide what your priorities should be. If you're overwhelmed at work, give your boss a list of your work projects
and ask her to assign the priorities.

It may take some practice to say no. If you need to stall
when asked if you can do something, say, "I don't know. I'll get
back to you." Then if you want to say no, rehearse your answer
in front of a mirror before you call the person back. Remember
that you don't have to give a reason. Simply saying "I can't" is
sufficient.

THOUGHT FOR THE DAY

*Remind any teenagers in your house that if they are old enough to
drive, they are old enough to be responsible for their own laundry.*

The two most beautiful words in the English language are "check enclosed."

DOROTHY PARKER

When credit cards are used wisely, they're used for convenience, not credit. The bill is paid in full every month. If your monthly statement is catching you by surprise lately, start thinking of your credit cards the same way you think about your checking account — that making a charge is the same as spending cash.

Begin by placing all your credit cards on a table. Cut up and throw away any that you're not currently using, then phone or write to the creditors requesting your account be closed. Take another look at the ones you do use; then pick the one that is widely accepted by the companies and stores with which you do business. Destroy the rest, close these accounts and pay off the balance as soon as possible. Your goal is to pay no interest but if you get behind in your payments again, you will be paying on only one credit card instead of several.

Now wrap a piece of paper around that one remaining card and use it like your check register to keep a running total of your spending. Every time you make a purchase, write down the date, store name, what you bought and the amount you charged. If you know you won't be able to pay it off when the monthly bill arrives, don't make the purchase. When your statement arrives, pay it on time. Otherwise you'll incur extra interest charges.

∾ THOUGHT FOR THE DAY ∾

Some people use two cards — one for personal use and a second for business expenses. This makes it easier to keep those costs separate.

*"Let me put it this way," I said. "According to my girth,
I should be a ninety-foot redwood."*

ERMA BOMBECK

Are you carrying your extra weight in your middle? If you're a woman, stress may be a factor. A study at Yale University has shown that women who were heavy around their midsections were secreting more of a stress hormone called cortisol. The study shows that how you cope with stress is more important than the actual stress.

The researchers compared two groups of overweight women — those who carried most of their extra pounds in their midsections and those who carried their excess pounds on other parts of their bodies. They measured their levels of cortisol before and after being put in stressful situations. The women were given problems to solve and told they were failing, no matter what they did. The results showed that the women with large midriffs secreted much more cortisol than the control group. The researchers theorize that cortisol causes fat to be deposited on the stomach rather than on arms and legs.

If you have gained weight in your stomach, try some stress-reducing techniques. The easiest is to exercise on a regular basis — start by taking a daily walk. Of course, watch your diet, especially the amount of fat you consume. Taking care of yourself will make you feel in control and less stressed. And it will also help shrink your waistline.

∞ THOUGHT FOR THE DAY ∞

The next time you're in a stressful situation, take three or more quiet deep breaths. Let your face soften and your shoulders relax. You can clear your mind without others around you taking notice.

Our remedies oft in ourselves do lie.

WILLIAM SHAKESPEARE

More women work outside the home than ever before. As business and professional opportunities increase, so do the challenges of losing weight for the working women.

Being organized is as essential to your weight loss program at it is to your career. First, prepare a menu plan for yourself for everyday. When you're prepared, you'll be able to stay in charge of your eating, no matter how many crises arise during the working day. Second, be prepared for times in the day when you're most vulnerable to eating and snacking. Bring a snack for that midmorning or midafternoon slump rather than go to the coffee cart or candy machine. If you're usually very hungry when you get home, have a cup of juice or bouillon or fruit ready for snacking. It will take the edge off your appetite while you prepare a healthy dinner.

And last, be sure to take the time to exercise. You can walk at lunch time or close your office door and do some exercises and stretches. When you get home, go for a walk, putter in your garden, put on an exercise video or turn up the music and dance away your cares.

∾ THOUGHT FOR THE DAY ∾

If you're doing business over lunch, drink seltzer or diet soda instead of alcohol. Order a light meal, such as soup and half a sandwich with fruit for dessert. Or, let lunch be your main meal of the day and fix a bowl of salad greens when you get home.

I bend but do not break.

JEAN DE LA FONTAINE

Flexibility is your ability to move each joint in your body easily through its full range of motion. The benefits to stretching are more than keeping you limber. A sedentary lifestyle can result in your muscles and connective tissue tightening up, causing a decreased range of motion. Your hamstrings get tight, your shoulders hurt, your back gets stiff. Your movements become limited and you find that you're not moving as easily as before.

Working on flexibility keeps you aware of your body. You become more sensitive to its limitations and strengths. When you maintain your flexibility, you also prevent injuries due to limited joint mobility, for the more flexible a muscle is, the less likely you are to tear it in a slip or a fall. Flexible muscles are stronger muscles.

Work on making your body more limber so you can move more freely. There are several good books available on stretching Be sure to study the illustrations carefully to make sure you're exercising correctly. As you become more limber, you'll feel better, find it easier to relax and have a better sense of well-being.

∾ THOUGHT FOR THE DAY ∾

Yoga and swimming are excellent exercises for increasing flexibility. You can also ask a fitness specialist to set up a program tailored to your present needs.

Active minds are slow to quiet.

ARN SCHAPER, PH.D.

When you're stressed, you're often mentally fragmented. Your mind is going in different directions. You have too many obligations and too few hours in the day. You're in a whirl, turning here, turning there, yet feeling as though you're getting nowhere. What you need to do is stop and find your bearings. You can do this by meditating.

Meditation is a technique that teaches you to slow down and be still. You quiet your mind and focus on one thing to the exclusion of everything else. First make yourself comfortable, then close your eyes and breathe slowly and deeply, counting the number of breaths you exhale. When you reach four breaths, start over. Try to concentrate and think only about counting breaths. When your mind wanders, bring it back to counting. Do this as long as you like, but try to do this for at least five or ten minutes.

Meditation practice is deceptive in that it is not nearly as easy as it appears to be. In fact, most people are surprised at how much discipline it takes to do this simple four-breath exercise. They are also surprised that meditation works. With practice, the discipline of willing yourself to concentrate carries over into your everyday life. Where you once felt scattered and unfocused, you will soon find it easier to pick one task, concentrate on it until it's finished, then move all of your concentration to the next task. Once you have learned to quiet your mind, you'll feel more relaxed and have more energy.

THOUGHT FOR THE DAY

After lunch, close your eyes, turn on some music and try the breathing exercise. You'll begin your afternoon's activities refreshed and renewed.

Digestion is the great secret of life.
REV. SYDNEY SMITH

The number one recommendation for reducing stress is to exercise. But what you eat is just as important. Studies show that a high carbohydrate meal, for example, helps relax your body by releasing more serotonin. The Cooper Clinic, known for its research on aerobic exercise, says that what you eat can also affect your stress levels. Here are their suggestions on how to make sure your diet enhances your attempts to stay calm.

Be sure to eat regular meals. When you skip a meal, you get a buildup of stomach acid which makes you feel uncomfortable and jittery. Regular meals also control your blood sugar better, helping you to feel more relaxed. Be careful not to overdo meals or snacks. When you are stressed, your body will make more cholesterol, more fats and more sugar, so don't add to the problem with potato chips and ice cream.

Discover which foods make you feel relaxed and at ease. It may be your imagination but if you think coffee makes you sleepy, then it probably does. Be aware of any foods that cause discomfort. There's no need to upset your stomach with spicy foods if you're already stressed. And be particular about your "comfort" foods. Custard pie may be your favorite but a cup of chamomile tea can be just as calming and won't add any extra pounds.

When you take care to nourish your body, you are making an important contribution toward lowering your stress. Making good choices about the foods you eat helps you perform at peak levels and gives you a sense of control. Take care today to heed your body's signals.

∞ **THOUGHT FOR THE DAY** ∞

Remember to drink 6 to 8 glasses of water every day. If you are even mildly dehydrated, you will feel more tired.

MARCH 2

Bad excuses are worse than none.

THOMAS FULLER

Thinking about exercise can be more stressful than actually doing it. You may be more out of shape or ashamed of your body than you are willing to admit. When exercise is mentioned, you tune out or even leave the room. When pressed, you have countless excuses not to exercise: you need a partner, it's too hot at the gym, it's too cold outdoors, you get home too late from work. The list is endless and you have used them all at one time or another.

If you restrict when, where and how you exercise, you're also limiting the benefits it gives you. If you "don't like" to walk or "can only" work out at a certain time of day or at a certain place, you're setting the stage for failure.

Be honest with yourself today. If you are resisting exercise because it's too hard, remind yourself that any activity is better than none. Get up from your chair and stand tall. Reach your arms up high, stretching out from your shoulders. Flap them like a bird a few times. Walk around the room twice before you sit down. You just exercised and it was easy.

Tomorrow, walk out your front door to the nearest telephone pole. Touch it, then go back inside. You just took a walk. Each day, add another pole to your walk before turning toward home.

∾ THOUGHT FOR THE DAY ∾

Get a balloon and play with it. Bat it around the room, keeping it from touching the floor like you used to do when you were a young child. Let this balloon remind you that physical exercise doesn't have to hurt or cause shame. It can really be fun.

MARCH 3

Who knows the thoughts of a child?

NORA PERRY

Children, like adults, want to feel that they count. They like their parents around. Dave posts his weekly schedule on the refrigerator so his children will know which nights he'll be home early. Ellen calls home every afternoon to hear the highlights of her children's school day, then gets the details over dinner or before bedtime. When John is out of town on business, he phones every morning to touch base before his children leave for school.

As parents it's natural to question instead of listen. Allow your children to tell you what's happening in their own way, in their own words. If you're pressed for time and start to question, your children may feel like they're being given the third degree.

If you are a working parent, be aware of your emotions. If you feel bad about not spending enough time with your children, you might assuage your guilt by bringing home gifts but your children are liable to sense that the gift has more to do with you than them. Children like to feel they have earned the gifts you give them. A small gift is just as meaningful as a lavish one. Spending money on toys is nice but your children will always prefer that you spend time with them.

∾ THOUGHT FOR THE DAY ∾

One way to get your teenage children to talk is to play a game with them. While you're dealing a hand of gin rummy or shooting baskets or tossing a Frisbee, you might learn something new.

MARCH 4

Marriage is not a finished affair. No matter to what age you live, love must be continuously consolidated. Being considerate, thoughtful and respectful without ulterior motives is the key to a satisfactory marriage.

Pamphlet from the Chinese Family Planning Center

Partners have to work at their marriage or relationship to keep their life together healthy and happy. One of the things you can do to help your relationship is to treat your partner as you did when the relationship first began. Remember to say *please* and *thank you.* When you have been in a long-term relationship, it's easy to forget everyday courtesies. Familiarity begins to sound like hostility. You act as though you know what the other is thinking. You interrupt, finish each other's sentences and jump to conclusions, yet you're surprised when your partner accuses you of being impatient and angry. If you want your relationship to remain solid, you have to be willing to devote as much energy to it as you do to your career. Be as patient with your partner as you are with co-workers.

Housework can become a major bone of contention in a relationship. If both partners work outside the home, then they need to share chores equally. Agree to ignore the dust or hire a cleaning service. For the most part, household chores are not worth angry words. If you are arguing over dirty dishes or whose turn it is to vacuum, perhaps there is an underlying issue that needs to be addressed.

Remember that we all grow and change over time and as a result, your relationship will grow and change too. The changes each partner makes affect the relationship, often in a good way, by breathing new life into it.

∽ THOUGHT FOR THE DAY ∽

Develop and cultivate your own interests. Try to do something special apart as well as with your partner every week. It's unreasonable to assume that both of you will have identical interests all the time.

MARCH 5

"But wait a bit," the Oysters cried,
"Before we have our chat;
For some of us are out of breath,
And all of us are fat!"

LEWIS CARROLL

No one likes having any extra body fat but you can learn something if you pay attention to where your body is storing it.

The skinfold, or fatfold, test is an easy way to determine what percentage of your body is fat. Pinch a fold of skin on the back of the arm or below the shoulder blade or the side of the waistline, then measure its thickness with a specially designed caliper. The fat under the skin in these areas is proportional to your total body fat. When you gain body fat, the skinfold will increase; when you lose weight, the skinfold will get smaller. Most Ys or health clubs can take this measurement for you. They will have a chart to tell you how your body fat compares to other men or women your age.

If you have a large midsection, that may represent a health risk. Abdominal fat has long been linked to an increased risk of heart disease. One reason may be that when abdominal fat is used by your body, it goes directly to your liver where it is made into low-density lipoproteins that carry cholesterol.

∾ THOUGHT FOR THE DAY ∾

Let today be the day that you resolve to get rid of that extra weight.
You'll feel better as soon as you begin, secure in the knowledge that you
are on the road to a healthier and leaner you.

MARCH 6

No life that breathes with human breath
Has ever truly longed for death.

WILLIAM SHAKESPEARE

When you're stressed, your breathing sometimes changes. Instead of breathing in a slow and relaxed manner, you take short, fast, shallow breaths. This kind of rapid breathing is a clue that you are tense. The antidote is to do some deep breathing. Slow deep breathing is a good way to interrupt the stress response that your body is making. It will help you relax at the same time.

To start, exhale as much air as you can from your lungs. Purse your lips and blow out slowly through your mouth. Keep going until you feel that you have exhaled every bit of breath in your lungs. Hold that for a second or two, then begin to inhale slowly through your nose. As you inhale, you should feel your diaphragm expand. Your abdomen, not your chest, will begin to swell. Continue to inhale until you have filled up your lungs; then hold it for about five seconds. Repeat this exhale/inhale cycle four more times.

Deep breathing can be done anywhere—behind the wheel, in a meeting, listening to a teenager's complaints. Chances are no one will be aware of what you're doing. It's a quick and effective way to break the stress cycle. Use this technique to slow down and relax. You'll resume your activities with a better outlook.

∞ THOUGHT FOR THE DAY ∞

Use this deep-breathing technique just before starting a stressful task, such as making a difficult phone call or taking an exam.

*Remember that as a teenager you are at the last stage
in your life when you are happy to hear that the
phone is for you.*

FRAN LEBOWITZ

The telephone is often a cause of stress. You need telephones to communicate yet you resent phone interruptions and the time and money you spend on phone calls. Here are some ways to control your telephone and not let your telephone control you.

Start by investing in an answering machine or voice mail. Use it to screen your calls when you're home. Returning phone calls is more efficient than answering the phone every time it rings. If you have a lot of phone calls to make, take one or two hours after lunch and make all of your phone calls at once rather then letting them dribble along all day. When you're the caller, you can control the length of the conversation. It's easier to say good-bye when you're the one who made the call.

Don't be afraid to turn off the telephone ringer. Allow yourself uninterrupted time to play with your child, finish a good book or work without interruption. The odds of an emergency are small, so give yourself an hour or so of peace.

↾ THOUGHT FOR THE DAY ↿

*When you realize you've been called to listen to an
unwanted sales pitch, politely say you're not interested and
ask to have your name removed from their list. Telemarketers
now are legally required to abide by your request.*

MARCH 8

I always knew I would turn a corner and run into this day, but I ain't prepared for it nohow.

LOUISE MERIWETHER

There are always things that need fixing but because they are working at least marginally, you put them aside. It's only a matter of time, however, until a minor annoyance turns into a major difficulty because you put up with the problem rather than taking the time to solve it. For example, Eric never seemed to get around to replacing the windshield wipers on his car. But every time it rained, he was aggravated because he could barely see the road and knew he was making his commute unnecessarily dangerous.

Think about the petty annoyances in your life that could be fixed. easily. Perhaps your clock radio alarm fails to go off occasionally. If so, replace it now before you oversleep again. If you wear boots or shoes with laces, keep extra on hand. Put a pair in the glove compartment of your car or truck as well as at home. In winter, buy extra pairs of inexpensive gloves. Keep them in your car, your office, your closet, your coat pockets. Your hands need never be cold again.

There are plenty of big issues that are beyond your control but you can solve the small ones. Use whatever time you need today for solving small problems. The big problems will be there tomorrow.

THOUGHT FOR THE DAY

If a major appliance is old and won't last much longer, make plans to do something about it now. It's easier to get it fixed or replaced at your convenience instead of in an emergency.

MARCH 9

*But if one doesn't have a character like Abraham
Lincoln or Joan of Arc, a diet simply disintegrates
into eating exactly what you want to eat, but with
a bad conscience.*

MARIA AUGUSTA TRAPP

People who repeatedly gain and lose weight are often called yo-yo dieters. If you are a yo-yoer, you may wonder why each successive cycle of weight gain seems to be greater than the last time and why each round of dieting is harder and it takes longer to get the pounds off. The answer has to do with exercise and how it affects fat tissue.

The first time you lose weight, whether you exercise or not, you are probably losing both fat tissue and lean muscle tissue. But if you regain the weight, you'll put on mostly fat. In other words, you may weigh the same but there will be more fat than before. As your body fat increases, your metabolism slows down. This is because it takes less energy to burn fat. So the same number of calories that once allowed you to maintain your weight may now even add pounds.

How then do you lose the fat tissue? By exercising. When exercise is combined with a program of healthy and sensible eating, the weight you lose will be body fat, not lean muscle tissue. Exercise has other benefits as well. As your conditioning improves, you will burn fatty acids rather than glucose for energy Exercise also will keep your metabolism working faster for longer periods—even when you're resting.

∞ THOUGHT FOR THE DAY ∞

*The best fat-burning exercise is aerobic, moderately paced for 30 minutes
or more. Start by taking a brisk walk, perhaps with a friend.*

We are all of us failures —at least, the best of us are.

J. M. BARRIE

Every now and then each of us will fail. The issue to address, however, is not failure itself but your attitudes about it. Some people see failure as a personal deficiency, proof that they are indeed terrible, a disappointment, unable to meet their own expectations. But these people are not looking at failure in the right light.

Failure is a learning experience. Failure tells you what you need to focus on. It gives you feedback about yourself and how you do things. As you get older, you tend to succeed more because you learn from previous failures. The danger is that you begin to set standards for yourself that won't permit failure. You stick to what you know, what you've already mastered. Worse, you stop trying new things altogether. You let old attitudes and embarrassments keep you from trying one more time.

Take time today to think about what you have learned from past failures. Although you may not want to repeat those experiences, you can act upon what you learned.

∞ THOUGHT FOR THE DAY ∞

Take a more positive attitude about failure. Think of it as feedback, experience, practice. The real failure is when you don't try at all.

MARCH 11

Some people regard discipline as a chore. For me, it is a kind of order that sets me free to fly.

JULIE ANDREWS

You often motivate yourself by setting goals, something to strive for and achieve. One of the ways you can help yourself succeed at meeting these goals is to keep a record of your progress and monitor the steps along the way. If you are on a weight loss program, for example, you can keep a record of what you are eating. Make a table of food groups and check them off as they are eaten during the day or use your log to keep track of fat and fiber grams consumed.

Keeping an exercise log is a good way to track your fitness goals. Walkers, joggers and bikers often log distance and time. A log is a good way to watch your improvement if you are regularly doing resistance training with free weights or weight machines. If you belong to a health club, you may want to have a personal fitness evaluation done every six or twelve months so you can monitor your progress. That way you'll be able to see your improvement doing more sit-ups or push-ups or lifting a heavier weight on one of the weight resistance machines.

You may also want to set trackable goals that have to do with your behavior. You might choose to attend a support group on a regular basis—once a day, once a week, twice a month. You can keep track of how many compliments you give to friends or family members, perhaps aiming for a goal of one per day per person.

THOUGHT FOR THE DAY

Logs are useful for tracking many things besides exercise and food. You can keep tabs on routine auto maintenance, your monthly financial budget and how you're spending your time away from work.

*When your schedule leaves you brain-drained and
stressed to exhaustion, it's time to give up something.
Delegate. Say no. Be brutal. It's like cleaning out a
closet—after a while, it gets easier to get rid of things.
You discover that you really didn't need them anyway.*

MARILYN RUMAN

There are many situations where you have to put your needs on hold. You have young children, for example, or your significant other has been laid off and needs extra emotional support until he or she lands a new job. Sometimes, however, you ignore your own needs for so long that you're no longer sure what they are or whether they're important.

If you are waiting for the future to arrive, you often say things like "Someday I am going to do X." You're waiting for better health or a promotion at work or the day your youngest child graduates before you take time for yourself. In the process, you turn down opportunities for self-care.

Realize that taking care of yourself may cause other members of your household to complain. It's okay to decide that the rules need to be changed but a minor inconvenience to them may have become a major imposition on you. You're not the only one who can sort the laundry or push the vacuum cleaner. If you've been paying the household bills for the last fifteen years, maybe it's time to let go and allow your spouse to assume that responsibility.

∽ THOUGHT FOR THE DAY ∽

*Decide to start saying yes to your own needs today.
If you are at a loss as to where to begin, start with a
regret. Make plans to address it. Think how good you'll feel
when you can say, "I'm so happy I did that."*

MARCH 13

How many prompters! What a chorus!

WALTER SAVAGE LANDOR

When you're stressed, you're usually distracted. You're thinking about yesterday's car problem or tomorrow's visit to the doctor or the incomplete project that you have to tackle Monday morning. When your minds are on something else, you're more susceptible to eating triggers. Before you know it, you've eaten something without thinking, something you didn't want and didn't need. You were watching TV or talking on the telephone or walking by the vending machine at work.

Here are some steps you can take to help you eliminate triggers. First, make an effort to be consistent about when and where you eat. When you're at home, for example, eat at the same time in the same room. Pay attention to your internal hunger cues; when you're full, stop eating. If there's food on your plate, save it for the next day or throw it away. Finally, give more thought to when you do your grocery shopping. You'll buy more intelligently if you shop after a meal, not before. It's easier to leave the candy bars and chips at the store if you're not hungry.

Remember today that triggers are easy to avoid. You just have to be aware of where they are.

THOUGHT FOR THE DAY

If other members of your family insist on certain snacks that are trigger foods for you, let them do their own shopping. Then make them responsible for storing their snacks out of sight.

MARCH 14

At one time or another in your life, you will need the services of a lawyer. You may be preparing a will or buying a piece of property. You may need someone to represent you in traffic court or in a divorce or in a contractual dispute. *Consumer Reports Magazine* makes some recommendations to make sure your experience with a lawyer is good.

Start by shopping around. Ask for recommendations from friends who have used legal counsel for a situation similar to your own. You can also check with the American Bar Association office near you. Then interview several lawyers before hiring one. Ask about their experience in handling cases similar to yours. Get an idea of how long it will take to resolve your problem. Ask for an explanation of possible outcomes. Discuss how you will be kept informed as your case progresses. Communication is vital and you should feel at ease speaking honestly and openly. The lawyer you hire should be supportive of your problem and answer your questions clearly and courteously.

Be sure to ask about fees, including how often you will be billed, so that there will be no misunderstanding later. Check on any expenses in addition to the lawyer's fee. Ask for a written estimate of the total bill in advance. A good lawyer will be happy to answer your questions, for he or she knows that the more you understand, the more realistic your expectations will be. This will set the stage for a positive and productive lawyer/client relationship.

∞ THOUGHT FOR THE DAY ∞

Find out if there is leg work or research that you can do that will help your lawyer help you. If you can save time for your lawyer, you might be able to reduce the legal fees in the bargain.

Eat to live, and not live to eat.

BENJAMIN FRANKLIN

Take a few moments to examine your own attitude toward losing weight. Decide whether your approach is rooted in denial and punishment. If so, the odds of success are low. But if your attitude is positive, if dieting means you've decided to improve your physical health and sense of well-being, then you're off to a great start.

People who lose weight and keep it off pay attention to what they eat. But rather than limit and restrict their meals, they learn how to choose nutritious flavorful foods from all four food groups. They also accept that moderate exercise needs to be part of their daily routine. Bridget likes to wake up thirty minutes earlier every morning so she can take a brisk walk while the rest of her family gets dressed. "Getting up earlier was surprisingly easy," she says. "It was the idea that was hard."

Remember to focus your energy on making good choices just for today. It can be overwhelming to think about changing your eating habits for the rest of your life. But if you choose foods wisely, one day at a time, that's what will happen.

∾ THOUGHT FOR THE DAY ∾

Let today be the day you begin to make small, but permanent, lifestyle changes that affect your weight. Become aware of the power of words and work on being more positive in your self-talk. Instead of denying yourself a chocolate candy bar, be positive and choose a comforting cup of herb tea. Set short-term goals that are easy to attain and then celebrate each success.

When you're lying awake with a dismal headache,
and repose is taboo'd by anxiety,
I conceive you may use any language you choose
to indulge in, without impropriety.

SIR WILLIAM SCHWENCK GILBERT

Although headaches were long associated with stress or psychological problems, recent research shows that most headaches have a physical origin and are related to the level of serotonin, a brain chemical that regulates pain messages. When the serotonin drops, the blood vessels in your brain swell and touch off nerves which cause pain. Headaches can be mild or severe and last less than an hour to several weeks or months.

Hormones are also associated with headaches. Seventy percent of migraine sufferers are women (due to fluctuations in estrogen during the menstrual cycle). Food allergies are known to trigger headaches as well. Bananas and cheese in particular contain an amino acid, tyramine, which causes the blood vessels in the brain to dilate, resulting in a headache. Alcohol can have the same effect. Chocolate, sweets and preservatives like monosodium glutamate (MSG), nitrates and sulfites also cause headaches. Salad bars in restaurants are often sprayed with preservatives that can trigger allergic reactions and headaches.

If you suffer from headaches, keep a record. Write down when the headache occurred, how severe the pain was, how long it lasted. Include notes on your meals and activities too. If your headaches are persistent and intense, see a doctor because the real cause of the pain might be more serious than stress or diet factors.

∞ **THOUGHT FOR THE DAY** ∞

For most people, over-the-counter pain medications like aspirin,
acetaminophen (Tylenol) or ibuprofen (Advil) will be effective.

MARCH 17

*The echo began in some indescribable way to
undermine her hold on life.*

EDWARD MORGAN FORSTER

Making changes in your eating habits can be difficult. When people undermine your efforts to follow a healthy eating plan, you think of them as saboteurs. But you need to remind yourself that it takes two to be successful at sabotage—one to push food and the other to eat it. Ann recalls visiting a friend who kept offering her something to eat. "I guess I wasn't very convincing when I said no because by the time I left, I had had two helpings of chocolate cake."

It is important to learn how to deal directly with saboteurs. You may not want to hurt their feelings but in the end the person you really hurt is yourself. If you find it hard to say no, practice. Look in the mirror and say no. Watch your facial expression and listen to the sound of your voice. Keep saying no until you are confident you mean it. Ask a trusted friend to role-play those situations where you find it hard to say no.

Fill your own plate at the stove or counter. It's easier to control portions there. A serving dish on the table will only tempt you to have extra helpings, and unnecessary ones at that. When possible, eat with others. If you're enjoying an interesting conversation with friends or family, you may find it easier to eat less.

∞ THOUGHT FOR THE DAY ∞

You're more likely to overeat when you're bored. When you're finished eating, leave the table. Take the conversation to another room rather than sitting in the kitchen nibbling at the leftovers.

MARCH 18

When a person is down in the world, an ounce of help is better than a pound of preaching.

EDWARD G. BULWER-LYTTON

Kayla was very worried about her parents. Her father had recently suffered a heart attack and her mother was frail; they were no longer able to take care of themselves. Because of their resistance to her pleas, Kayla decided that health-care professionals would be able to convince them of their needs more easily than she could. She had them meet with a social worker and their family doctor, both of whom explained why her parents should no longer manage by themselves and needed to make other choices.

Kayla says this meeting was important for several reasons. First, her parents were more willing to listen to trusted professionals than to her. Second, her parents still were in charge of their lives. Although they were unhappy about the choices that were available, the decision was theirs and not Kayla's. Lastly, Kayla was relieved. Although she had to supervise their caretakers, she could rest easier, knowing that they were eating nutritious meals, their medications were being administered properly and their home and clothes were clean.

There are many professional services available to help senior members of your family when they are faced with a difficult decisions. Let these professionals help you evaluate the situation objectively. They can give you advice and refer you to other agencies that may help as well. If necessary, you may decide to let the professionals speak for you. A trained social worker can keep the discussion focused on the issue at hand.

THOUGHT FOR THE DAY

If a senior in your family seems to be failing physically or mentally, be sure to watch their intake of food and medications. Many situations will improve dramatically with proper nutrition and a better monitoring of prescription drugs.

MARCH 19

In youth we learn, in age we understand.
MARIE VON EBNER-ESCHENBACH

Role models are important, no matter how much experience and knowledge you have. You always benefit by knowing someone who has learned life's lessons better than you. The best role models, senior citizens, are often overlooked—older relatives, retired coworkers, long-time neighbors. They may have a great deal of wisdom to share with you. All you have to do is ask and be willing to listen.

Think today about the senior citizens that you know. Organize a family reunion at a time and place that will make it easy for the older members of your family to attend. Visit senior family members one at a time and interview them, recording it on a video camera. Invite older neighbors to accompany you on errands or ask if you can do the tasks for them. Talk to the senior members in your church or synagogue. Perhaps someone you know is taking advantage of his or her retirement to pursue a hobby full time.

Senior citizens have much to offer. They have lived longer, experienced more, learned more. Many have found peace serenity, and acceptance within themselves that you still may be searching for. Most will be happy to share what they have learned.

∾ THOUGHT FOR THE DAY ∾

Remember that many people turn out to be better grandparents than parents. So even if your relationship with your parents is strained, perhaps they can have a more loving and generous relationship with your children. Make sure you don't stand in the way.

A life spent in making mistakes is not only more honorable but more useful than a life spent doing nothing.

GEORGE BERNARD SHAW

Once you develop a plan for dealing with a problem, it's easy to cut yourself off from other solutions. You aren't interested in hearing about alternate approaches but if you get too close-minded, you may be passing up a chance to learn something new.

Sometimes you spend so much energy trying to be right that you deny yourself the opportunity to be wrong. Being wrong means you have the opportunity to learn, to grow, to discover something new. If you try something but it doesn't work, then you have given yourself a chance to figure out what went wrong. The possibility is there for you to think about the event, make some corrections and handle it better the next time.

Remember that most situations involve other people. It's important for you to be willing to look at it from other perspectives besides your own. No matter how right you think you are, perhaps the other people involved have valid points of view too. Sometimes the answer is that everyone is right.

Instead of trying to make others see things your way, first ask them to explain their points of view. Listen carefully because you might learn something new. You've just opened the door to a new approach. Keep it open long enough to find a solution.

THOUGHT FOR THE DAY

Remember that trying something new can be risky but the outcome is bound to be positive for you. You'll have the satisfaction of knowing you tried every avenue—and you might be surprised to discover some new streets that will take you where you're going.

MARCH 21

The more human beings proceed by plan the more effectively they may be hit by accident.

FRIEDRICH DÜRRENMATT

You know that planning is important for some things—where you're going on vacation, how you're going to celebrate the holidays and whether or not you'll need a new winter coat this winter. Planning can help you in everyday events too—for example, if you put gas in the car tonight, you'll save time getting to work tomorrow. Perhaps the daily planning you overlook most often is eating. You eat on the run, in too much of a hurry to plan ahead, too stressed to ask if you are eating healthfully and appropriately.

If you plan ahead, you can be sure to eat a variety of foods and have several alternatives on hand to choose from. If you find it difficult to plan meals each day, set up a meal plan for the week, including snacks as well as meals. Shopping will be easier because you'll know what quantities to purchase. With some planning, you can learn how much to eat by measuring your portions carefully. If you use a scale and measuring cups and spoons, you'll soon be a good judge of what constitutes an appropriate serving.

Sometimes you need to remind yourself that planning your meals is a good investment. It's easier to prepare a healthy meal when you stressed if you've done some advance planning. When you eat healthfully, you'll look and feel better. You'll be reducing stress—and calories—at the same time.

∞ THOUGHT FOR THE DAY ∞

Post your weekly meal plan on the refrigerator or the inside of a cabinet door. Keep canned ingredients on hand for emergency meals too.

Life itself is the proper binge.
JULIA CHILD

Sometimes when you are trying to lose weight, you get too caught up in what you are losing from day to day or week to week and forget that it's the long term changes that are important. If your weight loss is to become permanent, you need to learn to change your eating habits for good.

It's the new eating habits that you're after—knowing that an apple is more satisfying than a glass of apple juice and a plain baked potato with cottage cheese is more filling and lower in calories than a box of low-fat crackers. You start to realize that you can feel satisfied now with less sugar and more fruits. You accept that if you overly restrict your daily intake of food, you set the stage for problems. When you feel deprived, you'll soon find yourself overeating or bingeing.

It's the long term changes that make your weight loss permanent and will bring you satisfaction with your new lifestyle. If you eat healthfully every day, if you get the calories and nutrients that you need every day, you will feel satisfied. If you do this long enough, you'll find yourself in a new lifestyle—one that helps you look and feel better and leads to happiness.

∞ **THOUGHT FOR THE DAY** ∞

Remember that adding exercise to a program of healthful eating is important. Simply taking a brisk walk every day will help you lose inches as well as pounds.

*Bad men live to eat and drink, whereas good men eat
and drink in order to live.*

SOCRATES

When you're stressed, you tend to snack. Problems can start when you eat unconsciously, nibbling on food while your mind gnaws away at some other problem. Snacks are fine as long as they are nutritious and you include them in your daily food plan.

You should be aware of what textures and tastes are most appealing to you. You may prefer crunchy or smooth, sweet or spicy, salty or sour. You can keep snacks on hand that are reasonable, yet satisfying. Try rice cakes, peanut butter and crackers, reduced-calorie or fat-free hot cocoa, raw vegetables or nonfat yogurt.

You also need to identify *when* you are most likely to snack. Morning snackers find the snack truck or coffee cart irresistible. Afternoon snackers may prefer to sneak off to the candy machine before the work day is finished. You may be prone to eating half a meal while preparing dinner for yourself and your family, or you might admit to sitting down in front of the tube for an evening of nibbling.

Fit the snacks you like into the times that you prefer to eat. For example, anxious afternoon snackers might find rice cakes most effective, while those who like to nibble while cooking may need to keep plenty of raw vegetables nearby. At night you may want soothing cocoa or herb tea. Remember there's nothing wrong with a snack as long as you're realistic.

∞ **THOUGHT FOR THE DAY** ∞

*If snacking is a big problem for you, try changing your meal pattern
from three substantial meals to six or seven smaller meals per day.*

MARCH 24

His fame soon spread around — He carries weight!
WILLIAM COWPER

Charleen didn't have time or money for a health club but she did want stronger muscles. "I bought a set of free weights," she says. "They are three-pound, five-pound and ten-pound weights. It was the best — and probably the least expensive — health investment I'm made in a long time." If you want to increase your muscle mass, you can do it at home with free weights or dumbbells.

Hand-held free weights can be as light as a half-pound or as heavy as 50 or 60 pounds. Start by buying one or two pairs in the weight range that is best for you. Many people walk with small lightweight wrist weights. Ankle and leg weights are best for floor exercises like leg raises. There are magazines and books that can show you some easy exercises for using weights. As you get stronger, you may benefit from personal instruction from a trained fitness expert.

Rubber bands and rubber tubing are also good ways to do muscle strengthening exercises on your own; these usually come with an exercise book or video. Like weights, rubber tubes are easy to use and inexpensive. Get on the floor and do modified push-ups and sit-ups.

∞ THOUGHT FOR THE DAY ∞

Libraries are a valuable resource that is sometimes overlooked. Use your library for books and videos on working with weights.

MARCH 25

Wisely and slow; they stumble that run fast.
WILLLIAM SHAKESPEARE

You live in a fast paced, stressed out world. You move quickly and take shortcuts whenever possible. You're in a hurry to perform one more task before the day is over. You act this way so much that your behavior around food and at the table changes too.

Take notice of how often you eat while moving or standing. If you eat while standing at the counter, in front of the open fridge or on the move in the car, resolve to stop and sit down. Take a moment to arrange the food attractively on the plate.

Watch how rapidly you eat. Most overeaters gulp down their food and eat faster than average, so they can pack away more calories in the same period of time. Make yourself slow down while you eat. Put down your fork or spoon between bites. Then swallow before you reload and pick it up again. Better yet, stop for a minute or two between mouthfuls.

When you're finished eating, leave the table and go back to the business at hand. You'll feel good knowing you ate less and ate better than you usually do.

∽ THOUGHT FOR THE DAY ∽

Remember that there are more than just physical benefits to eating properly. When you take a few extra minutes to eat healthfully, you're also giving yourself a mental break. You'll feel refreshed simply for having treated yourself to a nutritious meal and a short break.

MARCH 26

The woman one loves always smells good.

RÉMY DE GOURMONT

Even though your sense of smell is generally considered to be the weakest of your five senses, it is still very important. Certain odors or scents bring back memories of your childhood, evoke food tastes or remind you of certain rituals or ceremonies. Often the last thing you do when getting dressed is to dab on some perfume. Place a drop behind your ears or on the insides of your wrists. Other pulse points are on the insides of your ankles, behind your knees, in the crook of elbow, at the base of your throat and between your breasts.

How long your fragrance lasts depend on what percentage of it is made up of essential oils. Perfume is the most intense and will last four to six hours; cologne is the weakest and usually lasts only a few hours. You can make up for weaker scents by using a shampoo, deodorant or powder in the same scent. Body creams and lotions generally contain intense concentrations of fragrance.

When shopping for perfume, remember that scent and taste are closely related. If you've just eaten, you won't be able to smell the fragrance correctly. You should not be wearing any other scents, including those in hair care products. Test only two in one day. If you sniff very many, you'll be hard pressed to tell the difference among them. Perfume has layers or notes. The top notes are what you smell first. As your body warms the perfume, you will become aware of other fragrances. You should allow a half hour or more to allow the scent to adjust to your body chemistry.

∾ THOUGHT FOR THE DAY ∾

Fragrance should be kept away from heat and sunlight. Once opened, it will last only a year or two — so use it every day, not just for special occasions.

One of those happy souls which are the salt of the earth.

PERCY BYSSHE SHELLEY

With all the concern over sodium, you may lose sight of the fact that salt is an essential nutrient. Your body needs sodium to maintain a normal blood volume and blood pressure and to keep your heart rhythm steady. Sodium also helps transmit nerve impulses and maintain normal muscle activity. The reason salt has gotten so much bad press, however, is that it is consumed in excessive amounts.

Most of the sodium you eat comes from highly processed foods that are high in fat and low in nutrients. The amount of sodium you consume is significant if you have hypertension. Although not everyone is sensitive to salt, some people are extremely sensitive and a small amount can elevate their blood pressure.

If you want to cut down salt, you should stay away from highly processed foods like certain cheeses, soy sauce, lunch meat, canned soups and canned vegetables. Prepackaged grain mixes, using rice, potato or pasta, are also extremely high in sodium. Check the labels carefully, as some brands have more salt than others; there are also low-sodium versions of many of these foods. Fried foods and fast foods are quite high in sodium. When cooking, omit the salt or only use half the amount called for in the recipe. At first, less salty food will taste bland but as you get used to it, you'll discover that food has many other flavors besides salty and sweet. Remember that salt is an acquired taste and can be unlearned.

∾ THOUGHT FOR THE DAY ∾

People who have a tendency to retain fluid should cut back on salt. To tell if you have excess fluid in your body, press your thumb into your skin near the shin bone. If there is a lot of fluid in the tissue, there will be a dent in your skin.

Growth itself contains the germ of happiness.

PEARL S. BUCK

When you're ready to lose weight or make any other change in your lifestyle, you can get yourself off to a good start by asking why you want to make these changes. Perhaps you want to look or feel better, improve your health or put yourself in a better position for a promotion at work. These goals should reflect your desire for permanent, rather than temporary, lifestyle changes. You need to ignore the numbers, such as what the scale shows, the size of our paycheck or how many objects you own. Instead you should pay attention to yourself, asking how you can benefit.

Accept the fact that occasional slips are normal. You should use these slip-ups, however, to your advantage. For each, you can make a decision on how you are going to handle the situation next time. You can devise a plan, then practice your response in advance. It's easier to say no to a pushy friend if you rehearse in the mirror.

Exercise is important. It will give you a greater sense of control over your body and your life. If you find an exercise you enjoy, you're more likely to stick with it. As you get stronger physically, you will find that you are stronger emotionally too.

If you're making big or difficult changes, it's helpful to join a support group. When you meet new friends who have the same interests or who are struggling to make the same changes that you are, you'll find that everyone can trade tips. You'll also meet people who have already accomplished a great deal so there's hope for you as well.

THOUGHT FOR THE DAY

Be sure to set aside time for exercise. Even busy people can make an appointment with themselves to work out three or four days each week.

MARCH 29

In hospitals there was no time off for good behavior.
JOSEPHINE TEY

One of the stresses that you may face is an illness serious enough to require a hospital stay. The doctor and medical staff do their best to take good care of your body but they may not address other related issues that concern you unless you ask them. Here are some things that you might want to discuss with your doctor:

Share with your doctor and nurses what you are uncertain about, what you are afraid of, what worries you. Perhaps you are unclear what some test results really mean or you are afraid of being in a lot of pain or you are worried about how much time you will miss from work. Let them help you put your mind at ease as much as they can.

Be sure you understand what caused your illness. If there's a specific cause, you may be able to do something to prevent it from recurring. If there is no clear-cut reason why you are suffering from a particular illness, it may relieve your mind to know that there is nothing you could have done to prevent it from happening. Regardless of the cause, try to determine what the chances are of this episode happening again. Remember, the odds may be much lower than you think. Heart attack patients often go home, anxious and afraid to resume normal activities because they are fearful of another attack. Keep asking questions until you are confident that you know exactly what is okay and not okay for you to do once you leave the hospital. The more answers you get, the more you will feel in control of your body.

∞ THOUGHT FOR THE DAY ∞

Remember that there may be several courses of treatment available to you. The wise patient asks what these choices are and why the doctor is recommending one over the others.

When it comes to eating, you can sometimes
help yourself more by helping yourself less.
RICHARD ARMOUR

You often think of fast foods as fat foods but that's not necessarily the case. While the original fast food meals had as much
as 40 to 55 percent of their total calories from fat—one meal
can contain as much as one day's allowance of sodium—
today's fast food chains have heard the consumer and most
have added low-fat and/or low-sodium alternatives to their
menus. Most of the chains also will honor special requests. It
may take a few more minutes to fill your order but the fat and
calories you save will make those extra minutes worthwhile.

If you're stopping for breakfast, have orange juice. Avoid
high fat meats such as bacon, ham or sausage. Carbohydrates,
such as toast, pancakes or muffins are better choices. Pass the
butter or margarine and reach for the jams, syrups and jellies.
Use these sweets sparingly, of course. A bowl of oat, corn or
bran flakes with skim milk is an excellent breakfast choice.

Later in the day, order a salad with reduced calorie dressing. Use only what you need from the packet; there's no need
to drown your salad in dressing. A slice of lemon squeezed
over the salad is a tasty, nonfat dressing. For a sandwich, ask
for baked fish or grilled skinless chicken; request no sauce and
use ketchup or mustard instead. Pass on the cheese too. If
there's a salad bar, stack the sandwich with extra onion, lettuce
and tomato. Stick with regular size sandwiches; larger sizes are
double and triple in fat.

Educate yourself and read the brochures or charts with
detailed nutritional information available in these restaurants.

∾ **THOUGHT FOR THE DAY** ∾

It may be hard, but try and pass on French fries and
hash brown potatoes. If you must have a taste, get the
smallest size and share it with your dining partner.

Our greatest foes, and whom we must chiefly combat, are within.

MIGUEL DE CERVANTES

When you start a diet, you intend to succeed. You're motivated, you're determined, you've made a commitment. Yet a few weeks later, you have sabotaged yourself. You're once again eating all the foods that you know you shouldn't, regaining the pounds you worked so hard to lose.

One of the ways that you make it difficult is to deprive yourself of the foods you love. The key is moderation. You should permit yourself to have an occasional serving of a favorite food. If you don't feel deprived, then you won't binge and abandon your weight-loss plan.

Another form of sabotage is to overdo exercise. You try to make up for the last five years of couch-based lifestyle in the first few workouts. Soon you're so stiff and sore that you stop completely. Again, the key is moderation. If you have been sedentary for a while, even mild exercise is beneficial. As you build strength, you increase the duration and intensity.

Last, you can sabotage yourself with boredom. There's nothing wrong with low-fat yogurt for lunch but if you eat the same thing every day, you'll find yourself looking for a new taste and seeking out old fattening favorites. The more variety in the foods you eat, the more likely you are to stick with your food plan.

∾ THOUGHT FOR THE DAY ∾

Instead of worrying about how thin you should be, think how healthful you should be. With the help of your doctor, determine a healthy weight range for your height and frame. Remember that "ideal" weight varies greatly from one person to another.

What is food to one, is to others bitter poison.

LUCRETIUS

With modern technology, you assume that food poisoning is a thing of the past. But it isn't and the most likely place to get food poisoning is in your very own kitchen.

When baking meat, poultry or fish, the oven temperature should be 325°F or higher. Use a meat thermometer to make sure foods are cooked well done.

After you've handled raw meat and poultry, make sure the raw meat doesn't come in contact with other foods, such as salad ingredients. Before you touch any other foods, wash everything—all utensils, countertops, cutting boards and, of course, your hands—with soap and water. Bacteria will thrive on cutting boards, so wash them in the dishwasher; glass cutting boards are easiest to keep clean. Marinate raw meat in a glass dish in the refrigerator and never reuse the marinade.

Contrary to popular opinion, canned foods do not have unlimited shelf lives. Although some can be stored for several years, high acid foods, such as tomato products, sauces, fruits and juices, should be used within one year. Cans should be stored in a cool dry place. Garages and outside sheds have temperatures over 85°F in the summer and below freezing in the winter. Never buy or use cans that are dented, especially along a seam. If the top is bulging or the can is leaking, toss it.

∾ THOUGHT FOR THE DAY ∾

Some foods are irradiated to destroy bacteria that causes food to spoil. While the USDA feels that this poses no health risks, if you're not comfortable with buying irradiated foods, note that they are clearly marked with a green label.

*Severe illness isolates those in close contact
with it because it inevitably narrows the focus
of concern. To a certain extent this can lead to
healing but not if the circle of concern is so tight
that it cannot be broken into, or out of.*

MADELEINE L'ENGLE

Many people believe that to be healed, you need to tap into the powers of your mind. They believe you already have within you the tools that you need for getting better. One of the tools is knowing how you best handle physical illnesses. Here are some things which can affect your recovery.

Some patients want to know everything and be very involved in planning their own care, while others prefer that their doctors make any necessary decisions and inform them after the choices have been resolved. Other patients want their families to be involved and kept informed about treatments because they feel family members can be trusted to speak on their behalf. Others, however, may feel that well-meaning relatives will hinder the process and may ask the doctor and medical staff to help keep family members at bay. Some people are able to tolerate a great deal of pain yet others are very fearful of suffering and want to be assured that any pain will be controlled with adequate amounts of medication.

Remember that each person has unique needs. Your spouse, children and doctor aren't mind readers, so if they have to guess what you want or need, they may very well guess wrong. It's your responsibility to make these decisions; it's theirs to help carry them out whenever possible.

∾ THOUGHT FOR THE DAY ∾

*Healing can be a two-way street. Be sure to ask
your doctor what is expected of you. Sometimes small efforts
on your part—such as taking your medications exactly
as prescribed—can make a big difference.*

APRIL 3

*Forgiveness is the act of admitting
we are like other people.*
CHRISTINA BALDWIN

There are many reasons why weight may be a problem for you. One could be connected to the role of food in your family. In some families, food was a reward or a bandage. Good grades, a birthday, a skinned knee or hurt feelings were rewarded or soothed with food. In other families, food was something bad. There was little money for food or the family chef didn't like to cook or a parent had an eating disorder and underfed the family. You may have learned to fear food rather than control it. Food may have been a source of shame where as children you were embarrassed by how your overweight parents looked. You may also have unconsciously learned that being loyal to the family meant you should be overweight too.

Obstacles may have been put in your path but they don't have to be permanent. It may be time for you to acknowledge these roadblocks and deal with them. Part of this work will be to forgive your parents. Even though they made mistakes, they did the best they could.

It may be easier to forgive your parents if you are a parent yourself. Then you can truly understand what it means to try your best.

∾ THOUGHT FOR THE DAY ∾

*Make a list of the positive things that your parents did for you.
Start with the obvious: they gave you life.*

APRIL 4

*Cheese that is required by law to append the word food to
its title does not go well with red wine or fruit.*

FRAN LEBOWITZ

Fake foods—nondigestible fats, sugar substitutes, replacement
meats, liquid meals—promise that they are easy, convenient
and as tasty as real food. You may also turn to fake foods
because you don't know how to cook. If you think preparing
real food is too hard, takes too long or costs too much, you've
been mislead. Real food is less expensive. Recipes are easy to
follow and require no skill other than the ability to follow simple directions. There are many cookbooks available that give
you menus that can be prepared in thirty minutes or less.

The real effect of fake foods is to encourage you to eat
more. You decide to have a second serving since there are
fewer calories. Sugar substitutes, for example, taste good but
they do nothing to lessen your craving for sweets. Fake foods
are expensive too. They are mainly used in convenience and
prepackaged foods. They may be low in fat calories but their
nutritional value is minimal. In the end, you'll save money and
gain nutrition if you buy real food.

Fake foods are not the magic pills you're looking for. Used
properly, they can be a tool to help control your weight but
they should never be counted on to replace real food or moderate portions.

∞ THOUGHT FOR THE DAY ∞

*Focus your energy on how to fit one serving of real chocolate cake into
your weekly eating plan instead of justifying the health benefits of an
entire low-fat chocolate cake.*

*Anger is a momentary madness, so control
your passion or it will control you.*

HORACE

When arguing, your opponent feels that he or she wasn't heard
or that you didn't understand his or her point of view. To avoid
this frustration, set ground rules before the argument. Agree
that before responding with your own point of view, you will
paraphrase what your opponent just said. If there is any misunderstanding, it can be clarified on the spot. If there truly was
a misinterpretation, your response will probably change.

Ending an argument requires compromise. Both parties need
to accept that neither can have the last word nor feel total satisfaction. It often helps to end the discussion by coming up with
possible solutions for both sides to think about. You can reconnect several hours or another day later to decide on a resolution.

Remember that the purpose of a fight is not to seek revenge
or say I told you so. The goal is to resolve a conflict so that when
a similar situation comes up, you'll know how to handle it.

∞ THOUGHT FOR THE DAY ∞

*No matter how self-righteous you felt when the
argument started, you may be shocked to discover that
your behavior and words are upsetting to your partner.*

*More children suffer from interference than
from non-interference.*

AGATHA CHRISTIE

When your loved ones are sick, you suffer right along with
them, so much so that sometimes you forget just who the
patient really is. You have to be careful to set appropriate
boundaries, keeping in mind that even if you are the primary
caregiver, the ailing body belongs to someone else.

Janet's daughter had scoliosis, a curvature of the spine that
required her to wear a back brace for two years. She recalled
that the doctor would answer her questions by talking directly
to her daughter. "He would say, 'Your mother is concerned
about such and so, but you can tell her that the answer is this.'
" At first Janet was annoyed, but she soon realized that the
doctor was trying to empower her daughter. "I realized that I
had started to preempt my daughter's condition and make it
my own like most mothers do. But the doctor was right. My
daughter was the one with the bad back and the brace, so she
deserved to be in charge as much as possible."

If you have a chronic limitation, take control of your own
situation. And respect the needs of disabled loved ones to do
the same.

∾ THOUGHT FOR THE DAY ∾

*Even if your children are healthy, it is a good idea to occasionally
review your relationship. As they grow up, you need to let go and let
them be responsible for themselves as soon as they have shown that
they can. Teens respond better to openness and trust than to continual
and excessive efforts at control.*

Striving for excellence motivates you; striving for perfection is demoralizing.

HARRIET BERAIKER

An important part of handling stress is to take control. But try to be as flexible as possible. A stressful period is not the time for an all-or-nothing approach. It's one thing to concentrate on diet and exercise so that you can feel in control, but it's another thing to set rigid, impossible goals. This is the time to change goals as the situation requires. For example, you may not have an extra hour or two to work out at the health club but you can take a twenty minute walk.

You need to keep things in perspective. When surrounded by problems, you tend to see only the negative parts of yourself and remember only the negative things that have happened. You may need to ask a sibling or longtime friend to remind you of the good things in your life and the positive things that you have accomplished. Make a list of all the good things that you have and the things that you appreciate in your life. And if you think back to other crises, you can remember that none lasted forever. The sun came out again.

THOUGHT FOR THE DAY

Trust your experience and you can continue to meet life's challenges. The older you get, the more wisdom you acquire, the more you know what works for you.

APRIL 8

*A man can be part of the design of your life, not
necessarily the redesign of your life.*

GLENN CLOSE

Extra weight can get in the way of dating. In some cases, people gain weight on purpose, even though they might not realize it. People who are afraid of being hurt or have a problem with intimacy may find it uncomfortable or difficult to have close relationships. Activities that revolve around food, romance novels and being alone in front of the television are predictable and safe. Your weight becomes a companion, giving you a false sense of protection. The extra weight creates a protective layer that guards you against the outside world.

If you start dating again, you may have some fantasies about what it's going to be like to date when you are thin. You may expect that being thin means you'll quickly find the perfect relationship with the perfect mate. But few things in life live up to those expectations.

Rather than wait for that knight or princess, concentrate on building self-esteem and gaining confidence. Losing weight will make you feel more attractive but you may still have deep feelings of insecurity or worries about imagined personality flaws. You lost weight slowly so you should be prepared to reenter the dating world slowly too.

∾ THOUGHT FOR THE DAY ∾

*Take advantage of a support system. Sharing your feelings about
losing weight is important. Talk to others who have had similar
experiences and learn how they reentered the dating world.*

APRIL 9

A soul, like the body, lives by what it feeds on.
JOSIAH GILBERT HOLLAND

You may have put on extra pounds because you have been feeding your body not your mind. You eat because you are bored, overwhelmed, stressed, unhappy or uncomfortable with whatever feelings you have. Then you go on a stringent diet but in a short time you regain what you lost.

If you are to change emotional eating patterns, you need to recognize that strict dieting is not the answer. The problem with eating less than 1,000 calories a day is that it isn't enough to keep you going. You aren't full so you get hungry and often-times start binging. If you're eating a balanced diet that focuses on complex carbohydrates, you'll be eating low-fat, high-fiber foods. These foods satisfy your hunger, give you that full feeling and make it easier to wait for the next meal.

Strict diets are far removed from what a normal diet should be. One of the tip-offs that a diet is unhealthy is that it is based on one, or very few, foods. These eating plans are temporary and when they end, you revert to your old, inappropriate eating patterns. You haven't learned new, healthful eating habits The secret of losing weight and keeping it off is to recognize when you have physical and emotional needs.

THOUGHT FOR THE DAY

When your mind needs soothing, pamper yourself with things besides food. Visit a spa, get a massage, take a yoga class, listen to music, do some deep breathing or take a bubble bath by candlelight.

APRIL 10

The ability to choose puts human beings
in control of their actions.
MILDRED PITTS WALTER

One of the things that makes illness difficult and stressful is that you feel like you have lost control, that some disease or syndrome has taken over and is now in charge. However, no matter how serious or long-term the illness is, there are still some choices available to you. And as soon as you start to become active in choosing what form of help will be best, you start to exert control.

Ask your doctor what you can do to be an active and participating member of the health care team. This is particularly important if you have a chronic illness. Join a support group, ask questions, pay attention to how others handle a situation. Learn how to take the best possible care of yourself.

One area that patients are hesitant to discuss with their doctor is the cost of treatment. Yet the financial implications of your care may make a difference in your recovery. For example, let your doctor know if days off from work for recovery also means no pay. If you're worried about rent and food, you might be better off returning to work rather than staying home and worrying. No matter what your circumstances, it is important to share your point of view with your doctor. Give yourself permission to say no to that which you don't want and to ask for that which you know will make you better.

THOUGHT FOR THE DAY

If you require long term care, work with professionals,
such as a home health nurse, doctor or social worker.
They can help you assess where that care will be best for
you—with help at home or in an extended care facility.

APRIL 11

*Though all afflictions are evils in themselves, yet they
are good for us, because they discover to us our disease
and tend to our cure.*

JOHN TILLOTSON

Arthritis is an inflammation of the joints, especially weight-bearing joints like knees and hips. But it can also affect your fingers and hands, making routine daily tasks difficult and painful. One way to control and manage this condition is regular exercise. Daily range-of-motion and stretching exercises will keep your joints flexible and will strengthen the muscle groups which support those joints. For example, if you have arthritis in your knees, it will help if you strengthen your quadriceps.

Here are some suggestions that can help you manage arthritis more easily. Whenever possible, sit instead of stand. Open a refrigerator door with a towel through the handle. Close plastic containers with snap-on lids by pressing with an elbow instead of your hand. Hold a plate with the palm of your hand instead of gripping the edges with your fingers. Carry the weight of a purse on the shoulder or near the elbow rather than with the hand and fingers. Look for self-help devices for opening a jar, getting dressed or cooking dinner. Learn how to simplify and combine tasks to conserve energy.

Arthritis does not have to get the best of you. It is possible to manage this disease and to continue doing what you want to do within reason. Once you've explored your options and accept your limitations, you'll realize that you can still have a full and complete life.

THOUGHT FOR THE DAY

*Learn to use your joints in the correct position. If you're going to wipe
off the counter, for example, it helps to keep your fingers fully
extended. You should learn to use your strongest joints and muscles as
much as possible in order not to strain the weaker ones.*

APRIL 12

There is no cosmetic for beauty like happiness.
COUNTESS OF BLESSINGTON

How you see yourself is reflected in how you dress and, in turn, how the rest of the world treats you. If you think of yourself as in control, then you're going to act and look that way. You will stand taller, speak with conviction and dress like a leader. If you think of yourself as attractive, you will wear nice clothes, smile more often and move with confidence.

Natalie is a large women but she is proud of her flawless skin and complexion. She always wears make-up, jewelry and stylish clothes in colors that enhance her appearance and personality. She started a very successful business, is devoted to her family yet manages to find time for a variety of other interests. Karen, on the other hand, wears no make-up and takes little pride in her appearance. She sees herself as a victim so she lets the world take advantage of her. Her sons don't obey, her husband is abusive, her boss insists that she work many overtime hours each week without an assistant.

It's time to become aware of and focus on your positive attributes. The message that you want to be sending about yourself is that you are worthwhile and deserve good treatment and respect from others. When you respect yourself, others will follow suit.

∞ THOUGHT FOR THE DAY ∞

Take some time today to pinpoint your best physical characteristic, then do or buy something that will enhance it.

But Mr. Jeremy liked getting his feet wet; nobody ever scolded him, and he never caught a cold.

BEATRIX POTTER

As you get older, your feet will change, probably getting a little wider and longer than when you were young. That's why you should measure your feet every time you buy shoes. When you're buying shoes, fit the front of your foot first. If the heel is too big, you can easily put a heel grip in the back. If you have corns and calluses, cushion them to alleviate the pressure. Drug stores have a variety of inexpensive aids.

At work, get out of those high heels. High heels eight hours a day will cause problems eventually. Instead, buy smart-looking, flat-soled shoes. At home, unless your feet require special support, go barefoot or wear socks or slippers for warmth. You'll then exercise your entire foot and your toes will spread out like they should.

Your feet take the impact of your entire body weight so extra pounds aggravate any foot problems. If feet problems interfere with walking or jogging, try an exercise that is non-weight-bearing, such as swimming or riding a bicycle. A soft-soled sneaker helps distribute weight across the entire foot. If you have heel pain, a heel cup may help too. If foot pain persists after you lose weight and start wearing shoes that fit, you should see a doctor.

∾ THOUGHT FOR THE DAY ∾

Decide today to invest some money in good shoes and treat your feet with the tenderness and loving care that they deserve. Although shoes can be professionally stretched, this is not a good solution for most people. If your feet are seriously deformed, consider ordering custom shoes.

APRIL 14

Through [my characters] I've lived many parallel lives.

MARGUERITE YOURCENAR

Samantha is director of an in-patient treatment center that specializes in substance abuse. The most stressful part of her job is "seeing the same people again and again." It is heartbreaking, she says, to watch those people who continually beat themselves up with drugs and alcohol. To handle the stress of her job, she likes "to get out of myself" and so once a week she becomes Sister Sam, a disc jockey for a radio show of reggae and African music.

Getting involved in a new activity can be a fun way to get away from the stresses of your daily life. Different roles enrich your life. You are reminded to think of yourself in new ways—as more than just a parent, employee or spouse. Matt is a baseball umpire for local games. Bob plays Dixieland jazz with a small combo. Wendy coaches a girls' soccer team. Gabrielle teaches embroidery. Felisha puts on her clown makeup and costume and performs at children's parties and civic functions.

Many adults find that some of the interests they now enjoy—interests beyond job and family—were with them all along. Think back to the memories that bring joy to your mind. Then explore them again in your adult life.

∞ THOUGHT FOR THE DAY ∞

Consider joining a club where you'll meet others who share a common interest. Or, take a special interest class at your local community college.

Children have more need of models than of critics.

JOSEPH JOUBERT

Amy recently became a single parent. Shortly after her divorce, she noticed that her daughter's eating patterns were changing. She ate snacks rather than sitting down to eat regular meals. The upheaval of a divorce is very often as hard on the children as on the parents. Young children may not understand what's happening and may feel that their own behavior somehow caused the breakup. When a marriage dissolves, parents are often distracted with their own emotions and have little energy to pay attention to their children and the children's eating patterns begin to reflect a need for extra attention.

Whether there is emotional upheaval in your family or not, keep a record of what your children are eating throughout the day for a week or more. To make sure their nutritional needs are being met, show this record to the child's pediatrician. Danger signs are when a child suddenly becomes extremely overweight, extremely underweight or stops growing.

Amy learned that instead of fussing with her daughter over food, it was easier to just give her daughter the attention that she craved. So they would read a book together, play a game or take a walk. Amy also realized that she had been snacking herself and her daughter may have been imitating that eating behavior. When Amy settled down and got back to eating three healthy meals a day, her daughter did the same.

∞ THOUGHT FOR THE DAY ∞

There is nothing wrong with frequent snacking as long as the snacks are nutritious like pretzels, air-popped popcorn or fresh fruit. A snacking pattern is fairly common among children who are in stressful situations.

APRIL 16

A woman obsessed with her body is also obsessed with the limitations of her emotional life.

KIM CHERNIN

You have a specific image of your body, which you most likely describe as a series of major flaws. Your arms are too heavy, your legs are too skinny, your nose is too large, your ears stick out, your behind is too big, too small, too flat or too droopy. But your self-image probably doesn't match what the mirror shows. Chances are your mind is locked into a subjective, rather than an objective, mental picture. Few people have a perfect body and yours is no worse or better than anyone else's.

You should ignore actors on television or models in ads. Instead, take a look at the people around you. Pay attention to real bodies, the ones you see every day in grocery stores, restaurants, on the street or in the hallway at work. You are surrounded by a variety of body types and your own is about average.

Whenever you criticize your body, you should stop and restate what you said, replacing your negative thought with a positive one. Instead of saying your tummy is too big, you should say your smile is wonderful. Instead of concentrating on your flaws, work on accepting and respecting your body just as it is today.

THOUGHT FOR THE DAY

Learn to see yourself as others do. Pay more attention to what's attractive about you. Make a list of your non-physical qualities — your sense of humor, your ability to get a job done and pay attention to details, the fact that you're a good listener and a good friend.

What can I do but move.

RICHARD PURDY WILBUR

The thought of moving can make any woman reach for the chocolate chip cookies. The very act of moving is stressful, hard work. It is physically exhausting to pack, move, carry, lift, clean and unpack. Moving takes an emotional toll too. It's hard to leave family and friends, familiar places and routines. But there are things you can do to survive the move and make it a little easier on yourself.

Before leaving town, be sure to have copies of the medical and dental records for everyone in your family. Check health insurance policies to ensure that you'll be covered at the new location. If you're moving out of state, you should get refills on any prescription medications that you take regularly. If you have children, you'll need their school records. Household pets should be up-to-date on annual vaccines. It's wise to get a copy of their shot records to have on hand for the new veterinarian.

Sometimes a move is not by choice. Perhaps your spouse was transferred or you need to be closer to an ailing parent or relative or you need a change of climate for your own health. You still have some options, however. You can feel sorry for yourself and be resentful, making those around you miserable. Or, you can look for the good that the move brings you and seize the opportunity to make some changes.

∞ THOUGHT FOR THE DAY ∞

Moving can also be difficult if you're moving from one climate to another. If possible, you should try to move during a time of year when the temperature changes are less extreme, usually spring and fall.

You should pray for a sound mind in a sound body.

JUVENAL

Tina started practicing yoga when she was going through a marital separation. She and her husband were having a difficult time, she recalls, and yoga class was the only time she felt good. Four years later, she is still doing yoga every day, even if it is only for 5 minutes. "Yoga is my gift to myself," she says, "because I am taking care of myself. Yoga balances me, focuses me, allows me to be myself."

Yoga is an activity that offers both emotional and physical benefits. The series of exercises and postures make you put your body into new places, make you use your muscles in new ways. You learn to concentrate on breathing, on elongating and straightening your body. Yoga exercises are done slowly, easily, gently. As you slow down enough to concentrate on your breathing and posture, you are also slowing down your mind. Tina says, "Yoga helps me forget about everything for a few minutes. When I am done, I am refreshed and ready to face the world again."

Yoga has much to recommend it. You can learn to stand and walk taller, breathe deeper and more fully, align and stretch your muscles and limbs properly. And as you develop a new language for your body, you can learn to clear your mind and focus on the present moment. You can find a new source of strength from within.

∽ THOUGHT FOR THE DAY ∽

Begin practicing yoga by taking a class. The instructor will be there to make sure you are learning at a proper and correct pace. The support of others in the class is helpful and fun too.

Walking is also an ambulation of mind.
GRETEL EHRLICH

Mickey suffered a mild heart attack when he was 47. The doctor told him it was a "warning shot across the bow," so Mickey vowed to lose weight, stop smoking and start walking. "Walking was a challenge," he said. "It took me a while to figure out how to keep my walks from being boring." Eventually his thoughts turned to music. He hummed his favorite songs and found that his walks were more enjoyable and lasted longer. As musical fragments of once forgotten lyrics and tunes came to mind, he found himself going home and listening to old records and tapes, refreshing his memory. What had started as a way to pass the time now became a new and gratifying hobby.

Another way to enjoy a walk is to look around and try to see things that you haven't noticed before. If you're walking through your neighborhood, look at doors as you go by. What colors are they painted? Do they have windows? How many different styles are there? Inhale deeply through your nose. What do you smell? Whether you're walking through a quiet woods or a bustling city, listen to the sounds around you. Pay attention to one kind of sound; then count how many different ones there are. Listen for bird sounds, horn sounds, voices.

You need to take care of your mind as well as your body. While you're exercising, use that time to let your mind focus on something pleasant and enjoyable. Soon you may find that you'll let those pleasantries become a part of the rest of your day as well.

∾ **THOUGHT FOR THE DAY** ∾

Look for a book of favorite show tunes or campfire songs so you can learn the words. Teach your children the ones that were your favorites or invite your friends over for an old-fashioned sing-along.

And all the loveliest things there be
Come simply, so it seems to me.

EDNA ST. VINCENT MILLAY

If your makeup hasn't changed in the last ten years, your look is probably dated. As you get older, skin tone changes and the colors and techniques that worked when you were younger may not be as flattering now.

Dab some makeup on the side of your neck or cheek, not the inside of your arm, then look at this test spot in sunlight. If the color is correct, it virtually disappears. Switch from heavy eyeliner to a matte eye shadow—earthy colors like brick, smoky brown or rich charcoal are always good choices. Thicken brows with matte powder; apply with an angle brush instead of a harsh pencil line.

The wrong color translucent powder can drain color from your skin and give your skin a chalky look. Choose a silky matte formula in a color that warms your skin tone and creates a more natural finish. Blush is always great as long as it's not too bright. The right shade should approximate the color of your cheeks after you've exercised. Apply blush with a big fluffy brush for a nice glow instead of that slash of color under your cheek bones. Finish your new look with lush lip color. First define lips with a lip pencil; the apply lipstick to cover.

∾   **THOUGHT FOR THE DAY**   ∾

Remember to use sunscreen year round to protect your skin from the harsh and dangerous ultraviolet rays of the sun.

Moderation in all things.

TERENCE

Sticking to a diet can be difficult since even the most determined person is bound to have setbacks and lapses. When these setbacks occur, you're often surprised. You may not have seen it coming but perhaps the cause was simply a lack of moderation. Remember that being too strict is just as extreme as having an all-out binge—in fact, one might lead to the other.

In an effort to lose weight quickly, you may have become a perfectionist—weighing every carrot stick, obsessing over every morsel, worrying about the excess calories in a radish. You start to limit the foods you eat, banning favorites by making a long list of forbidden foods. This kind of deprivation only makes overeating problems worse and soon will trigger a lapse or a binge.

Trust yourself enough to be moderate. It is easier to maintain control if you occasionally allow yourself to eat a small portion of a favorite food. Look for ways to modify your favorite recipes so you can have the taste but with reduced fat and calories. It's important that you eat every meal instead of skipping one. When you try to lose weight gradually, you will be more successful.

∞ THOUGHT FOR THE DAY ∞

Remember that there is much more to who you are than what you weigh. Your personality, your outlook, how you help other people, what you do with your life is just as important. Self-esteem can be independent of the scale.

A hobby a day keeps the doldrums away.

PHYLLIS McGINLEY

Julie is a registered nurse and her days at the hospital are often tiring and stressful. On her days off, she makes hats and other accessories from vintage clothing. "When I'm making hats," Julie says, "I can forget about my troubles and concentrate on being creative." Julie also designs with other women. "It's the energy of many minds and creative spirits working together that is most enjoyable," she says.

If you aren't sure how to get started, see if you can work for or apprentice yourself to someone whose work you admire. Olivia worked for a well-known quilter for several years and in the process discovered that she had good ideas for quilts herself. Curtis worked for an illustrator and photographer before venturing out on his own. You can also take a class. A local store might bring in teachers or know who does. A nearby community college may offer adult noncredit extension courses in your area of interest. Or attend a few meetings of a hobby group and ask others how they improved their skills and learned more.

Remember, however, to keep a healthy perspective and attitude in mind. Your goal should not be to turn your hobby into a business but simply to pursue the hobby.

∾ THOUGHT FOR THE DAY ∾

Try something new. Go up in a balloon, learn to tango, ride a horse. The only excuse you need is that you've always wanted to do it.

There is no failure except in no longer trying.

ELBERT HUBBARD

Changing your eating habits is quite a challenge. Because you're human, you sometimes help yourself to foods that aren't healthy or you overeat from time to time. It's important, however, that you accept any slip-ups and move on. Dwelling on past mistakes only makes them worse.

You may also need to remind yourself of the difference between a lapse and a binge. A lapse is a slight error, an instance of eating something that's not on your food plan or eating too much of an allowed food. Binge eating, on the other hand, is eating an amount of food that is obviously more than most people would eat in one sitting or in a short period of time. For example, eating two bowls of ice cream is a lapse but eating a half-gallon is a binge. Binge eating also is accompanied by a feeling that you have no control over what you're eating. Binge eaters feel that they can't stop, that is makes no difference what they're putting in their mouths, that they are compelled to keep going.

Before you beat up on yourself, remember that nearly everyone has binged a few times. Unless you're having binge eating episodes twice a week for six months or more, you're not in trouble. Remember that everyone loses control occasionally so allow yourself to be human. Learning new habits is a complex process and it is normal to give into temptation every now and then.

∞ THOUGHT FOR THE DAY ∞

Use past lapses as episodes where you learned what not to do. Use them to make you aware of better ways of coping, like taking ten slow, deep breaths, leaving the TV set for a brisk walk around the block or giving your neighbor the bag of cookies you sneaked into the kitchen this afternoon.

APRIL 24

*The United Nations is child's play
compared to the tugs and splits and need to
understand and forgive in any family.*

MAY SARTON

When you're making changes in your lifestyle, the group you most want to support you is your immediate family. Yet as much as they want you to succeed, they may not be able to help you. In fact, they may sabotage your efforts. You need to remember that changes you make for yourself affect others as well and how your new behavior impacts family members will influence how supportive they can be.

First, your lifestyle changes may start to interrupt a long-held family pattern. Second, your personal changes may trigger a power struggle within the family. As you get stronger and feel better about yourself, you may start to take a stand on issues that you used to ignore. Third, other family members may feel that they're under pressure to make the same changes you are: If they choose not to make these changes, they may feel guilty and antagonistic toward you. Last, they may resent that you're spending more time on yourself and less time on them.

It's very important to be aware of family issues and to realize that they can be difficult to handle. Even if you understand what is happening, it may not be possible to discuss these issues with other family members. When it's reasonable, you can try to minimize the negative effects on the family so that you can maximize their support.

∞ THOUGHT FOR THE DAY ∞

*When family confrontations arise, don't avoid them.
Hold a family meeting with yourself as the mediator;
then air any complaints or issues at hand.*

Tradition is a guide and not a jailer.
W. SOMERSET MAUGHAM

Certain celebrations always involve food. Holiday parties, bar mitzvahs, retirements, weddings and other events can't be avoided. The way to handle these situations is to remind yourself that there are things you can do to deal with these events.

You must prepare yourself ahead of time to avoid spending too much time at the banquet table. If it's an informal party or a family get-together, you can call the host or hostess ahead of time and ask what foods will be served. You shouldn't burden the hostess by requesting special foods but you can plan around her menu. Be open to bringing your own food.

If you're giving the party, you can make choices about shopping, cooking and cleaning up. Make a detailed grocery list, so that if you shop from the list, you'll avoid buying extra trigger foods. While cooking, have a plate of freshly cut vegetables nearby to nibble on. When the party's over, ask family members to clear the table and put away tempting leftovers.

When you take time beforehand to plan how to handle food-related events, it is easier to stay aware of your behavior later. If you start to slip, it's easier to get back to your plan. When you plan and rehearse, you're taking control.

∾ THOUGHT FOR THE DAY ∾

At a party, cut back on calories by choosing only non-alcoholic drinks. Focus on socializing, not eating.

Cheer us when we recover.

EDMUND BURKE

Being temporarily disabled from a broken bone, sprain or the like, can be annoying at best, a source of major depression at worst. Sondra had to have surgery on each wrist to ease the pain and discomfort of carpel tunnel syndrome. Afterwards, she was surprised to find that even everyday activities like bathing or preparing meals or doing the laundry became major projects that tired her out. "It took longer to recover than I'd originally thought," she says, "but I certainly learned how to plan ahead and do my chores in one pass around the house." In order to minimize lifting, she carried things with her in a carpenter's apron with lots of pockets. When she left the house, she used her son's backpack.

If you're expecting a lengthy rehab period, you may want to invest in useful gadgets from a medical supply catalog. Reachers, jar openers, plates and bowls for one-handed eating and holders to keep your book open can make your recovery much more pleasant. You'll feel better sooner if you can do things for yourself. Special benches for a tub or shower and handrails to help you step into the tub will make it easier to bathe. More expensive items such a wheelchair can be rented while you need them. If you know in advance that you will be laid up, it's also a good idea to plan ahead financially. You'll want the security of knowing you have money put aside to cover this time of reduced income.

No one wants to be disabled, even if it's only temporary. But if you plan ahead a bit, you can continue to be independent with a recovery that is pleasant and textbook smooth, easy on you and those around you.

⚭ THOUGHT FOR THE DAY ⚭

Healing time is also a time for contemplation. Think about your future and what changes you might like to bring about for yourself.

*I have been devoured all my life by an incurable and
burning impatience and to this day find all oratory, bio-
graphy, operas, films, plays, books, and persons, too long.*

MARGOT ASQUITH

When you're under pressure, it's common to have little or no
patience. You want everything solved right now, this instant,
immediately. You're hurried and harried and hate to wait.
You're looking for instant gratification. You watch television
and see that personal problems are solved in an hour or less.
You are uncomfortable with your feelings so you have a drink,
eat a piece of chocolate cake, pop a tranquilizer or smoke a cigarette to keep those feelings at bay.

Sometimes you need to remind yourself that instant gratification simply isn't possible. You are going to have to wait in
line at the grocery store so you might as well do it cheerfully.
You will have to cool your heels in the doctor's office so you
can bring a book to read or use that time to close your eyes and
meditate.

You may have to learn to delay spending money too. You
might not be able to afford what you want at the moment but
you can put a jar on your refrigerator and give it a label—new
sofa, new dress or vacation, for example. If you start putting
your loose change and extra cash in the jar, you'll be surprised
how quickly the money adds up. You'll also find that planning
and saving is an enjoyable part of the whole process.

You need to remember that life has its ups and downs so
you must learn to tolerate some discomfort. And learning to
tolerate and handle a setback is what makes you strong.

∞ THOUGHT FOR THE DAY ∞

*Learn to endure waiting. Read a book, write some thank you notes,
listen to your favorite music or to a book on tape.*

APRIL 28

Man is the only animal that can be bored.

ERICH FROMM

You may have certain foods that you eat daily, such as coffee and oatmeal for breakfast, soup and sandwich for lunch. When you repeat the same general pattern, you establish a routine that makes your planning easier. You may even be able to buy certain foods in large quantities to save money.

If you're not careful, however, you can become bored eating the same foods every day. If you no longer feel a contentment after a meal, it's probably time for a change. Try to become aware of which foods are no longer satisfying to your tastebuds; then target those foods for change.

You can switch from hot cereal to cold muffins, make your sandwich on a different kind of bread, try drinking juice instead of soda, add an exotic fruit to your salad and experiment with ethnic cuisines like Indian or Middle Eastern. Cookbooks are a rich source of information and fresh ideas. You can easily find tasty substitutes that will be about the same amount of calories as what you're presently eating.

∞ THOUGHT FOR THE DAY ∞

If you are on a weight loss program, reevaluate your menu plans. Make a concerted effort to include at least three new items in your week's food.

APRIL 29

[Old Mr. Turveydrop] was not like anything in the world but a model of Deportment.

CHARLES DICKENS

It is worthwhile to determine your individual eating patterns; the best way is to keep a food diary. You merely write down everything you eat for a week, noting the time of day and whether it's a meal or a snack.

Once you determine your pattern, evaluate it, asking yourself if it's right for you. One eating pattern is no better than another; the only important thing is whether or not it works for you. If it works, then you will feel that you have some control; your hunger will be minimized and your satisfaction will be maximized. You'll be happy with what you eat and how much you are eating. If you find that you get too hungry, then binge, your pattern needs to be improved. You can change the time that you eat, making sure that you eat before you get too tired or hungry.

Writing down your meals and snacks will reveal your personal eating style. Do you like a big meal in the middle of the day or a big meal for supper? Is your style three good-sized meals and a couple of snacks or several little meals throughout the day? Whatever works for you is fine. You merely need to know what it is; then set up a daily food plan that accommodates your eating patterns and styles.

∾ THOUGHT FOR THE DAY ∾

If you normally skip breakfast, you may want to rethink this behavior. Research shows that eating a good breakfast can jump-start your energy and metabolism levels. In fact, research shows that people who eat breakfast burn more calories throughout the day than breakfast skippers.

The body is a sacred garment.

MARTHA GRAHAM

When you are stressed, your body tightens up. After a long period, however, you may accept this body tension as normal. One way to counteract this tension is to do a body scan. This is a relaxation technique that will give you a heightened awareness of the difference between tense and relaxed.

Begin by stretching out on a bed or get comfortable in an easy chair. Close your eyes and take some slow deep breaths to get settled and quiet. Then as you slowly inhale, tighten the muscles in your toes. Now exhale slowly but relax those same muscles. Do the same thing with your feet and ankles. Inhale and tense; exhale and release. Continue your body scan, slowly working toward your head and scalp. When you are finished, let your body remain relaxed and still for as long as you like.

Practice this technique at least once a day. Most people find that after several weeks, they are able to relax more easily than at first. More importantly, they become aware of carrying excess tension in their muscles, tension that they used to ignore or take for granted. Let yourself discover the pleasure of relaxation. Your body will tell you right away how much better it feels.

∞ THOUGHT FOR THE DAY ∞

Try a body scan when you get in bed for the night. It's a good technique to help you fall asleep.

*You don't get ulcers from what you eat. You get them
from what's eating you.*

VICKI BAUM

Stress affects you more than just emotionally; it affects your
body. You feel tight, tense and stiff when you're under stress
because it causes you to hold tension in your muscles. Thus, it
is important to learn how to relax. Two good ways of relaxing
are deep breathing and visualizing, which can help slow down
stress-induced body processes so you can regain control.

Begin by sitting in a comfortable position. Inhale slowly and
deeply through your nose, keeping your mouth closed. Imagine
that you are trying to inflate a balloon in your stomach as you
inhale. Push the air all the way down into the diaphragm and
feel the balloon expand. Now contract the diaphragm and
image the balloon collapsing as you exhale very slowly. You
may find it helpful to exhale more slowly than you inhaled.

As you inhale, imagine that you are drawing tension into your
lungs. As you exhale, imagine that this tension is flowing out of
your body. Try this deep breathing for several more minutes.

Now, add visualization to this breathing process. Picture
whatever is peaceful and relaxing for you. You may be sunning
on a beach, sitting by a campfire, taking a hike or having a
massage. Try to picture this relaxation scene in great detail.
Smell the air around you, hear the sound of the ocean, smell
the pine in the forest, gaze at the color of the sky and take in
the scent of the flowers that are on the path near your feet.

This place that you are visualizing is a safe place for you.
Let your mind return to it whenever you need to go there.

∞ THOUGHT FOR THE DAY ∞

*Visualize a different scene each time you do this exercise.
When you find one that is especially relaxing and
comforting, return to it as often as you like.*

MAY 2

*Communication is the largest single factor determining
what kinds of relationships he makes with others and
what happens to him in the world about him.*

VIRGINIA SATIR

Learning to speak up for yourself takes some practice but it's
particularly important if you are on a weight loss program. It
can be hard at times to ask for the food that you want and it
can be even harder to turn down food that you know is not
good for you. You may also have to ask for time to exercise or
to go to a support meeting. Or perhaps another person's
behavior is affecting you. Whether the effect is positive or negative, you may want to talk to that person about his or her
behavior. You will want to send them a message in three parts.

First, you should describe the person's behavior in a non-
judgmental way. For example, "When you ask me if I'm eating
something that's off my diet . . ." or "When you tell me how
good I look . . ."

Second, you should describe how the other's behavior
makes you feel, keeping in mind that your feelings aren't right
or wrong. For example, "When you ask me if I'm eating something that's off my diet, I feel angry . . ." or "When you tell me
how good I look, I feel encouraged to stay on my diet . . ."

Last, you should describe how that other persons' behavior
affects you. For example "When you ask me if I'm eating something that's off my diet, I feel angry because I want to be
accountable only to myself." Or, "When you tell me how good
I look, I feel encouraged to stay on my diet because I know my
weight loss is starting to show."

∾ THOUGHT FOR THE DAY ∾

*Remember that all it takes to have your needs met is
simply to ask for what you want. Most friends and family
members will be willing to respect your wishes, particularly
if you ask in a way that is not judgmental of their behavior.*

Sense of injured merit.

JOHN MILTON

When you feel that you are undeserving, it is very difficult to make changes in your life. You pass up opportunities for growth and change because you feel you're not entitled to good things in your life. This attitude undermines your efforts to bring about changes.

One way you do this is to put other people's needs ahead of your own. You won't do anything for yourself because it might interfere with someone else's activities. A friend invites you to go together to a weight loss program but you turn down the invitation because that one evening out will disrupt your family life. You feel that time spent on yourself is time that should be spent on someone else.

You need to work on changing your attitude so that you can feel that you deserve more and that you deserve to change. One way is to find a role model. Think of someone you admire who handles situations well; then put yourself in that person's mind. Think about how your role model would act; then try and act that way yourself. How would your role model ask for a raise? Behave at a party? Say no to that extra drink or gooey dessert? When you try to imitate a person you admire, someone who is worthy of your admiration, you will soon begin to become more like that person.

Today, tell yourself that you deserve to be healthier, that you deserve to make changes that will make you feel better about yourself. And because you deserve good things, you will let them happen to you. You will take as good care of yourself as you do of everybody else.

∞ THOUGHT FOR THE DAY ∞

Think of something simple and pleasant that you can do for yourself—have coffee with a friend, go to a movie, take a walk in the park—then do it today.

Seeing's believing, but feeling's the truth.

THOMAS FULLER

When you are stressed, you unconsciously tense your muscles. The tension may be subtle but it's there nonetheless. After a while, your body begins to ache. You have a hard time sitting still; you move and shift about because your back aches, your shoulders are hunched and sore, your neck feels stiff. You need a massage.

When your muscles contract, so do your blood vessels. Your circulation slows and waste products start to collect in your circulatory system and muscle tissue. Massage helps dilate your blood vessels and improve your circulation. It stimulates your lymph glands and improves your body's ability to eliminate waste and debris. When your circulation is stimulated, then there will be more nutrition for your muscle tissues. When there is a better interchange of substances between the blood and tissue cells, you'll have more energy and less ache.

If you suffer from a chronic muscle tightness or other problem, perhaps from stress or an old injury, you might want to investigate the therapeutic benefits of massage. You'll be pleasantly surprised at how much better you'll feel afterwards.

∾ THOUGHT FOR THE DAY ∾

Many athletes schedule regular massages to help their muscles recover after a hard workout or competition. But you needn't be a competitor to reap the benefits of massage. All you have to do is make an appointment.

Yes I have a pair of eyes . . . but bein'
only eyes, you see, my vision's limited.

CHARLES DICKENS

When you look at the world around you, you sometimes have selective vision. We focus on one aspect and ignore the rest. When you're stressed, it's easy to focus on the negative. Melissa recalls that in response to a compliment about her weight loss, she replied, "Oh! I still have 20 pounds to lose," forgetting for a moment that she had already taken off a monumental 60 pounds. If you have felt bad about your excess weight and have carried it for a long time, you may find it difficult to accept the fact that you really have lost weight.

Selective vision might also cause you to set down too many rules that have to do with the way you "must" behave and the way those around you "should" behave. These rules create anger, guilt and resentment in everyone, even yourself. When you're trying to lose weight, you may prefer that friends and family don't offer you a snack when they're having one. But being offered a cookie is fine. It doesn't matter what the rest of the world does; what matters is what you do. The person offering the snack is being polite. It's not up to them to read your mind and know that you would prefer that they not offer it. It's up to you to refuse it.

Remember that no one is perfect. Instead of saying, "I was bad" or "I am terrible," you should say, "Next time I will do better." There are plenty of big things in your life; try and let go of the small things. It's easier when you can give yourself a break, shrug off small setbacks and get on with your life.

∾ **THOUGHT FOR THE DAY** ∾

Remember to reward yourself for small achievements.
If you withhold rewards until you have accomplished
your goals, you're being unfair to yourself.

MAY 6

Gluttony is an emotional escape,
a sign something is eating you.

PETER DE VRIES

When you're stressed, you may turn to food to give you solace, to help you cope with a situation or person that is difficult for you to handle. When you use food in this way, you are eating to satisfy your emotional hunger. You should eat only to satisfy your physical hunger, which is easy to recognize. Physical hunger is when your stomach is growling or when you feel a little light-headed or slightly nauseous because you haven't had food for several hours. Emotional hunger, however, has nothing to do with the bodily needs; it's when our psyche is in need of nourishment.

Everyone has many habits associated with food. The telephone rings, so you might reach for a cookie while you talk to a friend. Or you might be annoyed about the constant yapping of a neighbor's dog but you don't want a confrontation so you stuff down your anger with a piece of pie.

Most of the time when you use food inappropriately, you are using food to deny your feelings, numb an emotional hurt or soothe yourself. Sometimes the intensity of your feelings, such as unbearable sadness or overwhelming anger, is hard to accept. The goal is to learn how to manage your feelings without using food.

∾ THOUGHT FOR THE DAY ∾

The next time you put food in your mouth, ask yourself if your body really needs nourishment. If you're not sure whether you're hungry or not, wait 20 or 30 minutes. If your body needs food, the physical signs will get stronger. If it's your mind that's reaching out for food, the physical signs will get weaker. And you'll know you need to take care of your heart and soul.

Every why hath a wherefore.
WILLIAM SHAKESPEARE

Everything you do has a consequence, so it's worthwhile to think about what happens when you behave, think or talk in a certain way. The reason you should think about consequences is that they may not be what you have been telling yourself they are. Once you see what is really happening, you may find it easier to change your own behavior.

For example, if you overeat, you need to ask yourself if there's a payoff. If the payoff is that you're going to escape unpleasant feelings caused by another, you need to think about the consequences more realistically. You need to think about what overeating does—whether it gets rid of those feelings forever or merely numbs the unpleasant feelings temporarily. You need to also think about the consequences of your behavior on others. If you behave in a certain way, will the other person change? Probably not.

You need to remind yourself that your own behavior is more likely to influence yourself than anybody else. So you should take a fresh look at what is happening when you overeat or give into someone else's desires. Then you can focus on what you want. You can ask yourself if your old behavior has lead you any closer to your goals, if it is working in a positive way for you. If not, then perhaps you should think about some new behaviors. If the same old thing isn't working, it's time to let go of the old and try something new.

∞ THOUGHT FOR THE DAY ∞

*Just because you don't look or feel a certain way,
doesn't mean that something is wrong. What's wrong
may be the way you expect to look or feel.*

MAY 8

Healing is a matter of time, but it is sometimes also a matter of opportunity.

HIPPOCRATES

Touch can be healing. The simple act of quietly and softly placing your hands on another tends to soothe that person. You are likely to reach out for a friend's hand when that friend is in physical or emotional pain. When a parent picks up a fussy child, the parent can often calm the child by gently rubbing the back or stroking the head and hair.

A person trained in massage can also be a healer. Tracy, a massage therapist, feels that when she is working on someone's muscles, she is also opening up emotional connections as well. "It's not unusual for someone to shed a few tears during a massage," she explains, "especially when that person's muscle tension is a result of emotional stress." Sometimes your muscle tension can act like a wall, keeping your emotions at bay for a while so you can get through the crisis with a clear and rational mind. But you need to remember to release this tension and your emotions at some point so that you can truly be done with the crisis and get on with your life.

Remember that there are different kinds of healing touch. Massage can be invigorating or relaxing, it can be soothing to help you heal after an injury or it can be more intense for deep muscle tissues. A good therapist will be trained in several methods and can help you decide what will be best for you at this time.

∞ THOUGHT FOR THE DAY ∞

A gift certificate for a massage is a wonderful gift to give to a friend or loved one—or to yourself.

Change is not made without inconvenience,
even from worse to better.

RICHARD HOOKER

When a change is recent, you may look fondly back to the past and wonder if you've done the right thing. You may find it easier to focus on what you have given up rather than what you have gained. In a weight loss program, you may put more energy into thinking about the piece of chocolate cake you passed up instead of the smaller dress size you now fit into. You may have ended an abusive relationship, yet fondly recall only those rare good moments you once had together, forgetting that what you've gained is a sense of peace, safety and self-esteem. You may have changed or improved your work situation, yet you focus on all the friends you left behind rather than the stimulation of working on new projects and making new friends.

Change can be scary. In order to have new and better environments in your life, you have to leave behind or give up certain things. You can't have the chocolate cake and the new dress size. You may need to grieve your losses but you shouldn't torture yourself with them. You should move on, focus on what you have now and what you intend to gain by making these changes.

Congratulate yourself for having done the hardest part—making the decision to change. Take a moment to remember the feelings that motivated you to make this change. There was a reason you made this change—a good reason. Try to remember it.

∞ THOUGHT FOR THE DAY ∞

Look around with gratitude and see how much you
have right now—a roof over your head, the sun in the sky,
good friends whose company you enjoy.

MAY 10

You can be pleased with nothing when you are not pleased with yourself.

LADY MARY WORTLEY MONTAGUE

Whenever you try something new, you want to excel and succeed. One of the things that determines whether you succeed or fail is your motivation and simply believing that you can do what you set out to do. Believe that you can be successful. If you don't expect success or you're not sure about your abilities, then you've just reduced your chances of being successful.

Ask yourself if you have any negative beliefs about yourself, such as "I'm not smart enough to do this" or "The last time I tried this, it didn't work." You might also be giving yourself self-destructive messages like "I don't really deserve this success" or "I always give in to my relatives." You need to be careful that your past doesn't determine your future. You should give yourself permission to try again, to make some changes, to work toward success and achieving your goal.

Make a list of the changes that you've already made. Every little change itself is a success, even the minor changes. Instead of looking at how far you have to go, take a look at the progress you've made so far. Be proud of every single accomplishment you have made. Acknowledge your progress to yourself. Share your pride with your friends. Perhaps many of them are on the same path as well.

∾ THOUGHT FOR THE DAY ∾

Support groups are good because you'll be with others who understand and appreciate the importance of small steps. Sharing successes reinforces the idea that you can be successful too.

MAY 11

*There's nothing on earth to do here but look
at the view and eat. You can imagine the result
since I do not like to look at views.*

ZELDA FITZGERALD

When you're on a weight loss program, holidays and vacations
can be a big challenge. Losing weight takes time and energy and
it can be hard to stay on track when you're on the road. If you're
not careful, you'll gain weight and lose your motivation. But
even during challenging times, you still have choices. You can
continue to lose, you can maintain your current weight or you
can ignore the issue altogether and accept the consequences.

Rather than gain weight unconsciously, you need to make a
decision. If you're willing to gain weight, that's okay. But if
you've been doing well and would prefer to maintain your current weight, you need to do some planning.

Losing weight and keeping it off really means making a
lifestyle change, so holidays and vacations are opportunities for
you to learn and practice new eating and lifestyle habits.
Remind yourself that there are fun things to do that don't
involve food. There are many ways to celebrate that will bring
good feelings without eating. In order to stick to your decision,
decide what steps you can take to help yourself. If you belong
to a national support group, you may decide to attend meetings
while you're out-of-town. If you're on vacation and off your
food plan, decide what day you plan to resume your weight loss
efforts. Remember that holidays and vacations are supposed to
be fun. So have a good time, confident in your ability to handle
the challenge of healthy holiday eating.

THOUGHT FOR THE DAY

*Bring healthy snacks like individual packets of pretzels or low-fat fig
bars with you when you travel by car so you're not at the mercy of
hotels and roadside restaurants.*

> *The sign of an intelligent people is their ability to control emotions by the application of reason.*
>
> MARYA MANNES

If you have a hectic life, you may have forgotten how to relax. You feel burdened by your responsibilities and are anxious that you can't quite keep up. Renee knew she needed to relax but she found it nearly impossible to do. Then she tried biofeedback using galvanic skin resistance (GSR). "Biofeedback appealed to my rational side," she says. "The GSR machine gave me a way to measure my stress and it also helped me know when I was making progress at relaxing."

GSR measures very subtle variations in your skin that are controlled by your sympathetic nervous system. Measuring your GSR can help make you aware of the internal state of your mind and body. A GSR device is about the size of a computer mouse and fits under your hand in much the same way. Two fingers are held lightly onto the finger plates with elastic or Velcro. Some GSR devices emit a high tone; as you relax, the tone will decrease. Most GSR devices can also be attached to a small monitor with a needle drops that drops as you relax.

Biofeedback is useful for many people. Learning to let go of tension means you have to become aware of subtle changes in your body. Biofeedback gives you immediate feedback so you can learn to recognize and achieve the results you want. Try it today. Relaxing might be easier than you think.

∞ THOUGHT FOR THE DAY ∞

Although GSR machines are relatively inexpensive, you might want to try one a few times before buying one. Ask your doctor or contact a stress reduction clinic in your area.

MAY 13

Failing to plan is a plan to fail.

EFFIE JONES

When you're setting goals, it's important to make them measurable so you have a way to tell whether or not you're on the right track. If your goal includes "how much" or "how often," then it's a measurable goal. If you're not sure what you can reasonably accomplish, then keep records for a week or so to find out where you are right now. Then set goals that are attainable for you.

Jocelyn likes to walk. She says her original goal was to walk regularly. "I was walking practically every day, but I never felt like I had achieved much. Then my friend suggested I set up walking goals that could be quantified. So I started tracking my distance." Her first goal was to walk ten miles in five days. "I accomplished that goal within two weeks so I was quite proud of myself." Recently she completed a 20-mile walk-a-thon to raise money for lung diseases. "I think it was possible because I kept setting distance goals that were within my reach. I just didn't realize I could reach that far."

Remember that you can measure behaviors other than exercise. You can measure how many times you raise your voice in anger, how often you say I love you to your spouse or significant other, how many minutes it takes to get ready for work in the morning.

∞ THOUGHT FOR THE DAY ∞

Your goal may be measurable but still too big. If you feel overwhelmed, break one big goal into several smaller goals.

It is easy to be beautiful; it is difficult to appear so.
FRANK O'HARA

No one has a perfect body but age and stress can contribute to poor posture. If you've lived a sedentary lifestyle, you may be slumped over, carrying yourself stiffly. Take a look in the mirror today. Your posture is a message from your body that it's time to get in shape.

Start with your head and work down. Pull your head back so it sits on top of your neck; if your posture is poor, your head is probably leaning forward. This will strain your upper back and neck. When your neck is straight, your ears will be in line with your shoulders and your chin will be level with the ground, not pointing up, down or forward.

Look at your shoulders and back. If your shoulders are hunched, you need to straighten your spine in order to take the strain off your upper and lower back. Your pelvic region should be tilted forward slightly. If your back is swayed, your abdominal muscles are weak and/or your lower back muscles are too tight. You may also be carrying extra weight on your tummy. Look at your legs and ankles. If your legs are straight, your knees will be directly over your toes. Your ankles should neither turn in nor turn out.

Remember that the better your posture, the less likely you are to injure yourself when doing work or any physical activity. As you start to exercise, your posture and body alignment will improve on its own. But it's okay to check the mirror occasionally to make sure you're standing straight and tall.

∞ THOUGHT FOR THE DAY ∞

One way to tell if you've been walking with rounded shoulders is that this posture tends to become exaggerated when you're climbing stairs.

MAY 15

To cure the mind's wrong bias . . .
Some recommend the bowling-green;
Some, hilly walks; all exercise.

MATTHEW GREEN

There are many health benefits to exercise. You tone your muscles and perhaps lose a few pounds. Another benefit is that exercise helps make your cardiovascular system stronger. While you're working your heart, you're also working other muscles so that the whole body develops endurance and becomes more efficient. As your body get stronger, you see more benefits. The stronger your abdominal muscles become, for example, the less pain you feel in your lower back.

Other health benefits of exercise are related to the psyche. You look better, your posture improves, you feel slimmer and trimmer. Exercise gives you more self-confidence. The more control you gain over your body, the more you feel it's time to get some control back into your life and reduce some of your stress. Your physical workouts help reduce the emotional and physical tensions that are associated with stress. You find it easier to relax so you don't turn to alcohol or cigarettes or food. Your overall level of anxiety decreases and bouts of the blues disappear.

Remember that cardiovascular endurance makes the rigors of everyday life seem easier and less strenuous. You can reach and bend because you are more flexible. You have more strength and endurance so the daily chores become easier. Take time today to take care of yourself by setting aside some time for a brisk walk or a workout at the gym.

∞ THOUGHT FOR THE DAY ∞

Exercise reduces your risk for developing many chronic diseases. Even a small increase in physical activity makes a big difference in your overall health, particularly when it comes to heart disease, high blood pressure, osteoporosis, some cancers and diabetes.

MAY 16

*The great difference between sport and art is that sport,
like a sonnet, forces beauty within its own system.*

RITA MAE BROWN

Swimming has a lot to recommend it besides being good exercise. It is a solitary activity and gives the swimmer's mind a rest while exercising. When you're stressed, it may take you a while —several laps or more —before you can settle into a comfortable easy rhythm.

Begin by concentrating on your breathing. Watch and listen to the bubbles you make when you exhale; listen to the quick sound of each inhale. Concentrate on a slow steady stroke until your breathing becomes rhythmic.

Pay attention to the temperature of the water. Are there warm and cold currents in different areas of the lake or pool? Think about how smooth the water feels on your arms and legs as you move through the water. Let the water soothe and caress your skin.

Try swimming a few laps today. You needn't be a competitive swimmer. Use your favorite and most comfortable stroke —perhaps your side stroke or back stroke —to propel you from one end of the pool to the other. You'll emerge refreshed in both body and spirit.

∾ THOUGHT FOR THE DAY ∾

*Swim for as long as you comfortably can. If you can
swim steadily for twenty to thirty minutes, you'll get a
workout that is both aerobic and relaxing.*

*No man is lonely while eating spaghetti; it requires
so much attention.*

CHRISTOPHER MORLEY

The old adage that carbohydrates and starchy foods make you
fat simply isn't true. It is not the carbohydrates that are the
source of calories but the fat that you add. It's the sour cream
on the baked potato, the butter on the vegetables, the rich
cream sauce on the pasta.

Here are some examples of how fat can ruin a perfectly
good carbohydrate. A 3 ounce plain baked potato is only 79
calories, but a big dollop of butter and sour cream more than
doubles the calories (now 178). A 1 ounce bagel is only 84
calories, but when a tablespoon of cream cheese is spread on
top, you've added 50 more calories. A cup of pasta, which has
very little fat, is only 190 calories. You can add a ½ cup of simple spaghetti sauce for only 35 calories but a rich white sauce
will add another 250 calories, bringing the total for pasta with
alfredo sauce up to a whopping 440 calories.

Remember that about half of your calories each day should
come from complex carbohydrates. These foods are your main
energy source because these are the foods that your body most
efficiently and most easily breaks down into glucose. Just
leave off the fat.

∾ THOUGHT FOR THE DAY ∾

*Complex carbohydrates like legumes, breads, grains, rice and pasta
are filling, lower in fat and often less costly than meat, poultry or fish.*

MAY 18

*Alcohol is an allergy of the body
and an obsession of the mind.*

RITA MAE BROWN

When you are stressed, you tend to do everything to excess. There is an over-the-top mentality to what you consume and how you behave. You eat too much, you smoke too much, you're angry too often, you cry too easily. It is especially important when you are under pressure to be aware of how much alcohol you drink because alcohol abuse and stress go hand in hand. After a hard day, for example, you decide to have a drink to relax. But because you're stressed, it takes several drinks. Before you realize it, your reflexes have slowed and your judgment is impaired. You're at risk for any number of accidents —from cutting your hand in the kitchen to driving your car into a ditch, or worse, hitting another car.

Excessive alcohol consumption also puts you as risk for some major diseases, including chronic liver disease, some neurological disorders, birth defects and certain throat and neck cancers. At the very least, alcohol adds unnecessary calories. An ounce and a half of hard liquor, such as gin or whiskey, has approximately 120 calories; a 12-ounce glass of beer averages 150 calories; a glass of white wine is about 90 calories. But don't be sidetracked by calories. Remember that a stein of beer, a glass of wine and a tall shot of whisky contain the same amount of alcohol. If you're going to use alcohol, make sure you do so in moderation.

∽ THOUGHT FOR THE DAY ∾

*If you suspect a loved one, or even yourself, is developing a problem
with alcohol, seek help. It's not healthy to allow your own or someone
else's substance abuse to add another layer of stress to your life.*

MAY 19

*We are under-exercised as a nation.
We look instead of play. We ride instead of walk.
Our existence deprives us of the minimum of
physical activity essential for healthy living.*

JOHN F. KENNEDY

If you're trying to decide what kind of exercise might be best, there's some good news—any exercise is great. To get the most out of your workout, you need to exercise at a moderate intensity. If you're breathing hard and fast, your intensity may be too high. If your breathing is quiet, you probably need to work a little harder. When you're working moderately, you'll be breathing through your mouth. You should be able to converse with a friend although you probably will be breathing too hard to sing a song. And you should perspire: after about 10 minutes of moderate exercise, you'll begin to sweat.

As long as you're exercising, you might as well burn fat. Choose activities that use large muscle groups like your leg muscles. Starting and stopping is okay but a steady and continuous exercise of those muscles will help you burn the most calories. Good fat-burning exercises are walking, riding a bicycle, dancing and swimming. Or use fitness equipment like an exercise bike, treadmill, or rowing machine.

To prevent injury you need to strengthen your muscles and improve your flexibility. Start exercising with a light intensity so you have a chance to warm up those muscles. When you're about done, slow down rather than suddenly stop. When you're finished exercising, your muscles will be nice and warm so take another few minutes and stretch out those muscles.

THOUGHT FOR THE DAY

Studies show that your own perception of how hard you're exercising is usually right on target. If you think your intensity level is too high or too low, it is. You live in your body. Trust what you know and feel.

*Whoever wants to know the heart and mind of America
had better learn baseball.*

JACQUES BARZUN

"Playing catch with Tony was the most fun I've had in a long time," says Robin, telling about a recent visit with her nephew. "While we were tossing the ball back and forth, he told me about school and how dumb all the teachers were and how cute his girlfriend was and how he kept a certain bully away from his younger brother. He talked and I listened and learned."

Like most kids, you probably played a little baseball or softball—in school, or on a neighborhood plot of dirt or in a more formal organization like Little League. You may not want to throw yourself around the bases anymore but you can still play catch. Ask a junior high or high school player to give you some pointers on your form so you don't hurt your arm and shoulder. Start out by throwing lightly and easily to your partner. With a little practice, you'll soon be throwing the ball farther and harder and faster.

Playing catch was fun when you were kids and it's still fun. Dig out that old ball and glove from the back of the closet and call a friend to come out and play.

∞ **THOUGHT FOR THE DAY** ∞

If you don't have a glove, use a softball. It's bigger and easier to use so you may like it better if you haven't played for a long time.

A mighty maze! but not without a plan.

ALEXANDER POPE

When you're working to improve the kind of choices you make about food, plan ahead by writing down what you are going to eat for the day. By planning ahead you stay focused on your goal. Planning helps you make a commitment that you are more likely to stick to that day. When you write everything down, there is less denial and unconscious eating. You become aware of what you are putting into your mouth.

Make a chart for yourself; then use it to plan and track the foods you eat. Plan ahead by writing down all your meals in advance. After each meal, check off servings from each of the four food groups—4-6 servings of bread or grains, at least 5 servings of fruits and vegetables, 5 servings of protein, 2 servings of milk or dairy products, 3 servings of fat. You could also record calories, fat grams and fiber grams. This helps insure that you eat enough of the proper foods throughout the day.

Make a commitment today to writing down what you eat. It's a good way to help you feel in control and in charge.

THOUGHT FOR THE DAY

Make a list of alternative foods to eat when you're on the go and keep it in your wallet.

MAY 22

*His body's taken on the weight his mind still
refuses to accept.*

TONI CADE BAMBARA

Nearly one-third of all Americans carry too much weight. If
you're one of them, this means you are increasing your risk for
heart disease, certain kinds of cancer and diabetes. In one
study of over 115,000 women, those who weighed the most
were four times more likely to have some sort of cardiovascular disease and twice as likely to suffer from cancer. One of the
surprising things that came out of this study was that women
who are only moderately overweight also had an increased risk
of major illness and premature death. If you're over 18 years
old, even a twenty-pound weight gain can increase your risk.

There are several excuses as to why some are overweight.
One of the more popular ones is that there is a genetic cause.
Although there is some evidence to show that some people are
predisposed to carry more fat than others, it's not your genes
that cause you to be overweight—it's your lifestyle. You don't
exercise very often, if at all. You chow down on foods that pack
a big punch in fat and sugar but deliver little nutrition or fiber.
In short, you take in more calories than you burn up in energy.

Think today about the choices that you've been making
about food and exercise. Resolve to start choosing foods that
are nutritious. Remember that when you eat right, you are
doing more than making a choice to lose weight. You are
choosing to live longer and in better health.

∾ THOUGHT FOR THE DAY ∾

*Open your cupboard and look inside with a stern eye.
Get rid of those candy bars and chips. You can still eat
a lot of food but now it's going to be the right foods.*

MAY 23

*To talk easily with people, you must firmly
believe that either you or they are interesting.
And even then it's not easy.*

MIGNON McLAUGHLIN

Many people know neighbors or coworkers who like to drop
by and socialize. The problem is that they sometimes stay too
long. Alison solved a problem with a talkative neighbor by
always keeping the front door closed so that her neighbor
would have to knock. Then Alison would step outside on the
front porch and talk to her there. "As long as I didn't invite her
in, it was easier to control the amount of time we visited. After
five or ten minutes, I would say I had to get back to work,
thank her for stopping by, then excuse myself and go inside."

You may have a problem when coworkers come to your
work station with a legitimate business discussion but then
stay to socialize. If a meeting is necessary, suggest that it take
place in someone else's office rather than your own. It's easier
to leave than it is to get someone out. Another way to shorten
a social conversation is simply to stand up and ease this person
toward the door. If necessary, have an excuse to leave your
office until your coworker moves on. Doug likes to listen to
music while he works but rather than distract his coworkers,
he uses a headset. He discovered that when he had the headset
on, fellow workers were less likely to interrupt him unless it
was essential to the business at hand. As a result he keeps his
headset on most of the day, even if the music is off, and especially when he has a deadline to meet.

THOUGHT FOR THE DAY

*If family members tend to interrupt you while you are working, set
aside time for them before or after your project. Just make sure that
you honor that time by refusing phone calls so that family members
have your undivided attention.*

MAY 24

Those whom we support hold us up in life.

MARIE VON EBNER-ESCHENBACH

A study by Dr. David Spiegel showed that women with breast cancer who were members of a support group lived longer and reported less pain than those who did not join a support group. In the caring atmosphere of these groups, the women learned and shared skills for dealing with all aspects of their illness. By sharing common experiences and emotions, they felt less isolated and more in control of their lives. In spite of a difficult disease, they could learn more about the treatment options available and learn how to gain control in other parts of their lives, in their relationships with friends and loved ones.

Scott's stroke left him physically handicapped. But in his support group, he met others with similar problems. He learned that in spite of his disabilities, he still had choices in how he lived. At the urging of friends in his support group, he decided to regain some independence. Although he could no longer drive a car, he bought a battery-operated cart so that he could leave his house, visit neighbors and shop at nearby stores by himself.

If you or a loved one is suffering from a chronic illness, consider joining a support group to meet others who are dealing with the same issues you are. Your choices may be different now but you can still choose how you live and how you relate to friends and family members.

∞ THOUGHT FOR THE DAY ∞

Remember that there are support groups for just about every situation imaginable but the goal is the same: to share a common interest, meet new friends and learn to accept and enjoy the challenges that life brings you.

Money can be translated into the beauty of living, a support in misfortune, an education or future security. It also can be translated into a source of bitterness.

SYLVIA PORTER

Shopping today has become too easy. In fact, shopping has turned into a form of recreation. Catalogs with beautiful pictures arrive in the mail. There are cable networks devoted entirely to shopping where models and actors display, demonstrate and sell products that you can order by phone. No matter where you live, a mall with many stores is within driving distance.

More than recreation, shopping can become a way to comfort and nurture yourself. If you shop a lot, perhaps you should take a look at why. If you have a closet full of clothes that you don't wear or if your house is full of things that you don't use, you're probably shopping for the wrong reasons. If you're in debt because of your buying habits, you're definitely shopping for the wrong reasons.

Ask yourself what shopping does for you. Perhaps it gives you a feeling of contentment or a rush. Problem shoppers say it's not what they buy that is important. It's the act of buying that fulfills them, at least for the moment. This kind of fulfillment invites problems, not the least of which is debt. If you are in debt, then resolve today to search for other ways to fulfill yourself. Invite a friend over, go to a movie, visit a museum, stroll through a botanical garden. If certain items are irresistible, then learn to make them. You'll find that the act and process of making something is infinitely more satisfying than the act of purchasing it.

THOUGHT FOR THE DAY

One way to curb your impulse buying is to write out a shopping list before you leave home. If those earrings or that sweater in the window is not on your list, you can't buy it, no matter how low the price.

*The greatest thing in the world is
to know how to belong to oneself.*

MONTAIGNE

Stress often distracts us. You're so busy attending to other people, other crises, other events in your life that you forget to pay
attention to yourself. When you exercise, however, you are
helping bring the pieces of yourself back together in one place.
You have to leave the rest of the world behind so that you can
concentrate on walking quickly or jogging steadily or not trip-
ping over your own feet in an aerobics class. Exercise helps
you get centered emotionally and physically.

Learn to respect and trust your body and spirit. If your
body is stiff, it's telling you that it needs exercise to limber up.
Then listen to your spirit to decide what is the best way for you
to exercise today. You'll know if you should be looking for others to exercise with, such as joining an aerobics class or meeting a friend on the tennis court. You'll know that on your own
it's going to be hard to stick it out for more than twenty minutes today. Other days, trust yourself to know that you need to
be alone, that a long solitary walk is what you need to exercise
your body and relax your mind at the same time.

Exercise helps put you back in touch with who you are and
whatever environment you're in right now.

∾ THOUGHT FOR THE DAY ∾

*If you travel regularly, be sure to pack a bathing
suit and shorts. Many motels and hotels have
swimming pool and exercise facilities for guests.*

Action is the antidote to despair.

JOAN BAEZ

As you set goals for yourself, you learn that you're more likely to be successful when you set specific, measurable goals that are relevant to your needs and lifestyle. When you are successful, when you meet each goal, it is important that you stop and reward yourself, acknowledging your good work. If you lose ten pounds, for example, you might want to treat yourself to a long distance phone call to an old friend. The reason rewards are important is that you need to remind yourself that you have been successful. You also want to stay motivated so that you can achieve the next step.

Sometimes, however, you fall short. You seem to get close to your goals but never quite grab the brass ring. When this happens, you need to figure out what why. Perhaps you have been listening to someone else's well-intentioned but bad advice. If you have been sabotaging yourself, then you need to address that issue as well.

You might also need to take another look at your goal—perhaps it was relevant last year but your life has changed and that goal is no longer practical for you now. For example, you may have less free time for exercise now because of a new job. So you may need to exercise in the morning instead of mid-afternoon or work out with a new partner or switch from an aerobics class to a treadmill. That doesn't mean you have to let go of your goal; only that you need to find a different route to get there.

THOUGHT FOR THE DAY

You can give yourself more rewards if you set smaller goals that are more easily achieved. Break a larger goal into little steps; then reward yourself at each stage.

*I am beginning to learn that it is the sweet, simple
things of life which are the real ones after all.*
LAURA INGALLS WILDER

Vanessa had a young exchange student from Japan live with
her for several weeks. She took her student to as many well-
known sights as they had time for. One evening they went to
the beach to watch the sunset and she realized the simplest act
can often bring the most pleasure. Vanessa brought along some
soap bubbles, attracting a shy little girl playing nearby. "All we
did was blow bubbles for an hour but the little girl was so
enchanting and the sunset was so beautiful that this was
Reiko's favorite memory of her time with me."

Take the time today to do something simple. Go to a nearby
playground and sit in a swing for awhile. If you're an early
riser, go outside and watch the dawn break. Listen to the
sounds of the world around you awakening and coming to life.
Walk barefoot in new spring grass, carve a sand castle in the
beach, shuffle through a knee-deep pile of autumn leaves or
roll a snowball and build a snowman or dinosaur.

You have a busy life, filled with responsibilities and duties.
The more complicated your days, the more you need balance.
The more you need to celebrate moments of simple pleasure.

∽ THOUGHT FOR THE DAY ∽

*Go for a walk today and bring back a rock, small branch or other
natural object that symbolizes an important aspect of your
personality. Display it artfully in a window.*

*Ask your child what he wants for dinner only
if he's buying.*
FRAN LEBOWITZ

If you are a parent, you are already concerned with giving your children nutritious meals. Start their day off right by making sure that they get a healthy breakfast. Studies show that children who eat a good breakfast do better at school. They feel good so they can concentrate better and their performance improves. Breakfast can be something besides a bowl of sugary cereal. A slice of pizza, a bagel with cream cheese or a peanut butter sandwich are all good breakfasts.

School lunches are more likely to be eaten if your child is involved in making his or her own lunch. Neil sits down with his son and makes a list of possible lunches—sandwiches, fruits, drinks, snacks—and lets his son pick his favorites. Freeze individual jars or boxes of apple juice, grape juice or orange juice. The juice will be thawed by lunch time and will help keep other foods cold until then. If your child likes yogurt, put some fruit, raisins or granola into a plastic sandwich bag to be stirred in at lunch time. Hot lunches can be sent from home too. A wide-mouth thermos is easily filled with soup, chili, stew or pasta.

It's important to teach your children good habits about food. One way to demonstrate good nutrition is to encourage them to choose color and crunch. Different colors of food—white milk, orange carrots, brown bread, green asparagus and yellow chicken, for example—generally indicate foods from different food groups. Crunchy foods like raw fruits and vegetables supply fiber and essential nutrients. Color and crunch is an easy message and kids will remember it.

∞ THOUGHT FOR THE DAY ∞

*Help your children discover new tastes. Peanut butter is just as good
with carrots, celery and apples as it is with jelly.*

The sleep of a labouring man is sweet,
whether he eat little or much; but the abundance
of the rich will not suffer him to sleep.

ECCLESIASTES 5:12

Getting a good night sleep is something that you take for granted, until you're plagued by tossing, turning, waking up too early or going to sleep too late. Although stress interferes with rest, there are some ways to improve the odds of a good-night's sleep.

The best sleeping aid is exercise. The body of a couch potato doesn't move enough to know the difference between activity and rest. If you get your blood pumping this afternoon, you'll rest easier in the middle of the night.

Reduce the amount of stimulants you use, especially caffeine and nicotine. Caffeine can work for as much as six hours after you've ingested it. Switch to decaffeinated coffee, herbal tea and caffeine-free sodas. If you're a smoker, sleep deprivation is another reason to quit.

Avoid depressants, including over-the-counter sleep pills. They may help you get to sleep faster but they generally lose their effectiveness if used over a long period of time. And you can become dependent on them. Alcohol and prescription sleep aids can also prevent you from getting a deep sleep.

Make your bedroom quiet, dark and cool. Turn off the lights, turn down the thermostat and shut out the noise. Use a white noise machine, if you have to sleep during the day or live in a noisy neighborhood.

∞ THOUGHT FOR THE DAY ∞

Sleep apnea is a common disorder where your upper air passages are blocked, causing breathing to stop for a few seconds. Narcolepsy is a disorder in which individuals experience sudden attacks of sleep or paralysis. If you suspect that you suffer from apnea or narcolepsy, make an appointment at a sleep disorder clinic.

MAY 31

*Honest bread is very well—it's the butter
that makes the temptation.*

DOUGLAS JERROLD

Whether it's chocolate, cheese or sugar cookies, many people crave one particular food more than any other. It's the ice cream treat you get up for in the middle of the night, the peanut butter that is your comfort food at the end of a difficult day or the bag of potato chips you use as a reward. Sometimes your craving for one item is the beginning of a binge. In the blink of an eye, you're noshing on everything in sight.

It's time to stand up to the trigger food in your life. It's time to say good-bye and give it up altogether. There are two surprises for those who do this. First, they find they have gained control over other foods. Second, doing it turns out to be easier than thinking about it.

Start by emptying your cabinets. Get rid of all your high-calorie snacks. If it's not in your kitchen, you won't be able to eat it. Stock your shelves with nutritious foods—whole grain breads, fruits and vegetables, pasta and rice. Now put an empty mayonnaise jar on top of your refrigerator. Make it a Dream Jar. Fill it up with the money that you used to spend on your favorite snack and start saving for your dream— perhaps a new car or cruise or your first year's membership fee at a health club. You'll be surprised how much those cravings cost you in money as well as weight.

∽ THOUGHT FOR THE DAY ∽

Eating regular meals helps control food binges. It's easier to say no if you've eaten a nutritious meal in the past few hours.

JUNE 1

*To be able to fill leisure intelligently is
the last product of civilization.*
BERTRAND RUSSELL

Losing a job can seem like the end of the world. You feel lost
and out of control. But while you're job hunting, you can use
your extra time wisely to take better care of yourself and
reconnect with your loved ones.

One of the best things you can do for yourself is to exercise
every day. Exercise helps keep your anxiety and anger at a
manageable level and it's a good treatment for depression without having to use drug therapy. If your old job kept you tied to
a desk for long hours, you may have had a sedentary lifestyle.
Use your time off to restore your fitness.

You also have the opportunity to spend more time with
your loved ones. Now that you're available, pick up the kids at
school. Attend all the extra-curricular activities that working
forced you to miss. Enjoy those after-school track meets and
band concerts. You can share a sunrise, catch up on old movies
and read the novels waiting by your bedside.

Keeping in touch with other people is essential if you hope
to maintain a positive outlook. You may want to become more
active in a church group, volunteer at a hospital, take a class at
the community center or join a support group.

Remember that losing a job doesn't mean that you've lost
everything. You still have friends and loved ones. Your talents,
skills and experience are intact. The cat still likes to sleep on
your lap. Although this is a period of uncertainty, you can use
it as a golden opportunity to rediscover yourself.

THOUGHT FOR THE DAY

*Take advantage of every resource, such as out-placement services and
computer networks, when you're researching job information.
Remember that the library has a wealth of information—and it's free.*

Words pay no debts.

WILLIAM SHAKESPEARE

When your next credit card statement arrives, take a good hard look at it. See if there are charges for items that you didn't really need. Take a moment to think about what you already own. Look in your closet and count the sweaters and pairs of shoes. Maybe it's time to cut back on your spending and start saving money for one of your dreams. Now take a good look at whether you're spending over your head. If you're withdrawing cash or using your credit cards to buy more than you can afford, you are financing yourself with debt not cash.

Calculate what you actually earn. From your take-home salary, deduct expenses that are essential to your job, such as child care, uniform costs or commuting fares. Include the cost per hour that you spend getting to and from work. Figure in taxes too. Remember that when you spend money, you have already spent energy to earn that money. Don't be surprised if half of your hourly salary is already accounted for before you spend a cent. That $10 an hour salary may really only be $5 an hour.

Remember that money equates with energy, your energy. The next time you are standing near a check-out register, ask yourself if the purchase you have in mind is worth your energy. It's important to keep track of every cent that you spend but more than that, you need to honestly decide if your purchase is worth the number of hours you have to work to afford it. The more you become aware of what you are spending in energy as well as cash, the more likely your expenses will drop.

∽ THOUGHT FOR THE DAY ∽

A major expense for most people is a car. Figure out how much you are spending each month in car payments and insurance. Find out if those costs will go down if you buy a less expensive car.

JUNE 3

Necessity is not an established fact, but an interpretation.

FRIEDRICH WILHELM NIETZCHE

Tanesha recalls a busy Saturday when a steady stream of friends and neighbors happened to stop by to say hello. "It finally occurred to me that I was not the only one in the family capable of carrying on a conversation. So I excused myself and let my husband and teenage children handle the social obligations while I finished my errands."

It is difficult at times to say no. As a result you find yourself burdened with extra commitments, obligations and work. You are afraid someone won't like you or that you'll hurt their feelings if you turn them down. However, by saying yes all the time you do hurt someone—yourself. You need to remind yourself that other family members are capable of cooking dinner, sweeping up crumbs, walking the dog, talking to a teacher and making an appointment. But they aren't going to assume any of these responsibilities if you continue to do it for them.

Start by setting some limits. Set aside time each day for yourself and honor it. Don't allow any interruptions. Use your answering machine and return phone calls later. Learn to yes to yourself even if that means saying no to someone else. If you lose a friend because you said no, then that person wasn't really a very good friend. If you don't respect your own needs, then no one else will either.

∾ **THOUGHT FOR THE DAY** ∾

Learn how to ask for help for yourself. It's unfair to expect others to read your mind and magically "know" what you need. It's your job to be clear about what you need and then ask for help when it's appropriate.

JUNE 4

Inner peace and outer peace are synonymous in the sense that without one, the other wouldn't happen.

YOKO ONO

Meditation makes some people think of bean sprouts, tofu and mystics sitting cross-legged. But meditation is simply a technique to relax your mind, a way to quiet your internal chatter.

Begin by making yourself comfortable somewhere that is private and where you won't be distracted or interrupted. Lean back on a pillow, sit down in a chair, relax in a warm bathtub or stretch out in the sunshine. If you're at home, turn off the telephone for a few moments while you relax. Now close your eyes and focus on a single word or syllable. It is enough to merely concentrate on the sound of your own breathing. The idea is to become very quiet and still, to let your mind empty. As thoughts intrude, push them away. Go back to listening to the sound of your breathing or continue repeating whatever word you're saying.

Do this for 15 minutes or as long as you want. When you are ready, resume your activities and get on with your day. You'll find that you have given yourself a nice break. You'll feel more relaxed, less tense, calmer and more serene. You have just finished a meditation session.

∽ THOUGHT FOR THE DAY ∽

Try focusing on an image when you meditate. Visualize an ocean beach and concentrate on the waves lapping the shore. Or, imagine a family of robins splashing about in a garden birdbath.

We are the children of your landscape;
it dictates behavior and even thought in the
measure to which we are responsive to it.

LAWRENCE DURRELL

If you live in or near a city, the sounds of a city may be around you most of your waking hours. If you commute to work by car, you may have to deal with traffic twice a day. If you commute by public transportation, you may have the stress of wondering if you can get a seat, if the weather will make you late or if mechanical problems will keep the bus or train from running at all.

What is important, however, is how well you accept the world around you and learn to function within it. If your environment is noisy, you can try to make your home as quiet as possible. Alicia, for example, decided to have soundproofing work done on the walls of her city apartment. She felt minimizing city noises was a worthwhile investment. You can use your commuting time to advantage too. Mario listens to books on tape while he is driving. "A good mystery is best," he says. Carole says she gets a lot of work done on the train because she is not interrupted with phone calls.

Think about the world you live in. Ask yourself what you might do to make it less stressful for you. Perhaps there are circumstances that you can use to better advantage. Notice what other people have done to cope with the situation. The best test of whether something works is to try it yourself.

∽ THOUGHT FOR THE DAY ∽

If you live in an extreme climate and find it hard to
adjust, your heating or cooling system is important.
Make sure it is in good working order so you can minimize
the stress of the outside heat or cold on your body.

JUNE 6

Procrastination is the thief of time.

EDWARD YOUNG

Procrastination is stressful. You put a task off and then you're stressed because suddenly the deadline is here and you have to get it done. So do yourself a favor and do tomorrow's job today. And do today's job right now. Here are some ways to get things done.

Give yourself an extra fifteen minutes in the morning by getting out of bed the first time the alarm goes off instead of hitting the snooze button. Plan to be at appointments ten or fifteen minutes early. If you're lucky and no traffic jams slow you down, use the time in the waiting room to make a list of errands. Later you can get them done in one trip instead of four.

Angela starts packing for a business trip three days ahead. "If I wait until the day before I leave, my favorite outfit is bound to need help. So I like to lay out my clothes early so there's enough time for any necessary mending or cleaning." If you have a plane to catch, be at the gate—not the parking lot, not the ticket desk—an hour before departure. If you don't need the extra time for an unforeseen delay, sit at the gate and catch up on some reading or writing.

Stop making excuses. No one really believes that your dog died or your car wouldn't start or you had a flat tire. Start telling the truth—that you have no excuse and the job isn't done. If you hear yourself apologize enough, you might stop putting things off and start getting them done.

∽ THOUGHT FOR THE DAY ∽

If you have a phone call to make that you're dreading, drop everything and make that call right now. The sooner you pick up the phone, the sooner you'll feel relief.

I frequently tramped eight or ten miles through the deep-
est snow to keep an appointment with a beech tree, or a
yellow birch, or an old acquaintance among the pines.

HENRY DAVID THOREAU

If you're a walker, you have already experienced the benefits
of taking a daily stroll. But if that daily walk is getting a little
boring, you might want to think about hiking up and down
some steep hills. A 150-pound woman will burn about 300
calories if she walks two miles in 40 minutes. But she can burn
520 calories if she hikes for an hour and her overall fitness will
improve dramatically.

When you hike, you need stronger leg muscles to manage the
hills and bigger arm movements to help keep your balance. The
more movement there is to your body, the more calories you
burn and the more toned your muscles will become. If you're
going for a longer trek and are carrying a 5-pound backpack,
you'll increase the calories you burn by another 15 percent.

Invest in a good pair of hiking books. Most hikers wear two
pairs of socks—a thin pair of synthetic socks that wick away
the moisture from the foot to help keep it dry and a second
wool or acrylic sock for cushioning—their hiking boots may be
another half-size larger than their regular shoes. Be sure to
wear both pairs of socks when fitting the boots to be sure there
is adequate toe room. The boot should cover the ankle for support and have a thick, steel-plated sole to protect the bottom of
your feet from rocks and other sharp objects.

∞ THOUGHT FOR THE DAY ∞

Include these essentials in your backpack—an extra pair of dry socks,
mole skin or bandages for blisters, Vaseline to coat the foot and mini-
mize friction and a first aid kit. Carry plenty of water—about one
quart for each hour you plan to hike. For snacks, pack peanut butter
and jelly sandwiches, fruit, raw vegetables, dried fruit and trail mix.

JUNE 8

*Change your life today. Don't gamble on the future,
act now, without delay.*

SIMONE DE BEAUVOIR

If you find yourself grumbling a lot, perhaps it's time for a change. If you're unhappy, uncomfortable, dissatisfied and disagreeable, others are probably getting tired of listening to you. Complainers constantly talk about their problems but often avoid taking any responsibility. It's time to take some action.

Start with your own behavior. Work on letting go of your negative attitude. Ask yourself if you're able to be more positive. If you feel you can't change, if you simply can't imagine thinking any other way, then pretend to be another person. The idea is to get out of your own head for awhile, long enough to discover that a new or different behavior is possible for you.

Adapt another person's behavior patterns instead of your own for a day or a week. Think of someone you admire and respect; then try to act like that person. Try to respond as that person would. Think of how another person might solve the problem; then try to imitate their solution. Depending on the situation, you might find yourself acting more gently or more assertively. Compare your new response to your old one and see if the situation has changed. If there is even a little improvement, you are on the right track. Continue what you're doing. And remember that by practicing a new attitude, it will soon become a real one.

∾ THOUGHT FOR THE DAY ∾

Write down each complaint on a separate slip of paper and put them in a basket. Draw one. This is the complaint to concentrate on. When you figure out a solution, you can throw the paper away.

We have become as poisoned as the eagle's eggshell.

CHRYSTOS

The environment can be stressful to your body. You might be allergic to certain pollens or plants or the air pollution where you live might be an ongoing concern. An allergy means your body is reacting inappropriately. Often your body overreacts and becomes hypersensitive to something that other people's bodies can handle with ease. For example, when the grass and trees begin to sprout each spring, they spew out pollen. If you are allergic to pollen, you may get a runny nose, itchy eyes and/or a sinus headache.

Allergies can be more stressful than you realize. Because your body is fighting the allergen, your immune system is working overtime and you are more likely to catch whatever cold or virus is going around. Over a long period of time, allergies can weaken or do damage to the system under attack, often your respiratory system.

There is help however. There are doctors who specialize in allergies. They can determine what your body can't handle so that you can avoid or desensitize yourself to those substances.

∞ THOUGHT FOR THE DAY ∞

There are many nonprescription remedies that can bring relief but these are often used excessively and inappropriately. If your allergies require medication, check with a doctor to make sure you're choosing the best treatment for you.

JUNE 10

Nothing is ours except time.

SENECA

One way to reduce the stress in your life is to give yourself time for enjoyable activities. It is very satisfying to work on the projects or pursue the hobbies that give you pleasure. These kinds of activities make you lose track of time and allow you to escape into something gratifying. Henry likes to play with his computer. Barbara sews, Tara gardens and Jeremy tinkers with his motorcycle. Research shows when you are doing pleasant work like this, your blood chemistry changes and your immune system is boosted.

There are cycles in your life, of course, when you really don't have much free time or energy to pursue a special interest. But chances are that's when your outside interests can serve you best. During those periods, your hobbies bring a bit of balance to your life. Although your spare time might be extremely limited, you should still find time to read a monthly magazine devoted to your hobby or take an evening off for a club meeting and guest speaker or attend a once-a-year exhibit on a weekend afternoon.

Take time today for a special hobby that gives you pleasure. Organize your fishing tackle box, sit at the piano, pull out that partially finished embroidery or head for the boat show this weekend. Allow yourself some fun for a while. Taking an occasional break gives you a chance to renew your spirit and restore your energy so you can return to the ongoing stresses of your life with a fresh outlook.

THOUGHT FOR THE DAY

Have a dance party for yourself. Close the door, turn up the music and dance like crazy for as long as you want.

JUNE 11

I generally avoid temptation unless I can't resist it.
MAE WEST

When eating out, it's tempting to overeat. But you can learn to eat out and still maintain healthy habits. Some decisions should be made before you leave home. Choose a restaurant that serves food that suits your taste and offers nourishing selections that fit into your food plan. If you are not familiar with the menu, call ahead and ask questions. Before you walk into the restaurant, decide what you are going to order. "I nearly always order fish when I eat out," says Ann, "because it's a dish that I rarely prepare at home."

Once seated in the restaurant, try to order before others so you won't be tempted by what someone else is having. Quickly push the basket of bread, biscuits, rolls and butter to the far side of the table so it is out of reach. Order a large tossed salad (without croutons) in place of an appetizer, especially if others are having hors d'oeuvres. Request a reduced calorie or fat-free dressing on the side. Lemon or vinegar is a tasty alternative and some people prefer to eat salad without any dressing.

Be aware of portions. Most restaurants serve twice as much as you'd give yourself at home. Ask them to wrap up half to take home before your order arrives. Although the occasional drink can be an enjoyable accompaniment to a meal, a glass of ice water with a slice of lemon or lime is equally refreshing. If you crave something fizzy, order seltzer or club soda.

∾ THOUGHT FOR THE DAY ∾

For your main dish remember the three Bs — broiled, baked and boiled are usually best. Foods that are steamed, poached, grilled or stir-fried are fine too.

*Cleaning your house while your kids are still growing is
like shoveling the walk before it stops snowing.*

PHYLLIS DILLER

Paige is the single mother of a young daughter. "Mornings
used to be the toughest part of the day," she says. "It was hard
to get us both up and dressed and out of the house on time."
Like other mothers, Paige learned that the day got off to a better start if she devoted a few minutes to getting organized the
night before. She fixes a bag lunch for both of them, makes
sure the diaper bag is ready to go and lays out their clothes for
the next morning.

Liza's sons are in junior high school and usually have homework so she sets aside time after school for them. In her house,
homework starts before supper so that they finish by the time
they eat. "While I'm fixing supper, I make sure that I'm available to help them. That means no phone calls for any of us—
even me. If I'm available and not distracted, the boys take
homework more seriously too."

Frank used to find it difficult to get his children to bed but
solved the problem with an evening ritual of bath, p.j.'s and a
read-aloud book. "The books are getting longer," says Frank,
"but that's okay. For one thing, they're more interesting. For
another, the kids are starting to read to me. Besides, I like to
curl up under a blanket and cuddle as much as they do."

∾ THOUGHT FOR THE DAY ∾

*Remember that a whining child is often in search of attention. Try
kneeling down to be at eye level with your child, offer a hug, then talk
and listen for awhile. Once your child gets the attention he or she
needs, the whining may diminish or stop.*

Give us courage and gaiety and the quiet mind.
ROBERT LOUIS STEVENSON

Meditation is sitting quietly and allowing your mind to become still. One way to meditate is to empty your mind of thoughts. Michelle sets aside "quiet time" for herself each evening. She likes to sit in a darkened room or at least have the lights turned down low. She says she imagines her thoughts to be "clouds floating through my mind and going away. When one wants to stick around, I try to put it on a balloon and watch it float away."

Try meditating for five minutes. To begin, find a comfortable sitting position in a chair or on the floor. Sit quietly and become aware of how your body feels. Let yourself relax, then close your eyes and concentrate on your breathing. Listen to the sound of air moving in and out of your body. If your mind wanders, bring it back to your breathing.

Remember that meditation takes some practice so be gentle with yourself as you begin. Your mind may seem to chatter incessantly; you may even find it hard to keep your body still. As you are learning, be still for as long as it is comfortable for you.

∾ THOUGHT FOR THE DAY ∾

As meditation becomes easier, you will be able to sustain it for longer periods of time. Many people find that twenty to thirty minutes is enough to achieve a pleasurable and worthwhile sense of relaxation.

JUNE 14

There are great joys which long to be ours.
God sends ten thousand truths, which come about
us like birds seeking inlet; but we are shut up
to them, and so they bring us nothing, but sit
and sing awhile upon the roof, and then fly away.

HENRY WARD BEECHER

A common stress is not having enough time and always wondering where the day went. One way to tackle this problem is to make sure that you are spending time on the things that are important to you. Start by keeping track of everything you do for one or two weeks.

Then write down all the things you would prefer to be doing. Compare this list with the first one. Are you spending time on things that are important to you? Certainly you have responsibilities that take up a great deal of your time. You work, you have family responsibilities, you have to maintain the house or apartment you live in. It really doesn't make any difference if the beds were made this morning. What's important is whether or not you took the time to listen to a child or share something silly with a friend. What's important is whether you took a few moments for yourself to still your mind, nourish your body or take a walk around the block. What's important is whether you briefly paused to appreciate the beauty of the world around you.

Remember that your second list is really a catalog of things that are important to you. Make sure that you do at least one of those things every day. Time is perhaps your most precious commodity. Once it's gone, it's gone forever. Make sure that you use each moment of your time wisely and well.

∞ THOUGHT FOR THE DAY ∞

If you're worried about those unmade beds and dirty dishes, do three
chores, then allow yourself an activity from your "important" list.

They can do all things because they think they can.

VIRGIL

The words you use to describe a situation can have a great impact on how you feel about that situation. Your own words can program your success or failure. For example, if you say *I can't help it*, you are saying that you have no control. But if you say *it's up to me*, then you are empowering yourself and taking responsibility for your actions.

When you decide to do something—lose weight, for example—do you make a promise or a commitment?

People who succeed make a commitment. They set measurable goals and make plans that include specific actions. Committed people also watch how other people behave—especially capable people; then start imitating others' successful behavior. Watching what is wrong isn't enough. They pay special attention to what another person is doing right. Successful people have a positive outlook—they see opportunities more often than problems. They expect success, not failure. People who achieve a lot understand that preparation and perseverance are part of the formula for success. They assume that rewards and promotions will be for hard work, not tenure. They also accept change and are willing to experiment. They readily try a new approach in case there's a better way of doing an old task.

∾ **THOUGHT FOR THE DAY** ∾

Take care today that you are programming yourself for success. Pay more attention to the words you use. Think about your attitude too. Be willing to work for what you want. When you begin to speak, think and act positively, opportunity and success will soon come your way.

JUNE 16

A little sunburnt by the glare of life.

ELIZABETH BARRETT BROWNING

A sun-kissed look gives you a healthy glow but be careful to protect your skin from too much sun. Damage to your skin from the sun is cumulative; most skin cancers start from excessive exposure to the sun when you are young. So today use a sun screen or moisturizer with an SPF rating year round to block dangerous UVA rays; an SPF rating of 15 or higher is recommended.

Apply sunscreen liberally—a dab on your nose or the top of your ears isn't enough—at least half an hour before you go outside. Reapply immediately after swimming, every hour if you're perspiring, every two hours as long as you're outside. Dry clothing, especially cotton, will protect your skin somewhat but hold your shirt and pants in front of a bright light to see how much light passes through. A wide-brimmed hat and large sunglasses will protect your eyes. After swimming, be sure to cover yourself with a dry shirt, not a wet one.

Protect your hair by putting sun screen on your scalp right after you shampoo; just don't rinse it out. Reapply sunscreen where your hair parts whenever you are putting sunscreen on any other part of your body.

∞ THOUGHT FOR THE DAY ∞

The sun is at its highest and harmful UVA rays are more concentrated between the hours of 10 A.M. and 3 P.M. so it's best to garden or walk the beach early in the morning or late in the afternoon.

JUNE 17

Life is not merely living but living in health.
MARTIAL

No one really knows whether vitamins can reduce stress, but it its known that a healthy body and a strong immune system can handle more stress. Recent studies suggest that large doses of vitamin C will improve your resistance to the common cold and boost your immune system in general.

The best way to get more vitamin C is to eat foods high in this nutrient. Good choices are strawberries, citrus fruits and tomatoes. Vegetables like raw green peppers and cabbage as well as cooked broccoli, cauliflower and other greens are good sources too. Just be careful not to load them up with empty calories and unnecessary fats such as butter and sour cream.

Some people can use more vitamin C than others. Smokers need more vitamin C because they metabolize it faster. Environmental stress, especially heat, taps your reserves, as do certain drugs, including aspirin and oral contraceptives. Elderly people, especially men, also need more. Be sure to check with your doctor if you think you may benefit by increasing your daily intake of vitamin C.

∾ THOUGHT FOR THE DAY ∾

The RDA (Recommended Dietary Allowance) is based on the amount that is metabolized in the body and what is considered necessary to maintain adequate body reserves. For an adult woman (who is not pregnant), the minimum RDA of vitamin C is 60 milligrams.

Who, except the gods,
can live time through forever without any pain?

AESCHYLUS

When Judy is under stress, her right leg begins to tense up. "The muscles in my thigh get tight and by the end of the day, my whole leg is in knots." Her problem persisted until she discovered how to break her stress cycle. She simply talks herself out of it. "All I do is tell myself how I want to feel," she says.

Take time today to make your body relax. Begin by visualizing yourself calm and at ease. Tell your body how it will feel. Then focus on one part of your body such as your leg. Tell your leg to rest and be still. Judy gives herself mental suggestions such as "My right leg is now relaxed." Concentrate until you feel your leg release the tension in the muscles. Do the same thing with your left leg. Tell your arms to feel light enough to float. Continue this process with the rest of your body, focusing on those muscles groups that are most tense. Finish with your mind, telling it to be still and calm.

People who try this technique are surprised at how well it works because it's so easy to do. "All you have to do is put your mind to it," says Judy. You've talked yourself into and out of situations. Today, talk yourself out of muscle tension caused by stress and talk yourself into relaxation.

∞ THOUGHT FOR THE DAY ∞

Talk yourself out of a bad mood. Simply tell yourself
how you want to feel—happy, contented, laughing.
Then concentrate on those feel-ings until your mind relaxes
and the pleasant feelings push away the negative ones.

JUNE 19

What is man, when you come to think upon him, but a minutely set, ingenious machine.

ISAK DINESEN

The set point theory of weight loss is based on the idea that each body has a preferred weight. So no matter what you do to try and lose weight, your body always returns to its set point weight. If you are overweight, however, this doesn't mean you're doomed to remain at this current overweight place forever. You can override your body's tendency to stay at one weight by doing two things: increase your activity level and decrease your calories. In short, you need to change your behavior so that you are burning more calories and making better food choices.

Your thermostat can be changed to a new setting. The catch is that once you lose weight, you have to maintain it for a while before your body adjusts to that new set point.

Decide today to override your thermostat. Eat better, move around more and you'll be able to maintain your weight loss. Then all those positive health benefits that you have worked so hard to get will be yours permanently.

∾ THOUGHT FOR THE DAY ∾

Once you have reached your desired weight, adjust your habits so that you can maintain (not lose or gain) this new, lower weight.

JUNE 20

When schemes are laid in advance, it is surprising how often the circumstances fit in with them.

SIR WILLIAM OSLER

Bringing your lunch or snacks to work isn't nearly as time consuming as you might think. On the weekend prepare a week's supply of vegetables: cut up celery and carrots, slice cucumbers, trim broccoli and cauliflower into florets, slice red and green peppers into rings. Divide them into individual packets or baggies. Place them in the bottom drawer of your refrigerator. If you are pressed for time, buy pre-cut fresh vegetables at the grocery store. Many supermarkets now have salad bars too.

If you are going to take your lunch to work, invest in an insulated bag. It will help keep your food cool and delay spoilage. If you're making a sandwich, wrap the lettuce and tomato separately so the bread won't get soggy. Add these trimmings to your sandwich when you're ready to eat.

An easy time-saver is to put tonight's leftovers into a plastic container when you clear the table. Tomorrow's lunch is now ready. Leftovers like soup, cooked vegetables, chili and casseroles make great next-day lunches. For a snack, bring an envelope of reduced-calorie hot cocoa mix, instant broth or a box of fruit juice.

∞ THOUGHT FOR THE DAY ∞

Remember that spending time preparing foods at home will save you money as well as calories. Keep a small cooler in your car stocked with diet soda, bottled water, fresh fruits and veggie snacks so that you won't have to stop for fast food when you're on the go and away from home.

JUNE 21

Health and good estate of body are above all good.
ECCLESIASTICUS 30:15

One of the most common physical reactions to stress is gastrointestinal distress. The muscle tension that you feel in your limbs is also happening inside your body too. Before long, you are complaining of diarrhea or constipation or an upset stomach. You may turn to over-the-counter or prescription remedies for immediate relief but for the long term, you need to reduce the source of stress.

First, eat enough fiber every day. Fiber adds bulk and holds water as food goes through your intestines. Fiber will alleviate your complaints by making your stools softer and larger, in other words, more normal. The easiest way to get more fiber is to eat whole grain breads and cereals along with five servings of fresh fruits and vegetables each day. Fresh foods of any kind have more fiber than canned or other highly processed foods.

Next, drink plenty of water—6 to 8 glasses a day. When you'll well hydrated, your kidneys and bowels work better. And last, exercise. When you move your body, you stimulate your internal organs to work more efficiently. A moderate walk is sufficient as long as you do it every day.

∾ THOUGHT FOR THE DAY ∾

Caffeine has also been shown to contribute to gastrointestinal distress. Most authorities recommend that you limit your intake to 200 milligrams a day—about one large mug of strong brewed coffee.

JUNE 22

Regimen is superior to medicine.

VOLTAIRE

When your muscles are strong, you can put some power into a push or a lift. But you need endurance too so that you can use your muscles for a long period of time without getting overly tired. When you were in school, you could carry armloads of books all day and still have plenty of energy left over for sports. But as you get older, carrying babies and young children puts your body to the test. And after more years go by, hauling bags of groceries from the car into the kitchen can be physically taxing.

The way to regain or improve muscle strength and endurance is resistance training. Any training will make a difference as long as you do it consistently. For endurance training, start with a weight that you can lift ten times without getting tired. Increase the weight only when you can lift it easily twenty times. Endurance comes from lifting a lighter weight for many repetitions.

If you are doing strength training, start with the heaviest weight you can lift seven or eight times. Increase the weight when lifting it ten times becomes easy. Strength comes from lifting a heavier weight for fewer repetitions.

∞ THOUGHT FOR THE DAY ∞

Good posture and form are important for resistance training. You want to make sure you protect yourself to avoid injury or accidents. Do the exercises slowly. Uncontrolled jerky motions are more likely to result in injury.

*Archly the maiden smiled, with eyes overrunning with
  laughter,
Said, in a tremulous voice, "Why don't you speak for
  yourself, John?"*

HENRY WADSWORTH LONGFELLOW

It is healthy to be aware of others' reactions to what you say,
think or do. This feedback is valid as long as you don't depend
entirely on others' opinions. You should trust yourself and
have confidence in your own judgment. You know how you
feel and how you should behave. Your opinions are as valid as
anyone else's. It's okay to like a movie that others hated or dislike a restaurant that is a local favorite. What you want to
avoid is jumping on the bandwagon too easily and getting
swept along by everyone else's opinion.

If you have trouble speaking out, you need to learn how.
You can start when you're around people who are your friends,
people who will support you no matter what you say or think.
As your self-confidence builds, you can begin to offer your
views to acquaintances. Find a trusted friend and practice
sticking up for yourself. This is a more important skill than
many realize. Some opinions are minor, such as where to eat or
which book to recommend or what movie to see. But other
opinions can be vital, such as decisions about your health care.

Although you should be responsive to the world around
you, you still have to be true to yourself. Certainly compromise
is a part of the picture and something that we all have to do on
a regular basis. However, trusting yourself also means you may
sometimes have to stand alone. The most popular people are
often the ones who are truest to their own beliefs.

∾ THOUGHT FOR THE DAY ∾

*If you've been accused of being opinionated and not listening,
perhaps you need to remind yourself that perhaps there are a
few things that you can learn.*

I don't need a man to rectify my existence.
The most profound relationship we'll ever
have is the one with ourselves.

SHIRLEY MACLAINE

When you are in need of advice, you may turn to friends, loved ones or your immediate family for an opinion. They give you unconditional support and understanding, making you feel good about yourself. But if you're relying only on one person, whether lover or friend, you may be asking too much.

The burden for solving your own problems and making yourself happy is yours and yours alone. You need to be sure you're not putting those responsibilities onto someone else. When you turn to just one or two people to meet your emotional needs, you tend to fall into familiar and predictable patterns which still may not give you the answers that you need. That's why it's important to have a wide variety of friends. A group offers many opinions and different ways of seeing as well as solving problems. You learn new ways of nurturing yourself and caring for others and fresh ways of dealing with life.

People will be attracted to you if you have your own interests but they will avoid you if they constantly have to pick you up and put you back together. When you widen your horizons and develop your own interests, you'll be more interesting to the best friend, spouse or lover.

∞ THOUGHT FOR THE DAY ∞

One way to meet new people is to get more active. Join a group
that is centered around a special interest, such as ballroom dancing,
hiking or miniature golf. Or, take an adult education extension
class and learn something new.

JUNE 25

*Lord Ronald said nothing; he flung himself
from the room, flung himself upon his horse
and rode madly off in all directions.*

STEPHEN LEACOCK

You're busy, on the run, harried and hassled. You eat too much, you eat too fast, you eat things that aren't good for you. It's no wonder that your stomach is upset. By incorporating some better eating habits, you can minimize this stress.

Take time to chew your food well. Chewing stimulates your body to produce more saliva, stomach juices and other enzymes that you need to digest food. Smaller pieces are easier to swallow and digest. Chili may be one of your favorite meals but you may need to go easy on spicy foods. Try to eat more often too. It's better to eat several small meals than one or two large ones. However, eating often doesn't mean eating more. Be sure to keep track of everything you eat or one cookie every now and again will add up to a dozen.

Remember to slow down. Take the time to pay attention to what you're eating and slowly savor every bite. Let mealtime be a time to relax and take a break. Use this time to nourish your body so that it functions continuously and well.

∾ THOUGHT FOR THE DAY ∾

Be aware of how much fat you're eating, as too much fat can interfere with your body's ability to digest food. High-fat diets are also associated with colon cancer, gall bladder disease and high cholesterol.

*You must know the story of your culture
and be proud of your ancestors.*

ROMANA BANUELOS

Most people have a very distinct eating style. You may be unaware of your own style but you probably have patterns as to when, where, what and how you eat. To learn more about why you eat the way you do, you should begin by keeping a journal—simply writing down what you eat over several weeks. The longer you keep a record, the better.

Some of your eating patterns come from various influences in your life. You may have been brought up with certain kinds of foods so you developed a taste for Italian, Asian, Hispanic or other ethnic cuisine. Extreme climates, availability of certain foods, formal education, religion and the amount of money you have available to spend on food will play a role in your choices. These factors can influence the amount of meat, cheese and fried foods you enjoy. If you're about to go on a weight loss plan, it's important to include foods that you like and are familiar with.

Your household situation—whether you live alone or in an extended family, for example, or whether a member of the household has any issues with food—is an important influence also. Remember that the attitudes about food that you grew up with will follow you into your adult lives. You should celebrate the cuisines that you love and appreciate the heritage these dishes represent.

∞ THOUGHT FOR THE DAY ∞

Age is a significant factor when it comes to food choices. Teenagers, for example, are still experiencing their last major growth spurt so it's not surprising their social lives often revolve around snacking. In your later years, however, your taste buds are less sensitive so food is not as enjoyable as it once was.

JUNE 27

*Within our family there was no such thing
as a person who did not matter.*

SHIRLEY ABBOT

If a member of your family is suddenly gaining an excessive amount of weight, you may want to help. But it's important that you not nag or hassle that person. Any discussion should be in private, away from other family members and away from the table. You need to be gentle and understanding when you broach the subject, taking care not to judge. An embarrassing or antagonistic confrontation will likely end in tears and denial and ultimately solve nothing.

You can help by preparing low-calorie meals and planning family activities that include exercise. You can fix healthy lunches or prepare an extra portion at supper to pack up for the next day. You need to be careful, however, not to single out that one person as the reason for these changes since you don't want to cause resentment from other family members.

You need to be sure you're being reasonable in your attempts to help, taking care not to overstep your boundaries or become domineering. Excessive restrictions will soon be ignored and disregarded by everyone, including yourself. You can encourage them to choose foods and plan meals but ultimately you have to let other people be in charge of their own eating. The most important support that you can give may be to notice their accomplishments when they make the decision to lose weight and compliment them as they change their lifestyle.

∞ THOUGHT FOR THE DAY ∞

You can also consider whether the weight gain is a symptom of another problem, such as stress, depression, boredom, lack of exercise or a new job. If you help your loved one deal with these issues, the weight gain may take care of itself.

JUNE 28

. . . yield to that suggestion.

WILLIAM SHAKESPEARE

When you're trying to lose weight, you cling to ineffective tactics, hoping for an easy answer. There are no quick fixes but here are some diet tips that really work.

Spread out calories throughout the day. If you starve yourself all day, trying to save up all of your calories for one blowout meal, you're likely to overeat and end up feeling bloated, miserable and guilty. Rather than disrupt your normal eating routine, you should eat on schedule. You can make allowances for a party later in the day but you shouldn't skip any meals completely.

Weigh and measure portions. When you use a food scale and measuring spoons, you learn what a normal portion size really looks like. When you're away from home, you can be confident that you're not overeating.

Be conscious of extra bites. Those bites add up, especially if you're not aware of what you're doing. For example, you'll pop 100 calories into your mouth with every two oatmeal cookies or a tablespoon of peanut butter or half a cheese danish or a glass of wine.

Your diet is no one else's business. The world is full of sneaky saboteurs, envious friends and nosy relatives. Some people mean well but if they don't know what you're doing, they can't influence you. Stick with a support group of like-minded people. They are dieters and leaders who understand the process and pitfalls, friends who are there to encourage your success.

∿ THOUGHT FOR THE DAY ∿

Before leaving for a party, eat half a sandwich or a small salad. You'll arrive at the party ready to dance instead of snack.

Getting company inside one's skin.
MAGGIE SCARF

When a woman becomes pregnant, her body is under great stress because it has to provide nourishment for both her and her baby. She will deplete most of her own body's reserves by the time the baby is born so it is important to be in good health before getting pregnant. During her pregnancy, she will need to increase her intake of all basic nutrients. The following guidelines are typical for the normal healthy woman.

In order to meet the demands on her system for energy, nutrients and extra protein needed for tissue building, she will need to increase her daily calorie intake 10 percent to 15 percent. During all childbearing years, women need to maintain adequate levels of iron. Iron is necessary to maintain a good supply of oxygenated blood. The mother's circulating blood volume will increase 40 percent to 50 percent—more if she is carrying twins. She will need about 66 percent more protein to accommodate the growth needs of her baby and the increased blood volume for herself. Protein has essential nitrogen, which is the nutrient basic to growth. Her calcium needs will increase by 50 percent—from 800 milligrams per day to 1200 milligrams per day. Calcium is essential for bones and teeth. She will need increased amounts of vitamins to aid in her own increased metabolism and the development of the baby's skeletal, nervous, vascular and muscle systems.

If you are pregnant, remember that vitamin and mineral supplements won't necessarily supply the nutrients lacking in your diet. The easiest way to meet these demands is to eat plenty of nutritious foods. And, of course, put yourself under a doctor's care.

THOUGHT FOR THE DAY

Moderate exercise is recommended for most women during pregnancy. You'll have an easier labor and delivery too if you're in shape.

JUNE 30

An active line on a walk, moving freely without goal.
A walk for a walk's sake.

PAUL KLEE

The biggest advantage of walking is that everyone can do it and walking is suitable for all fitness levels. If you're out of shape, you can start with a leisurely stroll to make sure you're using the right form. The well-known army posture is best — stand tall, head up, shoulders back and down, chest up and abdomen held in.

As your fitness improves, you can increase your walking speed and distance. Hold bent arms close to your body, then vigorously swing them. Some people like to walk with one- or two-pound hand weights. These should be carried in your hands or strapped to your wrists. Never use ankle weights; they can add unnecessary stress to your knees, ankles and hip joints.

You should protect your feet with good walking shoes. These should fit properly and offer heel support, a flexible forefoot and a wide toe box so your toes can spread out while you walk. For comfort, you may want padded insoles and arch supports. If you like to trek through woods or trails, walking poles are a worthwhile investment.

Wear loose-fitting clothes appropriate for the weather. Most walkers dress in layers so they can adjust for body heat as they walk.

∞ THOUGHT FOR THE DAY ∞

An added benefit to walking is that your legs get firm and shapely.

*But to look, even regularly, upon what you remember
and know you've forgiven is achievement.*

FAITH BALDWIN

If you have issues with food today, these issues may go back to what you learned about food from your parents. Ask yourself if you are still rebelling against your parents. Perhaps you are determined to be heavy if your parents were obsessively thin, or vice versa. Or you may prepare extra servings because there was barely enough food when you were young. You may also have picked up inappropriate messages about your body, such as being uncomfortable with your sexuality or having negative images about the way you look. You may feel that you should be accountable to your parents before yourself, that taking care of your own needs first is betraying them.

It's time to separate yourself from your parents. You need to change your own behaviors, replacing inappropriate behaviors with better ones. As you begin to change, you should also work on how you feel toward your parents. You need to accept that their mistakes weren't intentional, and you should learn to love them for who they are.

You also need to be patient with yourself. It took many years for these issues to become ingrained in your behavior and consciousness. These issues are also connected to how you feel about yourself, how you feel about love and what makes you feel secure. Just as it took a long time for these issues to develop in you, it will take a long time for them to change.

THOUGHT FOR THE DAY

*Remember that learning and practicing self-care is a wonderful gift
that you can give to yourself.*

JULY 2

They whose sole bliss is eating can give but that one brutish reason why they live.

JUVENAL

Your intentions about food may have been good in the beginning but sometimes eating can start to control you when you don't intend to. If you feel you are at the mercy of food, or if a close friend has suggested that you may have an eating problem, then perhaps you need to examine the way you think about food. There are certain behaviors that can signal trouble, warning you that you are starting to create problems for yourself.

When you start a diet, do you do so with a sense of urgency or desperation? Are you extreme about losing weight, calculating every calorie of every bite every day? Do you exercise to exhaustion or more than once a day, then calculate the calories that you burned up? Do you think about food morning, noon and night? Do you feel deprived that you're denying yourself? Do you feel hungry most of the time? Do you crave many foods because your diet is so stringent? Do you limit who you're with or where you go because you're trying to avoid food?

If you are falling into these patterns, you are very much at risk for an eating disorder. If you have all of these symptoms, you are probably already in a hospital or soon will be. But even one or two is a sign that you need help.

∞ THOUGHT FOR THE DAY ∞

Call your doctor, listen to your friend, get help. If there was ever a time to trust others, this is it.

Never lose sight of the fact that old age needs so little but needs that little so much.

MARGARET WILLOUR

In spite of the stress that you live with, you're living longer. In this century the average person's life expectancy has increased from 45 to 75 years. But even though you live longer, you still age and the aging process is its own stress. By the time you turn seventy, you'll lose 10 percent of your kidney and lung tissue, 18 percent of your liver tissue, 40 percent of skeletal tissue and 12 percent (men) to 25 percent (women) of your bone mass. One factor that can affect the aging process is the food you eat. Although aging varies greatly from one person to another, seniors should be sure they have a sound nutritional program and good eating habits.

In general, seniors need less protein, and more complex carbohydrates, fiber and calcium. Seniors eat more and better when they share their meals with family or friends. Senior housing complexes often have community dining rooms to promote fellowship and social interaction. Because many seniors have a diminished sense of taste and smell, it's important to serve foods with distinctive flavors and aromas. Many seniors are dealing with chronic diseases that require drug therapy, both prescription and over-the-counter. Because medicines can affect appetite and how foods taste, it's important to understand how these drugs work and why they were prescribed.

Getting older doesn't have to be a downhill slide. If you nourish your body and develop good eating habits when you're younger, you're more likely to enter your later years with a sound body and active mind.

THOUGHT FOR THE DAY

If you're a senior citizen, check with your doctor about how much protein your body needs. Too much protein can cause calcium to be excreted through the kidneys and hasten bone loss.

JULY 4

If some people didn't tell you, you'd never know they'd been away on vacation.

KIN HUBBARD

Like others, you may worry about vacations, fearful that you'll ignore your program of healthy eating and gain weight. One way to keep your weight under control is to plan a vacation with lots of physical activities, such as skiing, canoeing, biking, horseback riding or backpacking. Activities like these will keep your mind off food and you will be burning some extra calories too.

Camping is a good choice for the entire family. It's a nice change of pace, is relatively inexpensive and offers plenty of opportunity for exercise. It also allows you to plan meals and menus in advance, giving you control over what you eat. Camping is a good time to walk, hike, swim or play some family softball. For those evenings around the campfire, have a book of ghost stories ready so you can talk instead of eating roasted marshmallows.

You should plan your vacation so it is fun for you. Whether fun means sitting in the sand and reading romance novels or running up and down a mountain every day, that's what you should do. If your food program slips, you can resume your normal routine when you get home. The important thing is to have a good time. You want to remember your vacation by what you saw or did, by the side trips you made, not the weight you gained or what you did wrong.

∞ THOUGHT FOR THE DAY ∞

If there are several restaurants in the area where you're vacationing, take a walk and study their menus in advance. Or call ahead and ask if they feature any low-calorie entrees.

> *Let us never negotiate out of fear.*
> *But let us never fear to negotiate.*
> **PRESIDENT JOHN F. KENNEDY**

The art of successful negotiation is knowing what the limits are. For example, when a house is for sale, both the buyer and seller have established some monetary limits ahead of time. The wise buyer has decided on her top price; the wise seller has decided on her minimum price.

You negotiate for many things besides property or contracts. You negotiate to extend deadlines, increase job responsibility or get a pay raise. On a personal level, you negotiate to get more help from family members or for a quiet evening alone with your spouse. To negotiate successfully, you need to be able to identify real issues. Money issues are easy to clarify but personal issues get foggy, especially when several people are involved because each person has his or her own issues, needs and boundaries.

Try to be clear on what is required to resolve the situation. Usually everyone involved has a role. Then set some boundaries. Decide what the minimum requirements are and how far beyond this you are willing to go. These limits need to be reasonable but once set, then you cannot bluff. You know where you stand at all times so you are free to act within your own limits. So the next time you step over that pile of dirty laundry in the bathroom, decide what you are willing to negotiate for and then sit down and talk.

∞ THOUGHT FOR THE DAY ∞

If you set reasonable limits, you can be more confident.
You won't have to second-guess yourself or wonder if you
are doing the right thing. You can feel strong because
you know you stood up for yourself at the proper time.

JULY 6

Oh! The old swimmin' hole!
JAMES WHITCOMB RILEY

Nancy had never been a particularly good swimmer and now she was overweight and out of shape as well. But she decided to try swimming laps anyway. In the beginning, she could only swim half the length of the pool doing the front crawl, then she would have to switch to the backstroke. "It took a couple of months but finally I could swim two or three laps before stopping to catch my breath," she recalls. "Then all of a sudden, I improved dramatically. Soon I was easily swimming 15 laps."

Swimming is an excellent activity for those who are significantly overweight. The water makes it easier to exercise because it helps support your weight, keeps you cool and offers a gentle resistance for your muscles. Attractive bathing suits are available in stores that specialize in larger sizes. And remember: When you're in a pool, most of you is under water anyway.

If you haven't done any lap swimming for awhile, begin by concentrating on your swimming technique. When you're doing the front crawl, use a slow, steady rhythm. Reach forward on every stroke, keeping your fingers closed as you pull yourself through the water. When your arms come out of the water, your elbows should be higher than your hands.

Kick from the hips—three times for each arm motion. Keep your knees straight, but not locked and your ankles loose. Most swimmers breathe on the same side. When you take a breath, turn your head rather than lift it out of the water.

∞ THOUGHT FOR THE DAY ∞

If you swim in a pool and the chlorine in the water bothers your eyes, use swimming goggles. They're inexpensive and make swimming more pleasurable. Flippers also can help propel you through the water.

A place for everything and everything in its place.

ISABELLA MARY BEETON

Margo was getting tired of her husband's tendency to make clutter. She complained that when her husband got home after work, the first thing he would do was put his mail and other papers on the dining room table. "One of us has to move his stuff off the table before supper so every evening we're both annoyed."

Clutter can be more stressful than you realize. You forget where you put your car keys or you lose that scrap of paper with an important phone number on it. There are papers, magazines and bills in a pile on the coffee table. You forget appointments, your thoughts are scattered and unfocused, you live in visual chaos.

Margo solved her problem by "giving him his own closet by the front door." She added several shelves, then labeled baskets for him to sort his papers—Boy Scouts, soccer, bills, office papers, etc. "Now he is better organized and the clutter is out of sight," she says with a smile.

Take a moment to think about how you handle the clutter in your life. If you're using piles of magazines as end tables, perhaps its time to get a better system. Start small but keep plugging. Organize one drawer at a time rather than tear apart a whole room. Don't be afraid to toss. You can start by throwing away those old magazines.

∞ THOUGHT FOR THE DAY ∞

Organize that one drawer in the kitchen that you open most often. Everytime you open it, you'll be inspired to tackle other drawers, shelves and closets.

JULY 8

I believe that when all the dreams are dead, you're left only with yourself. You'd better like yourself a lot.

RITA MAE BROWN

When you have many reasons for wanting to lose weight, it's easy to confuse how you look with how you feel about yourself. If you don't like yourself in the first place and you happen to be carrying a few extra pounds, it becomes easy to say that if you lost the weight, you would feel better about yourself. In order to lose weight successfully, you have to learn to like yourself as you are right now—overweight, underweight, or just right.

When you lose weight, you will soon find out that you are still the same person as before. You still have the same shortcomings. People that were problems in your life are still there, just as troublesome as ever. You may be so disappointed that losing weight didn't fix these problems that you start to overeat again, giving up your hard-won victory over the scale.

There are plenty of reasons for wanting to lose weight, including wanting to look better, feel better and improve your overall health. But you need to remember that losing weight will be only one part of changing your life. You need to make sure your motives are healthy and realistic. When you have meaningful reasons that come from within yourself, you will be motivated to work on making permanent changes in your lifestyle.

Remember that making lifestyle changes is a long process but these changes can indeed be permanent. If you try to change your habits impulsively and dramatically, it simply won't work. But if you're reasonable with yourself, you'll discover that surplus pounds no longer have to control your life.

∞ THOUGHT FOR THE DAY ∞

If you're unhappy or sad, there may be other issues to deal with besides your weight. When you deal with those other sources of unhappiness, changing to a program of healthy eating will be much easier.

JULY 9

Eat, drink, and be merry, for tomorrow we diet.
WILLIAM GILMORE BEYMER

If you're playing hostess to a large family for the holidays, you may lose sight of your own weight loss program and find yourself overeating. But with a little planning, you can have a good time and not gain weight.

Start by planning the menu in advance. Decide what will be served at each meal, including snacks, drinks and desserts. You may need to remind yourself that it's okay to choose meals that meet the guidelines of your diet program. Although there are likely to be family traditions about food, you should allow yourself to start some new traditions too. Use your health-conscious cookbooks for recipes that update the family favorites in ways that are lower in fat and cholesterol than the originals.

Once your meals are planned, make a shopping list. Check to see what you already have on hand; then clear the pantry and refrigerator shelves and head for the grocery store. A big shopping trip can be time-consuming but it helps you avoid last-minute substitutions.

After the shopping, you can do preliminary preparation or cook in advance and freeze. Post the menu on the refrigerator so guests will know what you're planning to serve and won't be snacking on tomorrow's food. Since it's easy to eat anything in sight, put leftovers away as soon as the meal is finished.

Finally, make sure there's plenty of non-food activities. Get out the board games, rent videos, plan a visit to a local historical place of interest. The family will feel pampered, you'll be relaxed and everyone will enjoy the holiday.

∞ THOUGHT FOR THE DAY ∞

There is no rule that says the family can only get together over Thanksgiving or Christmas. Host a family softball tournament in the summer and have everyone sleep outside in tents. With this type of low-key event, the atmosphere will be more relaxed and fun.

JULY 10

Fuel to maintain his fires.
THOMAS CAREW

Many people wonder if it's possible to reduce calories without reducing energy levels. The answer is yes. Applying basic tenets of sports nutrition to your diet will improve your stamina, as long as you exercise on a regular basis. The secret is to know what and when to eat so that you fuel yourself for top performance.

To get more energy, you should be eating carbohydrates. Your body converts carbohydrates into glycogen, which becomes fuel for your muscles. High-protein/low-carbohydrate diets that focus on tuna fish and cottage cheese but no bread, potatoes or pasta, deplete your energy. You find it hard to exercise on a high-protein diet; you feel lethargic and heavy.

You need protein to build and maintain muscles but the energy to make your muscles work comes from carbohydrates. Athletes who regularly compete consume 60 to 70 percent of their calories from carbohydrates. You can do the same. The only difference is that your portion sizes will be smaller.

When you eat is important. Carbohydrates keeps your blood sugar at a normal level. When your blood sugar is too low, you feel light-headed, nauseous and tired. Carbohydrates provide energy for your muscles so it's important to eat before you exercise. You can exercise midmorning after you've had some breakfast or you can jog a couple of hours after your lunch or dinner meal.

∞ THOUGHT FOR THE DAY ∞

Complex carbohydrates are not fattening. Fat is fattening, such as the cream cheese on the bagel, the Alfredo sauce on the pasta, the sour cream, butter and gravy on the potatoes. Carbohydrates are only four calories per gram; fat is more than twice that at nine calories per gram.

JULY 11

*A community is like a ship; everybody ought to be
prepared to take the helm.*

HENRIK IBSEN

It's easy to get so caught up in your own life that you sometimes ignore the larger community that you live in. You expect
services from the community—maintained roads, police and
fire protection, clean water, to name a few. Paying taxes is not
the only one way you can give back to those around you. You
can also get involved in community activities. Volunteering
your time is a good way to contribute to others and enhance
the neighborhood you live in.

If you're a parent, there are many things you can do that
involve children. You can be a Scout leader, room parent or
chaperone school trips. You can join the high school booster
club and sell hot dogs at football games. When you're helping
in ways like these, you're also showing your children that you
care about their lives, that their activities are important too.

You can join a civic organization, such as Jaycees, Lions or
Rotary, that focuses on giving back to the community. You can
lend a hand to a local charity, perhaps one that is sponsored by
your place of worship. You can donate to a food pantry, take
meals to shut-ins and spend some time with a hospice patient.
You can help build a playground.

Remember that you'll probably get back much more than
you give when you join with others in your community. You'll
put some balance in your life. You'll make new friends. You'll
have the satisfaction of being a benefactor. And your community will be a nicer, more pleasant place to live.

THOUGHT FOR THE DAY

*When you support community theater, local art shows, school music
and drama, you're also supporting your community. And you'll be
entertained at the same time.*

JULY 12

Things sweet to taste prove in digestion sour.
WILLIAM SHAKESPEARE

Many people have a sweet tooth or an overwhelming craving for something sweet that seems to pop up without warning. A sweet tooth can work to your advantage if you faithfully remind yourself to reach for a ripe, delicious piece of fruit whenever you crave something sweet. But that sweet tooth works to your disadvantage when you comfort or reward yourself with sugary candy bars, cookies or other sweets.

Sometimes a sweet tooth is really a fat tooth in disguise. If you really wanted only sugar, you'd probably reach for a teaspoon of sugar right out of the sugar bowl. However, you are probably looking for fat—which makes food taste better with sugar. It's the rich creaminess of fat that you crave. Fat and sugar combined give you the delectable taste of chocolate ice cream. If you're after sweets only, try a hard candy or a breath mint. If you're after fats, you should choose a low-calorie treat that tastes rich and creamy, such as non-fat frozen yogurt or pudding made with skim milk.

When that sweet tooth attacks, try to wait it out. Sometimes food cravings will pass in fifteen or twenty minutes. Eating something sour, such as a dill pickle, takes the edge off too. If you must satisfy it, make sure that you do so in moderation. Satisfying a craving doesn't mean permission to overindulge.

∞ THOUGHT FOR THE DAY ∞

You should also be aware of the time of day that your sweet tooth usually acts up, so you can be ready. If you crave sweets late in the afternoon, you'll need to have fruit on hand. If you are inclined to head for the cookie jar the minute you get home from work, have an apple on the way home so you're not ravenous when you walk in the door.

A happy family is but an earlier heaven.

JOHN BOWRING

Family gatherings can be great fun and there's usually a table full of great food. These are occasions where all the family cooks prepare their favorite recipes. Aunt Mary bakes two custard pies, Uncle Max makes his famous homemade ice cream and everyone begs Aunt Lizzie to bring her fried chicken, biscuits and gravy. It's easy to overeat at these events but there are some tricks to make it easier on yourself.

The advantage of several people making food is that you can bring special servings for yourself. If cake is going to be served, for example, you can make sure that you have a healthier dessert substitute on hand. You can buy a low-calorie, low-fat version of a favorite food from the grocery store. When you get home, you can cut the cake into portions, wrap them individually, then pop them into the freezer. When it's party time, you can bring your own serving.

If you are hosting the party, leftovers can be a calorie problem. Instead, you can make sure that every guest goes home with a generous portion of whatever is left over.

∞ THOUGHT FOR THE DAY ∞

If the celebration is in your honor, you can ask for fresh flowers instead of food. Fresh flowers may not last long but they will probably be in your house longer than the chocolate cake.

JULY 14

Things do not change; we do.

HENRY DAVID THOREAU

Stress can produce a lot of energy, but you don't always use that energy appropriately. You see threats where they don't really exist. You make a big deal about issues that aren't really important. Or, you do the opposite—a threat does exist and you ignore it or a loved one's behavior is inappropriate and you deny that there is a problem. Before you react, you need to ask yourself what's really going on.

Some situations, such as the clutter in the house or whether your shirt and socks match, aren't worth fussing about. Yet other situations deserve some attention. Perhaps you purchased something that was too expensive. If your credit card bills show that your personal debt is rising, if you can't pay off your credit cards in full every month, then you have a problem. You have a right to be upset because you understand that the issue is not one purchase—but one in a series of purchases. It's time to hammer away at the problem.

But there are some situations that simply won't change. A family member is determined to be miserable. You're getting older. Your children are growing up and leaving home. You need to stop yammering, let go of your feelings and get on with your life.

You want to make a difference and the the best way is to use your resources where you can make a difference.

∾ THOUGHT FOR THE DAY ∾

Be glad that you want to make a difference in a situation. Focus your resources where you can make a difference.

JULY 15

*I like to walk about amidst the beautiful
things that adorn the world.*

GEORGE SANTAYANA

One of the advantages of walking is that you already know how to do it. But like anything else, there's probably room for improvement. Bob Anderson, in his book *Stretching*, gives some good pointers on how to walk properly.

Balance your head on top of your body. Keep your upper body tall but relaxed. As you walk, make sure you're not leading with your head or leaning forward. Let your arms relax and swing naturally from your shoulders. They should move straight forward rather than across your body. Your wrists and hands should be relaxed—not floppy, but not stiff either. Your fingers will have a slight natural curl. Your arms and legs move in opposition, that is, right leg/left arm forward, then left leg/right arm forward. Point your toes forward. The length of each step should be natural and comfortable for you.

You don't need any special equipment although most walkers recommend you get a good pair of walking shoes that fit properly, offering good shock absorption and cushioning for your feet. They should support your heel to minimize sideways roll, yet be flexible.

The only thing that's left is to take a walk. Invite a friend to join you if you need some motivation and encouragement. It's a good opportunity to visit without focusing on food.

∞ THOUGHT FOR THE DAY ∞

*Many malls sponsor walking clubs, opening indoor concourses early or
posting measured mile courses around the perimeter.*

JULY 16

*The world is a book, and those who do not travel,
read only a page.*

ST. AUGUSTINE

As difficult as moving is, it is also an opportunity to start over. As long as you're packing, you can sort and get rid of stuff. Moving offers you the chance to throw away those fat clothes and other junk that's been accumulating in the bottom drawer of your dresser for a long time. If there's ever a time to hire outside help, this is it. Hire a professional mover or someone to help carry furniture and boxes. You can pack the first couple of boxes yourself so that you'll know where the things are that you need right away. You'll want to find bed linens and towels, the pots and pans you use everyday, the children's favorite toys and anything you'll need for your new job.

Once you've arrived at your new location, you'll need a street map and a phone book. You can then locate nearby places that you'll need, such as a grocery store, hardware store, shopping mall, gasoline station and the like. If you used a real estate broker, that person can probably recommend a good restaurant and a safe place or a nice park to walk. If you plan ahead, you'll know whether your Y membership can be transferred. You can start exploring—on foot, of course. The best way to resettle is to get involved with your new community as soon as possible. Call the local Red Cross, animal shelter or hospital and work as a volunteer for a while. If you have kids in school, you can volunteer some time as a room parent or with the PTA.

∞ THOUGHT FOR THE DAY ∞

*If you're planning to job hunt after you move, get your résumé in
order before you leave. Save yourself long-distance phone charges by
confirming your references before you leave town.*

JULY 17

Not to be sneezed at.

GEORGE COLMAN THE YOUNGER

You're surrounded by harmless, often invisible substances such as pollen, dust, mold spores and animal dander. Some handle these airborne allergens with ease but others have an immune system that overreacts to these substances. If you are allergic, you may have symptoms such as sneezing spells, watery eyes, runny nose, tickling in the throat, blocked ears and asthma.

Seasonal allergies are fairly obvious because they come and go at specific times of the year. You may be allergic to grass or trees in the spring or ragweed in the fall, for example. Other allergens are with you year round. These can be harder to recognize because you may have a mild but overlooked symptom every day of the year. These allergies are caused by dust, dust mites, some fabrics, animal dander and animal saliva. The only way to be sure is to consult a medical specialist and undergo testing. In the typical skin test, a small amount of the suspected allergen is injected under the skin on your upper arm or leg. If a red welt appears, you're allergic to that substance.

Mild allergies can be ignored but once they begin to interfere with your daily routine, you need to see a medical doctor who specializes in allergies and environmental medicine. Treatment is important because untreated allergies put unneeded stress on your body.

∞ THOUGHT FOR THE DAY ∞

If you're having trouble pinpointing the allergen, consider the chemicals in the products that you use every day. You might be allergic to formaldehyde, ethanol, perfume, glycerin, tobacco, perfume or house cleaning chemicals. Speak to your doctor about getting tested.

JULY 18

An act worthy of reward.

JOHN BROWN

As children, many people learned to associate food with rewards or special events. You fell down and scraped your knee and Mom gave you a cookie. You were brave when you got a penicillin shot and the doctor gave you a lollipop. You played the sheriff in the school play and afterward you celebrated with a banana split. Now that you're adults, you have to relearn a few things, including your attitudes about food. You have to learn that the main role of food is nourishment.

Post on the refrigerator door a list of rewards that aren't foods, rewards that give you satisfaction. Include things you like such as a favorite mystery or romance novel, an item you want to purchase, a place to go, a movie to see. Write down ways to pamper yourself such as carving out time alone to listen to a favorite album, sit in solitude or spend time with a good friend. Keep adding to the list whenever a good idea comes to mind.

As you look at this list of rewards, you can ask yourself what it means to you. If the reward means nothing, then it should be crossed off the list because it won't be satisfying. Then pick out a good reward to match a specific goal. For example, if you exercise after work every day this week, you can treat yourself to a special movie this weekend.

∞ THOUGHT FOR THE DAY ∞

Be careful what you teach your children. You don't want
to pass on any inappropriate attitudes about food. A hug,
a new pair of sneakers, an uninterrupted board game with
Dad and the chance to choose what movie the family watches
this weekend are all appropriate rewards for youngsters.

JULY 19

*In the fields of observation chance favors only
the prepared mind.*

LOUIS PASTEUR

When you were a student, you may have had an "exam" dream that sprang from anxieties about taking tests. When finals drew near, Joseph often dreamed he couldn't find his classroom in time to take the exam. But he recalls that when he had been studying well, the dream occurred less often.

The act of preparing gives you a feeling of control. You are doing something that will help so you tend to settle down and relax a little, once you start getting ready. You may be out of school now but the same principles still apply. If you're giving a party, it helps if you make a To Do list several weeks ahead. If you have a deadline at work, you need to work out a schedule so you know all the components will be in place when you need them.

No matter how carefully you prepare, the end situation may still be stressful. You may be faced with a new or unusual combination of events. The exam may be essay questions instead of multiple choice, the refrigerator may break down on the day of the party, your boss may want your project completed a week early.

Part of everyone's life is being faced with a new, unusual or unexpected combination of events. But if you take the time to get ready, you will be more likely to perform well and come up with creative solutions or shortcuts. You no longer have to worry about how you'll do under stress. You know you'll do just fine.

∾ THOUGHT FOR THE DAY ∾

*Put a big calendar on your refrigerator to keep track of family
commitments like Scout meetings, dentist appointments, business
travel and car pool driving days.*

JULY 20

Every man is the architect of his own fortune.

APPIUS CLAUDIUS CAECUS

The best laid plans sometimes go astray, and that includes plans to lose weight. When you have a lapse or setback, it's easy to feel terrible. You're ready to give up because you don't know what to do or how to go about getting back on the program. Here are some strategies that can help.

You need to take responsibility for your own actions. Even if your friends may have been eating ice cream in front of you, your lapse is not their fault. You ate the ice cream too. You should admit what you did, then remind yourself that you can do better next time. You don't have to beat yourself up by getting too critical, too full of self-loathing. Rather than give up, it's better to ask yourself what can you learn from this experience. Rather than feel there is no hope, it's better to remind yourself that no one is perfect all the time.

You need to get back on your program immediately. Now. Not tomorrow or Monday or next January. Your next meal is only a few hours away, so you can get out your food plan. If there is no food plan, you can make one right now. You can decide what you're going to eat at your next meal and when that next meal will be.

∞ THOUGHT FOR THE DAY ∞

Learn from every setback. Once you recognize a personal high-risk situation, you can plan ways to handle it the next time without overeating.

JULY 21

*The fullness of life is in the hazards of life.
And, at the worst, there is that in us
which can turn defeat into victory.*

EDITH HAMILTON

When you're trying to make changes in your behavior, you may need to remind yourself that there are some circumstances that are high risk. These may be specific events or people, uncomfortable feelings, time of day or other occasions that trigger inappropriate behavior such as an urge to eat even when you're not hungry. The problem with these risky situations is that one lapse often leads to another.

How you think about lapses is significant. If you view a lapse as temporary, then you expect that you can and will get back on your program. However, if a lapse triggers overwhelming feelings of guilt, if you feel as though you were completely out of control or if making changes seems too difficult, then you're liable to give up on your program and you won't get back on track until tomorrow or next week or next month or next year.

You need to recognize your own high-risk circumstances. Even when you feel positive, powerful and in control, these situations can suddenly trigger feelings of inadequacy that will make you want to behave or eat inappropriately. Those are the times that you have to use every trick you know to stay on track. If you know what your high risk situations are, then you can prepare. You can stay in control because you are ready, thus lessening the chance that you will lapse or relapse.

∾ THOUGHT FOR THE DAY ∾

Taking care of yourself means you are realistic about what you can and can't control. You can evaluate situations honestly and make good choices for appropriate behaviors.

JULY 22

Healthy families are our greatest national resource.
DOLORES CURRAN

When you're on a weight loss program, the temptation is to insist that everyone in your family follow the same program. But there's likely to be at least one person who isn't interested. If you do the cooking, the challenge is to improve the family's eating habits without encouraging resistance.

Start by making changes gradually. For example, even if you want more meatless meals, the family may not. One solution might be to feed them one meatless meal a week. Over several months you can decrease the amount of meat you prepare.

When you begin to experiment with new foods and dishes, the reaction of your family might be indifferent. But that doesn't necessarily mean they dislike it. Ask them what they think. If they say it's different, but okay, they'll probably learn to like it.

It always helps when the family participates in meal planning. For example, you can ask them to choose whether it's white or brown rice, spaghetti or macaroni, peas or carrots. Ask them to select the vegetable with tonight's chicken dish. The more you involve them, the more likely they are to accept the change.

It may help to let others in the family know that these changes will benefit them. But you need to be realistic and anticipate some resistance. Although you have decided that the changes you're making will benefit everyone, these changes need to happen slowly. Remember that you were resistant to making changes in your food choices too, so be patient. Just as you have learned to change your tastes, so can they.

∞ THOUGHT FOR THE DAY ∞

Accept the fact that some differences are never going to be resolved. If you force your decisions on everyone else, they'll merely resent you. Treat others the way you want to be treated. Offer suggestions; then let them decide.

JULY 23

Work! Work! Work!

THOMAS HOOD

Sometimes when you have a big task to do, you are overwhelmed. There are too many details, too many decisions, too much pressure and not enough time. Dana prepares catalog material on scientific instruments. "The hardest part of the job is dealing with constant interruptions—a co-worker has a question, the phone rings, a vendor stops by, there's a staff meeting," he says. "I'm always losing my train of thought."

One way to deal with a big project is to break it down into smaller pieces. Dana looks at what is due each month and then breaks it down by week. "It's easier for me to think about preparing a few pages a week than many pages a month."

What task is weighing heavily on your mind today? Think about how you can turn it into several easy jobs. Clean house one room at a time; sort your laundry at home before you take it to the Laundromat; do several errands in the same trip; shop for groceries weekly instead of daily. Remember that ants can move dunes but they do it one grain of sand at a time.

⸎ THOUGHT FOR THE DAY ⸎

Take advantage of your answering machine or voice mail. It's more efficient to return phone calls than to answer them because it's easier to end the call quickly and politely if you're the caller.

JULY 24

Vision is the art of seeing things invisible.
JONATHAN SWIFT

You usually have plenty of notice if there is an event or celebration coming up that will feature food. If you are concerned about how you are going to enjoy the celebration and still keep to a program of healthy eating, you need to think about the details of the occasion. Visualize your behavior step-by-step, seeing yourself having a wonderful time and picturing yourself making positive choices about food.

You can make certain choices in advance such as driving instead of taking a train or making arrangements to sit with people who exercise control over their own behavior. You can make up your mind what you are going to drink and how much. If there is food near you, you can picture yourself moving to a table on the other side of the room. You can see yourself standing instead of sitting, moving around the room, meeting new people and conversing with old friends. You can imagine the buffet as a glorious spread of food that is probably going to be irresistible to you. Knowing this, you hear yourself asking a trusted companion to fill your plate for you, knowing that person will make better choices than you will. But you don't want to feel deprived either so you can visualize yourself saving your calories and fat grams for the occasion.

You see yourself flushed with the pleasure of the evening, happy that you know how to handle a party successfully and use behaviors that are appropriate for you. You picture yourself finding your coat and leaving for home. You take a deep breath as you step outside, a breath of power and strength. You enjoy your new success.

THOUGHT FOR THE DAY

Rather than feel sorry for yourself that you can't enjoy yourself at an upcoming event, save calories and fat grams so you can enjoy a guilt-free piece of cake or glass of wine.

Out of the strain of the Doing,
Into the peace of the Done.
JULIA LOUISE WOODRUFF

When you're on a weight loss program, it's important that you make sure that the right tools and foods needed for success are accessible to you. This is not as hard as it seems. After all, the wrong foods have been accessible for some time. You just need to do some replacing.

First, you need to think about how you spend your time so that you can do things that will support losing or maintaining weight. You will need to plan, make a shopping list, decide what you're going to eat for the next day or two, perhaps prepare some dishes in advance. You may decide to join a weight loss program, one with a sensible eating plan. You will need to find some time for physical activities. If you have some high-calorie snacks in the cupboard, you need to get them out of the house and replace them with low-fat, low-calorie foods. You can put your food scale and measuring scoops on the counter so you'll use them. You should be willing to take healthy lunches and snacks to work or make sure that the right foods are available there. You need to choose restaurants that will accommodate your food needs.

The supportive behaviors on this list are easy to do. They only require some thought. Then all you have to do is decide that you're going to follow through.

∾ THOUGHT FOR THE DAY ∾

Be sure to keep a food diary to keep track of what you eat. Writing down every bite makes you aware and minimizes unconscious nibbling.

We all need money, but there are degrees of desperation.

ANTHONY BURGESS

Debbie had problems with money. In fact, her money problems had taken over her life. Although she was only 23 years old, she owed more than $20,000 on her credit cards. She worried about money constantly yet she couldn't seem to stop spending it. It was only when she began to get creditors' phone calls at work that she had to face up to the fact that her spending was out of control.

Compulsive spenders spend money to get emotional relief. Many feel that they deserve something because life hasn't treated them well. Spending money is a way to keep emotions at bay. Mary describes coming home from a shopping spree with armloads of packages, having no idea what she bought. As the pattern of overspending increases, spenders become nervous and irritable when the subject of money comes up. As their financial worries get more serious, they become defensive about how they are spending money. They feel confused and guilty. Spenders will make a budget, but it is difficult for them to stick to it. They continually make new resolutions about their spending habits but can't follow them for very long.

Debbie wised up and got help. She went to a consumer credit counseling service and got financial guidance at a nominal charge. If you need to learn some money management techniques, take advantage of services like these. Debbie did and she is debt-free today.

∾ THOUGHT FOR THE DAY ∾

If your spending patterns are unhealthy ones,
look for relief by getting sound financial assistance.
Your bank can recommend legitimate sources of help.

JULY 27

Peace is when time doesn't matter as it passes by.
MARIA SCHELL

Your home is often a refuge from the stresses of your life. When you're at home, you can find some peace and quiet. You have choices that you don't have at other times during the day. You can answer the phone or not. You can prepare a delicious meal or you can eat leftovers or you can call a friend and go out. Home is a place where you feel safe and in control. For others, the workplace is a refuge. If your job is enjoyable, it is a place to get away from family problems.

Depending on the circumstances of your life, you choose different places of refuge, places of security and peace. You can sit at the beach and watch the ocean for as long as you need to. You can walk down a tree-lined boulevard or wander through a museum. You can sit in the library and read. You can take a ride on a ferry and watch the sea gulls.

What is important is to know that these places of peace exist. Search them out for yourself and go there when you need to refresh your spirit.

∞ THOUGHT FOR THE DAY ∞

Visit your place of worship for peace and tranquillity. You may find it restful and soothing to sit quietly by yourself when no one is around.

*Observe due measure, for right timing is in all things
the most important factor.*

HESIOD

You have long been encouraged to keep a food diary and write
down what you eat. Keeping track of what you eat is a good
start but you are probably underestimating portion size. If you
are trying to lose weight, initially you should weigh and measure portion sizes carefully. Although it can be distracting to
do this, there is a good reason.

Studies show that overweight people tend to underestimate
their food intake by 500 to 1000 calories per day more than
people of normal weight. If you think your calorie intake is
about 1000 calories a day, you might be guessing low. Maybe
it's really closer to 1500 or 2000 calories per day. If that is the
case, no wonder you're not losing any weight; no wonder
you're frustrated.

Weigh and measure your food carefully; then write it down.
It's best to weigh and measure food with the proper tools—a
food scale, measuring scoops, cups and spoons. These are specially designed to help you keep track of portion sizes.

❧ THOUGHT FOR THE DAY ❧

*Compare portion sizes to your hand for some quick estimates. Your
fist is about one cup or 1 medium whole fruit. Your thumb is the size
of 1 ounce of cheese or meat. Your thumb tip equals 1 tablespoon; a
fingertip equals 1 teaspoon. Your cupped hand will hold 1–2 ounces of
pretzels or nuts. A piece of cooked poultry or fish the size of your palm
(minus fingers) is about 3 ounces.*

The talk that filled the kitchen those afternoons was highly functional. It served as therapy, the cheapest kind available to my mother and her friends.

PAULE MARSHALL

There are many feelings associated with stress—fear, anxiety, and panic, to name a few. You may feel there are so many emotions bottled up inside you that you are about to explode. You may not know where to turn or how to deal with your stress. You don't know what to do.

One surprisingly effective way is simply to release those feelings. Expressing your feelings, in an appropriate way, can do a lot to improve your mood. Some people like to write in a diary, journal or notebook. When you see those feelings in black and white, it often gets easier to step back and get perspective. You may realize you are overreacting or you may suddenly find that there is a different way of looking at this situation. Once your feelings are on the page, you can often write your way out of the feelings and into a solution.

Another equally good alternative is to share how you feel with another person. A good listener will help you listen to yourself. Anytime you are talking, you should listen to the words that you're saying. It will help if you try and step aside and listen to your words with some objectivity. You may talk yourself into a new approach, especially if you try and process your feelings. You can say this is how I feel or this was my reaction. You can ask yourself if there is a better, more appropriate way for you to handle the situation.

❧ THOUGHT FOR THE DAY ❧

A friend can give you support and encouragement but a qualified professional therapist is more likely to give you a new way of looking at the situation and offer positive suggestions to help you deal with the situation better the next time around.

Just say no.

NANCY REAGAN

If you're on a weight loss program, you don't always know what to do when someone pushes food at you. If you find it hard to be assertive, then staying on your eating plan becomes a definite challenge. Here are some ideas to help you stay on your program when you're dining in a restaurant or are a dinner guest in someone's home.

You need to be aware of your food needs. If you want your foods prepared a certain way, you need to tell the waiter or hostess ahead of time or you can bring your own food. You might need to tell your hostess that you have had enough when second helpings are offered. You may also need to tell your dining partners that you don't want to share or taste their desserts.

You should practice new behaviors whenever necessary. You can take one small bite and leave the rest, if you think you are capable of that. You can ask to take the food home to eat later; once home you can give it to a neighbor or your dog or throw it in the garbage can. You can also practice saying no in a firm but gentle voice. You can practice saying that you would appreciate their help in not tempting you with more food than you really want to eat.

After you return home from the restaurant or party, you can think about how you did. The idea is not to judge yourself but rather see what you learned from the experience. Perhaps you need to practice some more refusals or maybe you deserve a pat on the back for the good progress you've made. Remember that speaking up for what you need may be difficult at first but it gets easier every time you do.

∾ THOUGHT FOR THE DAY ∾

Many people find it helpful to keep a small notebook handy. They keep special phrases they can use to make it easier to ask for those needs.

Nobody has ever measured, even poets,
how much a heart can hold.

ZELDA FITZGERALD

When you are stressed, you react physically as well as mentally. Your blood pressure increases, your heart beats faster and more blood goes to your muscles for extra energy. Your body is getting ready to do battle or run fast—the fight-or-flight response.

However, if you don't expend this extra energy, you can damage your heart. Over time, the muscle wall of the heart can become thicker but your heart will not make extra blood vessels to feed this muscle wall. So the heart muscle can become flabby and dilated and will have a harder time doing its job of moving blood through the body.

So what do you do to protect your heart? Exercise. Aerobic exercise makes your heart stronger so that it has to pump fewer times per minute to circulate the same amount of blood. To exercise aerobically, you want to push your heart to 60–75 percent of its maximum. Although there are Target Zone charts in any health club or Y with recommended heart rates for your age group, here are some easy guidelines to follow. You want to push your heart and body a moderate amount. If you're excessively winded and sweating profusely, you're working too hard. If you're just breaking a sweat, you're probably about right. You should be able to talk while exercising without gasping for breath; if you can sing, you're not working hard enough.

∞ THOUGHT FOR THE DAY ∞

Start with a comfortable 20 minute walk three times a week. As your
conditioning improves, you'll find that you need to walk longer or
faster to get your heart rate up. When this happens, congratulate
yourself. You've increased your fitness already.

Nothing is good or bad but by comparison.

THOMAS FULLER

The rate at which people lose weight varies a great deal from one person to another. Many things influence how you will lose weight. Men generally lose faster than women. Weight comes off faster when you're younger than when you're older. The more weight you have to lose, the longer it will take. People who exercise lose weight faster and are more likely to keep it off permanently.

You have to be careful and try not to compare your weight loss progress with someone else's. When you compare, you start getting competitive. If your friend loses weight a little faster then you do, for whatever reasons, suddenly you feel there is something wrong with you. You need to focus on your own goals, your own achievements and resist the temptation to compare. The more personal you make your weight loss effort, the more successful you're going to be.

You will also be more successful in losing weight when you lose weight for yourself, not for another person. You need to allow yourself to lose weight at whatever rate is right for your particular body. You should take care to pay attention only to your own accomplishments and not to someone else's. You need to celebrate your own milestones, not the next person's. You all lose weight at different rates but the only weight loss that counts is your own.

∾ THOUGHT FOR THE DAY ∾

Select a weight loss program that recommends that you lose no more than one or two pounds a week. A slow and steady loss is more likely to become permanent because it reflects positive changes in your lifestyle.

AUGUST 2

As cold as cucumbers.

FRANCIS BEAUMONT AND JOHN FLETCHER

If you're on a weight loss program, it's worth the time to give your kitchen and pantry a makeover—not a remodeling but a food reorganization. By keeping high-calorie and high-fat snacks out of the kitchen, or at least out of sight, you minimize temptation and eat more appropriately. Try these tips for reorganizing your refrigerator.

Start with the freezer. Put high-fat treats like ice cream in the back, out of sight. Put healthy treats like frozen bananas or seedless grapes in the front. Stack frozen vegetables with frozen beans, hamburger or chicken; this is a good reminder that proteins and vegetables go together at a meal.

Now reorganize the refrigerator. Put water, flavored seltzer, skim milk and orange juice in the front on the top shelf. This makes it easier to drink enough liquids during the day. Use the second shelf for snacks. Keep sliced veggies next to a jar of salsa.

On the bottom shelf, keep quick meal ideas together. For example, put tuna, tomatoes and fresh green beans next to each other or place fat-free cheeses and sauces alongside cooked pasta. Keep dinner ingredients in the crisper. That way you'll add spinach to your lasagna or when you're making meat loaf, you'll be sure to add onion, green peppers and rice. Stash foods that you want to keep out of sight in the fruit bin like cookies, candy in a jar or peanut butter. Finally, keep fresh spices and bottles of flavorings in the refrigerator door.

THOUGHT FOR THE DAY

Count the number of times you open the refrigerator, other than when you're preparing a meal. Remember, every time you look inside, you're inviting temptation. By counting the times your hand is on the handle of the refrigerator, you'll become aware of how many times you look inside even when you don't want to eat.

AUGUST 3

One sword keeps another in the sheath.
GEORGE HERBERT

If you're bored with the same old aerobic classes, think about taking a self-defense course. Few people would know what to do if mugged or attacked but there are some simple kicks and shoves that any person can learn. Basic self-defense courses teach you how to yell, hit your attacker with the full force of your body, then get away. Form helps but what's most important is to repeat the moves over and over so that your muscles will remember in an emergency. Here are some moves that are easy to learn and very effective.

1. If grabbed from the front or side above your elbows near your shoulders, use your legs and your knees to hit your attacker's abdomen or ribs. Lift your leg up and inward as though trying to hit the side of the attacker's body.

2. If grabbed from the rear and the attacker has hold of your upper shoulders, use your elbow. Aim for the center of your attacker's body which will be right behind you. Step to the side, make a fist to tense your muscles, and shove your elbow backward at waist level.

3. If attacked from the front and very close to your face, use your elbow, bending and raising it to shoulder level. As you twist, your elbow is free to hit the attacker's side, ribs, abdomen and possibly the neck and face.

The best self-defense, of course, is to not get in situations where you're liable to be attacked like walking alone on dark streets.

∾ THOUGHT FOR THE DAY ∾

Walk with a strong purposeful stride. If you don't look like a victim, the chances are good that you won't be one.

AUGUST 4

*I think dogs are the most amazing creatures;
they give unconditional love. For me they
are the role model for being alive.*

GILDA RADNER

Jake's doctor was surprised at the good improvement in Jake's health until he learned about Sadie. Sadie was Jake's new dog and he had been taking her on a long walk twice a day. "Actually," Jake explains, "Sadie walks me." He says that their early morning walks are the best. "That's when I do my best thinking. I use that time for mulling over problems and planning my day. By the time I get back home, I feel organized and in control." At night, he likes to walk after dark because it's peaceful and quiet.

Dogs can be trained to help people with sight, hearing and other physical handicaps. Dogs also give their owners a feeling of security because they will bark at strangers and display other protective behaviors. Let your dog help you get in shape. Dogs need plenty of exercise so a daily walk or two is good for both owner and pet.

If you're thinking about getting a dog, size the dog to your lifestyle and space availability. Dogs require more attention and care than some other pets but they are loyal and faithful companions in return. After a long hard day at work, it's reassuring and soothing to be greeted with a friendly bark and a wagging tail.

THOUGHT FOR THE DAY

If your dog is difficult to control, remember that dogs respond well to training so obedience school is a good option to consider.

Patience is bitter but its fruit is sweet.

JEAN JACQUES ROUSSEAU

Each of us has different eating styles. For example, some prefer three meals a day, while others are happiest with five or six very light meals throughout the day. One eating style is as good as another as long as you cover certain bases.

It's best to distribute calories evenly throughout the day. If you're trying to change your eating pattern, aim for three meals a day and a couple of snacks. A low-fat, high-fiber diet that includes a variety of foods will meet your nutritional needs. Most experts also recommend that you eat more of your calories in the beginning or the middle of the day. If you eat a light dinner, you'll be hungry in the morning and in the mood for a good breakfast.

When preparing foods, you'll add less fat if you poach, grill, steam, bake, boil or broil. If you eat sensibly every day, you can have the occasional special dinner or dessert without feeling guilty. What you want to avoid is the all-or-nothing approach where you starve all day and then eat one big meal at night. The problem is that one big meal is liable to turn into a binge.

You should be patient with yourself while you learn to create circumstances that make it easier to eat more healthfully. You know what to do but it really does take practice to put your knowledge to work.

∞ THOUGHT FOR THE DAY ∞

Get a diagram of the food pyramid from the library or a home economics teacher at your local high school. Post it on the refrigerator and use it as a starting point to make this week's shopping list.

Man is a tool-using animal.

THOMAS CARLYLE

You may own more cooking gadgets and time-saving devices than your grandmother but you're probably doing a lot less cooking. You're spending less time preparing meals and you're cooking fewer meals. If you're like most people, as much as one-third of your food budget is spent in restaurants or on take-out food. Many grocery stores are now offering salad bars, expanded delicatessens and gourmet take-out dishes.

To cook a healthful meal, you need a few good tools—a paring knife, vegetable peeler, cutting board and a few bowls. To make healthier meals in less time, try these shortcuts.

Purchase fresh vegetables and salad fixings that have been pre-cleaned and cut or frozen vegetables without sauce. Buy lean beef already cubed for fondues or stew. Choose skinless boneless chicken already cut into strips for stir-fries or use ground turkey in your next batch of chili. Bake potatoes in the microwave and make quick-cooking rice. Serve fresh fruit for dessert.

Whenever possible, prepare and cook double portions; then freeze leftovers in single portions in containers that can go from the freezer into the microwave or oven. Use the electric slow cooker for great stews, soups and casseroles; pop in the ingredients before you leave for work and dinner will be ready when you get home.

∾ THOUGHT FOR THE DAY ∾

Get the family involved to help wash, slice and chop.
Even youngsters can use a salad spinner.

> *Change gives you branches, letting you*
> *stretch and grow and reach new heights.*
>
> PAULINE R. KEZER

When you're trying to lose weight, be realistic about personal limits. If ice cream is a weakness, you should not walk into the ice cream parlor. When you decide to treat yourself, write it in your diary before it goes in your mouth. "I am consciously and willingly choosing to have this banana split." It's more difficult to sabotage yourself when you see it in writing. You may even make a different choice at that point. "I am consciously and willingly choosing to have a child-size sherbet cone."

Make lifestyle changes quietly and slowly. Prepare a few meals each week using low-fat cooking methods—poach, bake or broil instead of fry. Start choosing restaurants that offer healthier options. Suggest non-eating activities to your friends like going to the movies or taking a walk. They'll probably be happy to join you. If they are unaware you're trying to lose weight, the saboteurs will leave you alone.

Remember that fat-free foods still have calories. If you want foods that can be eaten in unlimited quantities, reach for fresh fruits and vegetables. Remember that the focus of your diet should be not fat-free foods but fresh foods such as grains, fruits and vegetables. These automatically save you calories and most are free of fat and additives.

Lighten up. Assume that a bad day will creep in every now and then. If you backslide a bit, you're only human and you shouldn't beat yourself up. If you get back on your program, then it will be an isolated incident and you can move forward to the next healthy meal.

∞ THOUGHT FOR THE DAY ∞

Learn to read food labels. No more than 30 percent of the food you
eat should get its calories from fat.

AUGUST 8

Serenely full, the epicure would say,
Fate cannot harm me, I have dined today.
SYDNEY SMITH

Everyone reacts to stress in different ways. One person's reaction isn't better or worse than another's; it's simply different. Justin and Felicia were in a car accident. Although neither were seriously injured, their car was totaled and it was a stressful event for both. "Once we were safe at home," Felicia recalls, "I cried from relief. But Justin wolfed down a large pizza!"

When you are under stress, you may find yourself eating inappropriately. If you use food to calm down, that dish of ice cream becomes a tranquilizer. A chocolate candy bar soothes your hurt feelings after an argument. Those three doughnuts on the way to work help ease the tensions of a high-stress job.

If you turn to food when under stress, remember that food is a poor solution to the problem. Substitute something else. Use physical exercise to release energy and tension. Listen to music, call a friend, have a good cry, read a book, take a walk, meditate. There are many healthy ways to respond to stress — and most are calorie-free.

THOUGHT FOR THE DAY

If you must chew, reach for an sweet crunchy apple or a bowl
of air-popped popcorn (without butter, of course).

*So the legs are a little short, the knees
maybe knock a little but who listens?*

GERTRUDE BERG

Beautiful legs are one reason many women start walking. They
want to get their legs firm and in shape and grooming makes
them more appealing.

The best time to shave your legs is after a shower or bath.
The water has softened your skin and plumped up the hairs. It
is better to lather your legs with a special shaving cream or gel
rather than soap. The aloe in these gels will soothe your skin
and keep the hair hydrated so that it's easier to shave. Shave
diagonally upward on the shins. Take special care because the
shins are the easiest part of the leg to nick and cut. Never
shave sunburned skin. Use moisturizer and sunburn balm and
let the irritation heal before you shave the skin. You shouldn't
shave your legs immediately before sunbathing either, as your
skin will be especially prone to burning.

Use a brush or pumice stone to exfoliate the dead dry skin
on your feet. Foot scrubs are good for heels and calluses. A
beauty salon pedicure is a nice treat but a home pedicure after
a bath or shower is just as nice. Use clippers and cut toenails
so that the corners are squared off; this will help prevent in-
grown toenails. Shape and smooth with an emery board; then
rub lotion into cuticles to soften and moisturize them. If
desired, you can push back cuticles with an orange stick
wrapped in cotton. Then apply a coat or two of a favorite color
nail polish. Finish by massaging your feet and legs using moisturizer or baby oil.

∽ THOUGHT FOR THE DAY ∾

*To get calves in shape, stand with feet hip distance apart. Rise up on
the balls of the feet, hold, then lower heels to the floor. Repeat ten times.
Another good exercise is to pick up marbles with the toes of one foot
while balancing on the other.*

AUGUST 10

The rainy days a man saves for usually
seem to arrive during his vacation.

KIN HUBBARD

Vacations are supposed to be a time to relax, renew yourself and have fun. But if you overeat, you'll return home depressed, guilty and overweight. But if you plan ahead, you can have a wonderful vacation without packing on the pounds.

Remember that vacations are not an excuse to go wild and binge on food. Good exercise and good eating habits should follow you wherever you go—whether it's a day at home or a vacation day far away.

If you are traveling by car, pack a cooler with diet soda, fruits and crunchy vegetables for snacks. If you are flying, you can request a special meal when you make your reservations. Before signing up for a tour, you can check to see if they can accommodate any special dietary needs that you have.

Travel books will tell you a lot about the area you are planning to visit. You can decide which regional cuisine dishes will best fit into your food plan. Some people find it easier to stay in control if they keep a food diary during their trip.

Cruises can be great fun. You can take advantage of the on-board fitness centers, swimming pools and exercise classes. Extras like massages and spa beauty treatments are sometimes available, too. Since cruise ships tend to have food out all day long, you can plan to be busy during most of the meals or request a later seating to minimize evening nibbling. Most cruise ships now offer low-fat, low-calorie choices, but you should make sure before you finalize your reservations.

∞ THOUGHT FOR THE DAY ∞

If the cruise ship buffet is irresistible, you can ask your traveling companion to fill your plate for you, if you're sure he or she will make better choices than you might. Or, use the rule of four: \Circle the entire buffet table; then select only four items.

AUGUST 11

How soon unaccountable I became tired and sick.
WALT WHITMAN

If you feel tired all the time, there could be several reasons. Pay attention to your body and try to figure out the cause.

When you are under pressure, your body releases stress hormones, including adrenaline, which increase your pulse rate and blood pressure. You breathe harder and faster—which is fine if you're about to fight or flee. The problem is you do neither but those hormones are still flooding your body. The only way to get rid of them is to exercise. A 20-minute walk will do the job but it must be a very fast 20-minute walk. Without it, the stress hormones will wear you out. Relaxation techniques will help your stress response shut down too. You can sit quietly, listen to the sound of your breathing or tense and release each major muscle group until your body relaxes.

Exercise can tire you out too. If you're exhausted after you exercise, you did too much. When you work at a level of intensity that your body can handle, you'll notice an increase in energy within a few days. Then you can gradually increase your exercise until you're happy with your fitness goals. The problem may be simply that you need more sleep. If so, a weekend on the couch may not be enough to catch up. You'll need an extra hour every night for a month or more to recover from chronic sleep deprivation.

Try these suggestions and see if you feel more energized. Sometimes small and seemingly minor lifestyle changes can make major lifestyle differences.

∾ THOUGHT FOR THE DAY ∾

Remember that you do not have to be as frenetic as everyone around you. If you are calm and tranquil, others will be coming to you for advice on how to slow down and gain control.

AUGUST 12

Great wide, beautiful, wonderful world,
With the wonderful water round you curled.

WILLAM BRIGHTY RANDS

Have you tried water aerobics yet? This is a fun variation of the traditional aerobics class, except classes are held in a pool instead of the gym. Pam, a quilt store owner, started attending water aerobics classes last year after recovering from back surgery. "I was out of shape and run down," she says. "Exercising in the pool was a safe exercise for me. And after a long day in the store, it's a great way to unwind too."

Although you may not feel like you're working as hard—the water keeps you cool and there's minimal impact to harm your joints—the cardiovascular benefits are plentiful. Water provides resistance for your whole body, not just your legs. And because you're buoyant, it's easier on your joints. Moves that are high impact in the gym, such as jumping jacks, are low impact in the pool. Some classes utilize special belts that let you float in a upright position without touching the bottom of the pool. Water dumbbells are made from styrofoam but when you are pulling and pushing them under water, there is a great deal of resistance so your arms and abdomen get a good workout.

All you need is a bathing suit or swim trunks and the willingness to try something new. Try a water aerobics class today. It might be the most fun you've had in a long time.

THOUGHT FOR THE DAY

If the bottom of the pool irritates your feet, try some water shoes
or sneakers specially designed for water workouts.

There's no sauce in the world like hunger.
MIGUEL DE CERVANTES

To be a smart food shopper, you need a shopping list. Its purpose is to keep you focused on what you need so you can avoid impulse purchases and ignore the specials at the ends of the aisles. It's not a great buy if it's not on your list.

A healthy food should have no more than 30 percent of its calories from fat. That means no more than 3 grams of fat for every 100 calories. Here's a table that will make it easy:

THIS MUCH FAT, MAXIMUM	FOR THIS MANY CALORIES
3 grams	100 calories
6 grams	200 calories
9 grams	300 calories
12 grams	400 calories

Do most of your shopping along the outside walls of the supermarket. You'll find fresh fruits and vegetables, milk products, meat and other essentials. Leave your cart when you step into the inner aisles for grains, such as breads, rice, cereals and pasta. What you want to avoid is aimlessly wandering through the entire store, filling your cart with impulse buys. The best time to shop is after you've eaten so that you're not hungry when you walk in. You'll also shop more intelligently if you have sufficient time. With a little organization you'll only have to shop for staples every two or three weeks and the rest of the time will be short trips to pick up milk, fresh produce and bread.

∞ THOUGHT FOR THE DAY ∞

If you want something crunchy, the best choices are pretzels and air-popped popcorn. If chips are a must, buy corn tortillas, cut them into wedges and crisp them in your oven.

AUGUST 14

Never does nature say one thing and wisdom another.
JUVENAL

When you're stressed, it's easy to get caught up in your own world, your own problems. You forget that there are other worlds besides your own. One way to slow down and get some perspective is to pay attention to nature. Find a park or a plot of ground and sit down. Be still and listen to the sounds. Listen to the wind blowing, the leaves rustling, the birds and insects chirping. These are the sounds of the world that sustain you, nourish you, and give you life.

Look at the colors around you. Green is the color of growth and renewal: the grass and pine needles, the color of moss on the north side of the tree, the color of algae in a nearby pond. See how many different shades and tints of green you can find. Look carefully and see that each green is different from the next. Some are yellow, some are brown, some are blue yet at a glance they look like the same green.

If you sit as still as you can, you will soon become aware of how lively the natural world is. Plants and trees sway, birds swoop from branch to branch, squirrels and chipmunks scurry about looking for food, small insects carry enormous loads back to their hiding places.

You need to think about your place in this natural world and respect the lessons it has to offer you. You need to remember that your personal world is quite small and other worlds exist alongside your own. Let the natural world be a place you can return to, a place to regain perspective, a place of peace, a place that is there for eternity.

∞ THOUGHT FOR THE DAY ∞

Use your powers of observation to take a new look at what goes on at home. Look and listen for new messages from other family members.

One cannot think well, love well,
sleep well, if one has not dined well.

VIRGINIA WOOLF

When you are stressed, you may be so burned out and exhausted that you wonder if you're ever going to get your energy back. The good news is that it's possible to stay energized even in the throes of a crisis. When your body needs energy, it first uses the glucose in your blood stream, then it turns to the glycogen in your muscles and liver and converts it to glucose. When you are out of glycogen, your body finally looks for fat to burn.

What you eat is of primary importance. The more stress you're under, the more glycogen you need. The best source of this fuel is complex carbohydrates—foods like pasta, rice, potatoes, breads, cereals, fruits and vegetables. Complex carbohydrates are more stable than simple carbohydrates like sugar or honey. They're absorbed more slowly so your energy level is steady. For an energy boost, reach for a piece of fruit; have a sweet potato for lunch and rice for dinner. You can also eat lots of vegetables without eating too many calories. Your energy stays up and your stressed bodies continue to run efficiently.

What you don't want are simple carbohydrates such as sugar or corn syrup, molasses or honey. Although simple carbohydrates are stored as glucose, they only give you a short-lived energy boost soon followed by a letdown feeling.

∾ THOUGHT FOR THE DAY ∾

If you've had a stressful morning, have a low-fat lunch with a little lean protein, such as broiled fish or a salad with tuna or chicken breast and lots of complex carbohydrates. A high-fat lunch will cause you to fade in the middle of the afternoon.

Let him step to the music which he hears.

HENRY DAVID THOREAU

Step aerobics are low-impact exercises that involve stepping on and off a platform, or step, that can be raised or lowered with risers. Most instructors use a step and two sets of risers, making the bench 6 inches off the floor. Beginners, however, should start with the lowest platform height—or even no platform at all—until they are comfortable with the moves.

The basic move is to step on, then off the bench one foot at a time, right foot up, left foot up, right foot down, left foot down. The variations are easy. For example, step and lift your knee or step across the top and walk around to the front again. Just be sure to step onto the bench with your whole foot. If you let your heel hang off, you can injure your Achilles tendon.

Stay close and keep an eye on the bench, especially in the beginning, to avoid a misstep and possible fall or twisted ankle. Add the arm movements after you're comfortable with what your feet are doing. Most classrooms have full length mirrors so it's easy to see what you're doing. Just be careful not to overdo. If you feel dizzy or out of breath, march in place or move around in the back of the room until you feel better.

Step aerobics can be a great way to get in shape. They're easy and fun to do, especially if you're taking a class. So if you've gotten bored with regular aerobics, try this easy, low-impact exercise. Then step your way to good health.

∽ THOUGHT FOR THE DAY ∽

If you want to practice by yourself, rent a video and try it at home first. A step bench isn't necessary. You can simply do the moves on the floor.

AUGUST 17

Much smoking kills live men and cures dead swine.

GEORGE D. PRENTICE

One of the reasons that smokers hesitate to quit is that they are fearful that they will gain weight. In fact, many smokers do maintain a slightly lower weight because their bodies must work hard to get rid of nicotine, a toxic substance. This increased metabolism also interferes with the body's ability to store fat. When you quit smoking, your metabolism slows down but it is simply returning to normal. The average smoker may gain only 5 to 10 pounds when he or she stops, a small price to pay for living 8 years longer.

To keep your weight gain to a minimum, you should eat like you used to smoke, slowly savoring each bite and tasting every morsel. The slower you eat, the calmer you'll feel. You can put down your fork, chew your food thoroughly, sip some water and have a leisurely dinner and conversation with a friend. You want to avoid eating fast, lest you stuff down extra helpings that you normally wouldn't eat.

When you quit smoking, you need to be easy on yourself and not get too discouraged. It may take a few weeks or months before you feel normal or have any confidence that you can say no if a cigarette is offered. Most of your friends have quit and so can you. Quitting smoking is a gift to yourself and your family. You can congratulate yourself for having the gumption to give up an unhealthy habit. Once you've quit, you will feel an enormous relief, knowing that you finally did what you've been fretting about for so many years.

∞ THOUGHT FOR THE DAY ∞

Smokers also harm the people who live with them. Children whose parents smoke have many more bouts of bronchitis and pneumonia and their spouses have higher rates of lung cancer even if they don't smoke than spouses of nonsmokers.

AUGUST 18

These . . . times call for the building of plans.

FRANKLIN DELANO ROOSEVELT

Hannah is a first grade teacher. Before school starts each September, she uses her weekly planner and marks the end of each marking period for the coming school year. Then for each subject, she records in her planner where she wants to be in terms of the material that she has to teach. As the school year progresses, she has little reminders of what the academic progress should be. If she is falling behind, she can make plans to catch up. If she is ahead, she can use the extra time for special enrichment activities.

Hannah decided to use her planning skills in her personal life too. She felt that too many years had passed and she hadn't accomplished what she wanted to. She decided this year she would do three things: lose weight, clean out every closet and save money. She used a personal planner to set out an easy and reasonable schedule that would help her accomplish her goals by the end of the school year. She wrote down a date by which she had to start attending a weight-loss support group and a date by which she had to start exercising. She gave herself monthly reminders as to how much money she should have saved so far, how many closets she should have cleaned and how she should be doing on her weight loss program.

Use this technique. A planner is an easy way to keep your goals in focus and remind you of where you want to go. It also reinforces the fact that you're getting there.

∾ THOUGHT FOR THE DAY ∾

Remember to set realistic goals. Losing 200 pounds, saving $100,000 and winning the lottery are fantasy goals. But you can easily lose one or two pounds a week and save 5 percent or even 10 percent of your take-home pay if you plan carefully.

By means of water, We give life to everything.
THE KORAN

Once you are on a regular exercise program, you should find that exercising energizes you. If not, perhaps you need to pay more attention to the foods you eat. But if your diet is sound, then you need to look further. Perhaps your lethargy is due to dehydration.

Your body require six to eight glasses of water every day. If you're exercising regularly and actively, you may need more. When you're exercising, you perspire to cool your skin and keep your body temperature down. But sweat is also a sign that you're losing water. If you sweat a lot, you might be well advised to weigh yourself before and after exercise to see if you're dehydrating. Each pound of sweat you drop while exercising means a 10-ounce water loss. If you lose more than 2 percent of your total body weight, you will get overheated. For example, a 150-pound person is dehydrated if more than 3 pounds are dropped while exercising. Another way to tell if you're dehydrated is to look at your urine. It should be clear and excreted in large quantities. If you're dehydrated, your urine turns dark and very little is excreted.

It's best to drink plenty of fluids throughout the day and especially during or after exercise. Plain water is best; sports drinks merely add extra calories—as many as 60 to 80 calories per 8 ounces. Many people find the easiest way to drink enough water is to put a big pitcher on a countertop or desk and then sip all day.

∞ THOUGHT FOR THE DAY ∞

Buy yourself a pretty carafe and water glass. Fill the carafe in the morning and make an effort to empty it by the end of the day.

AUGUST 20

Your blood vessels are surrounded by muscle tissue. When you're stressed, your muscles tighten and constrict your blood vessels at the same time. Your blood pressure rises. This serves you well if you're in physical danger because you'll be able to run faster and fight harder.

The problem is that long-term stress can lead to chronic high blood pressure, causing small cracks in the interior walls of your blood vessels. They become scarred and thickened with fat and calcium deposits. Scar tissue forms and these arteries become narrower and less elastic. After many years, you are diagnosed with arteriosclerosis.

Remember that your body causes your blood pressure to rise in order to give you more energy. So if you're not going to fight or flee, you'd better exercise. Exercise uses up that extra energy and keeps your muscles and blood vessels elastic. Your muscles work and your blood vessels dilate. Afterwards, in fact, your blood pressure will be lower than before the stress event.

∾ THOUGHT FOR THE DAY ∾

Here's another reason to stop smoking. Cigarette smoking contributes to rigid, inelastic blood vessels —and, therefore, high blood pressure.

*Life is a process of becoming, a combination
of states we have to go through.*

ANAÏS NIN

When you decide to make some major changes in your life, you often are motivated by outside influences. Your doctor tells you that it's time to lose weight or you have a class reunion coming up and you want to look your best. This external motivation gives you a jump start and you're off. But a few weeks later, you hit a plateau.

How you handle plateaus is critical. If you react with frustration, you may end up back where you started. The way to deal with plateaus is to start looking inside yourself and find your own inner motivation.

It is important that you focus on the process of losing weight instead of the result. You'll begin to realize that the process of weight loss gives you more energy. Once you start to appreciate the inner changes, you'll usually feel encouraged enough to outlast a plateau. With improved self-esteem, you'll find the strength to continue the program you started.

Joining a support group is helpful when you're on a plateau. It's a chance to compare notes with others to get ideas when your own motivation is lagging. You can reward yourself for sticking it out too: a new pair of earrings, that novel that you've been wanting to read, an herbal scented pillow. As you continue to substitute new behaviors for old, you won't be bored and you will no longer feel deprived. You'll be energized and excited about your program.

∞ THOUGHT FOR THE DAY ∞

Make a contract with yourself today. List the reasons that you've decided to lose weight or get in shape. List the specifics of how you're going to do it. Even though this is a contract with yourself, treat it like any legitimate contract. In other words, it should be honored.

AUGUST 22

The body never lies.

MARTHA GRAHAM

Your immune system is a wonderful defense system. It's a complex network of specialized cells that defend your body against harmful invading bacteria. If a foreign substance like a harmful bacteria or virus enters your body, the immune system kicks into action. First, the invader is attacked by a scavenger cell called a macrophage. The macrophage then calls the white blood cells into action. White blood cells, also called T-cells, bring more immune cells to the attack. They track down infected cells, stimulate B-cells and finally your body produces antibodies that attack and overpower the foreign microbe.

When your immune system is not working properly, diseases appear. Allergies, arthritis, cancer and AIDS, for example, are among the diseases that have been linked to a deficiency in your immune system. Immune deficiencies often appear because your body has already been busy fighting off another sickness. That's why it's important to rest when you're sick so that you don't get one infection on top of another. Stress can also cause immune deficiencies, causing the number of T-cells and B-cells to drop. It also causes the adrenal glands to release corticosteroids. These chemicals are major suppressers of the immune system. In fact, they are used to prevent rejection after an organ transplant.

You protect your immune system the same way you protect your body. You need regular exercise, good nutrition and proper rest. You also need to develop strategies and behaviors that keep your stress level under control.

∽ THOUGHT FOR THE DAY ∽

Give your immune system a boost by taking a daily multi-vitamin. If you're interested, ask your doctor about other supplements that might be helpful.

The good man is the man who . . .
is moving to become better.
JOHN DEWEY

One way to take charge of your life is to set some goals. Goals are important because they help you find purpose. Short-term goals, such as making an appointment to have your teeth cleaned, changing the oil in the car or completing an important project at work help you organize your immediate future. Long-term goals are important, too, though it's easy to lose sight of them. Then you feel frustrated because another few years have flashed by and you're not sure you utilized your time well or accomplished what you had hoped to accomplish.

Take time now to focus your attention on long-term goals. You can start with asking yourself what you would like to accomplish in the next twelve months. Perhaps you've been dreaming about a special vacation or a big purchase that you are ready to save money for. Maybe you need to get your résumé together and begin looking for a better job. You should also address goals for the rest of your life. Some of these might be related to finances or decisions about retirement.

But you need personal goals too. Learning, for example, should be a lifelong goal. You might want to become fluent in another language or build a boat and learn to sail it. Some of your goals should be related to fun. You might want to join a community theater group, do a little acting or spend some free time as a stage hand. Go to trade shows and see the latest in computers or motorcycles. Read travel magazines to spark your interests. Take a cruise and see a palm tree or an iceberg.

∾ THOUGHT FOR THE DAY ∾

Make sure one of your goals is to get in shape. The rest of your life will be more enjoyable if you can spend it in a healthy and fit body.

AUGUST 24

And on his back the burden of the world.

EDWIN MARKHAM

When you're stressed, it shows in how you hold yourself. You are tense, in a hurry, your mind on the zillion things you need to do. You walk fast but you're holding your body tight, leaning forward as though gale force winds are trying to blow your feet out from under you. Your back is rounded; your shoulders are hunched. You bend over and grab a heavy bag of groceries with one hand and a fretful child with the other. Women tote large purses; men carry heavy briefcases and tool boxes. It's no wonder that so many of us suffer from chronic back pain.

The everyday activities of bending and lifting can take a toll on your lower spine. But a few simple changes in how you do these things can protect your back and prevent further injury. First of all, try to stand tall and erect. Imagine you're a marionette with a thin rope strung from the bottom of your feet through the top of your head. Pull on that string and your back becomes straight. Pull your shoulders back and down to open up your chest.

When lifting, bend your knees and keep your back as straight as possible instead of bending at the waist and rounding your back. The idea is to keep the weight of your body or whatever you are carrying centered over your legs and feet. To lessen the load on your spine when carrying something, try to hold it close to your body.

Take a few moments throughout the day to be mindful of your back. Be sure you're standing or sitting straight and tall with your abdomen pulled in. Caring for your back is another way to care for yourself.

∞ THOUGHT FOR THE DAY ∞

An easy way to practice good bending and lifting techniques is to drop a pencil on the floor, then pick it up as though it were a large parcel.

AUGUST 25

Sloth, like rust, consumes faster than labor wears, while the used key is always bright.

BENJAMIN FRANKLIN

When you're in a couch potato mode, you love to hear stories about people who injured themselves while working out. "Ah ha," you say, "exercise is bad for your health." You decide there's no point in risking life and limb by exercising. What you conveniently overlook is that you're more likely to sustain an injury when you're out of shape.

Most exercise-related injuries are preventable. They are caused by overusing a muscle or joint, such as doing high-impact aerobics when you're out of shape. Another cause of injury is poor flexibility due to inappropriate training or not warming up properly. Muscles and tendons become irritated and are prone to injury unless they are properly stretched before and after a workout. Poor technique is another cause of injury. One common example of this is wrist and elbow problems caused by using an incorrect grip on racquets and free weights.

Probably the biggest reason for injury is that you exceed your ability and take on more than you can handle. This is an easy mistake to make because your pain response might be delayed by a day or two. Being overweight simply adds to the injury. When you're in poor shape, your extra pounds put additional stress on your tendons, muscles, joints and ligaments. If you listen to your body and use a little common sense, you'll get in shape faster than if you overdo it the first time out.

∾ THOUGHT FOR THE DAY ∾

If you have any doubts about how much exercise you can or should do, check with your doctor.

I like to write when I feel spiteful:
it's like having a good sneeze.

D. H. LAWRENCE

If you are suffering from allergies, there are some ways to minimize your exposure and reduce the stress that allergies place on your body. The most important room to consider is the bedroom. This is where you spend one-third of each day so it should be as allergy-free as possible.

It's time to kick Kitty and Bowser out of the bedroom unless they are stuffed toys that can survive a weekly ride in the washing machine and dryer. Keep the door closed during the day so pets can't use your bed for their afternoon nap. If you have a cat, a family member without cat allergies should be assigned the task of keeping the litter box clean. You should wash the bedding where your pet sleeps at least once a week.

Keep your bedroom free of anything that collects dust because where there's dust, there are also dust mites. Dust mites are microscopic insects. They are found in bedding, mattresses, pillows, upholstery, carpeting and the like. They are impossible to see and impossible to eliminate completely. To keep the mite population under control, replace heavy drapes with blinds. Remove all upholstered furniture. Leave floors bare except for small carpets that can be washed every week. Take care to vacuum and dust at least once a week. Remember that knickknacks and dried flower arrangements hold a lot of dust so move them into another room. Cover the mattress, box springs and pillows before putting on the bed linens.

∞ THOUGHT FOR THE DAY ∞

Mites also like humidity. In the summer, use a dehumidifier or air
conditioner to keep the humidity below 50 percent. In cold weather,
avoid using a humidifier at all. Clean the filters on your heating and
air-conditioning systems regularly.

Green how I love you green.
FEDERICO GARCIA LORCA

Food presentation is an art form. One reason a meal at a restaurant is so appetizing is that it's appealing to your eye. So take the time with a meal today and try and present it in a pleasing way. The most important factor in eye appeal is color. To keep vegetables a deep intense color, cook them until they are tender but still crisp. When vegetables are overcooked, the color fades. Green beans, broccoli and asparagus are a sumptuous bright green when cooked properly. Dressings slide off wet lettuce — oil and water don't mix. Apple slices turn brown fairly quickly, once exposed to air. But brush on lemon juice and the slices will stay fresh-looking and juicy. Saffron is a tasty spice that adds a brilliant yellow color to rice and chicken dishes.

Some foods also grow in colors that you don't normally try. Instead of green peppers, try red, yellow or purple peppers. Instead of a white baking potato, try one with yellow or even purple pulp or a sweet potato. Red-skinned potatoes are excellent for soups or cold salads. Leave the red skin on for added eye appeal and extra taste.

A garnish will complement your food by adding flavor, color and texture. Glazed onions or carrots encircling a roast make a pretty garnish and add extra flavor. Try sprinkling vegetables with a garnish that contrasts in color and texture, such as diced red pepper on broccoli, white sesame seeds on asparagus or pale tofu on dark greens. Add fresh fruit on top of a pie or cooked fruit dessert. Choose vegetables that look appealing alongside the meat. A potato looks good next to dark meat; green beans complement fish or poultry.

∞ **THOUGHT FOR THE DAY** ∞

Color is a clue to nutrition. The more colors you have on your plate, the more likely it is you have included foods from all food groups and served a meal packed with nutrients.

The more one smokes, the wretcheder one gets.

GEORGE LOUIS PALMELLA BUSSON DU MAURIER

If you're a smoker, you probably think about quitting more than you're willing to admit. If you need some extra motivation to make that final step and throw away your cigarettes, here are some facts to keep in mind.

Ninety per cent of lung cancer cases can be attributed to cigarette smoking. As more women smoke, there are increased numbers of deaths from lung cancer among women. The more you smoke, the more likely you are to have a heart attack or coronary artery disease. In fact, the risk of coronary artery disease doubles for each pack of cigarettes you smoke per day. Sudden death is five times more likely among smokers than among nonsmokers. Smoking speeds up the atherosclerotic process—in short, your arteries will get harder sooner if you smoke. Cigarette smoke includes many compounds that have been shown in lab animals to be carcinogenic.

Smokers have higher than normal levels of carbon monoxide in their blood. Because nicotine stimulates the heart, smokers have faster heart rates and higher blood pressure. Their hearts need more oxygen but the ability of their blood to carry oxygen has been diminished by the effects of carbon monoxide.

If you stop smoking for good, the excess risk of developing cardiovascular disease will drop dramatically within two years. And after ten years, ex-smokers are in the same statistical pool as nonsmokers. So do yourself and your loved ones a big favor right now—stop smoking.

∞ THOUGHT FOR THE DAY ∞

Call your local health center and ask about classes for quitting smoking. It may be easier if you have the support of others who are also making the commitment to give up cigarettes.

Success is never a destination—it's a journey.

SATENIG ST. MARIE

Making progress is not always a predictable or steady affair. You hit plateaus, your motivation comes and goes, unexpected situations get in your way. But you can still be successful.

Success can be defined in many ways. If you're on a weight loss program, for example, there are more ways to show success than how many pounds you have lost. You are successful if you have learned how to handle frustrations and challenges better than before. Success today might mean simply showing up for a group support meeting; next week, success might mean dropping another two pounds. Changes in your behavior also mean changes in your attitudes and feelings. To keep yourself motivated, you need to reinforce these changes in a positive way.

Reevaluate your own success. An early success might be the day you asked for help or the day you decided to start exercising or begin a weight-loss plan. Write down each and every accomplishment—dropping one dress size, jogging one mile, receiving a compliment from a coworker. It's good to be proud of your accomplishments. Recognizing your success is one way to stay enthusiastic and stay aware of your new positive behavior. The more success you recognize in yourself, the more motivated you're going to be.

∞ THOUGHT FOR THE DAY ∞

Sort out your list by days, weeks, months or years, depending on how long you've been actively involved in your own process of change. Put a star next to important milestones. The first twenty-four hours is sometimes as big a milestone as the fifth year.

*Food is a human necessity, like water
and air, and it should be available.*

PEARL S. BUCK

Foods are neither good nor bad. There are merely foods that promote good health and foods that don't. We all have foods that are difficult to pass up, foods that we yearn for and crave. These foods are more difficult than others to control but your control can vary with the day, the time or the season. Try dividing the food that you eat into three categories: green light, yellow light and red light.

Green light foods are those foods that you can eat and still maintain control. You're satisfied with a moderate portion because these foods don't trigger overeating. Fruits and vegetables are green light foods for most people. *Yellow light foods* are those that you can control under some, but not all, circumstances. For example, you might be able to eat one piece of pie in a restaurant but if the pie were on your kitchen counter, you'd eat the whole thing. *Red light foods* are the foods that you should avoid, foods that sing a siren song to you. For some, chocolate or sweets are your downfall. For others, salty, crunchy chips can trigger a setback.

If you're not sure which foods go into which category, then keep a food diary and write down everything that goes in your mouth. Soon you'll start to recognize foods (and situations) that you should avoid.

∾ THOUGHT FOR THE DAY ∾

*Remember that green light foods are best so try and maximize
the variety in this category.*

*There is nothing which we receive
with so much reluctance as advice.*

JOSEPH ADDISON

People who are working to make changes in their lives often get together with people of similar interests in a support group. Some of these support groups are rather informal and members of the group take turns being the discussion leader. Other groups have a leader and a specific topic to discuss at every meeting. There are support groups from everything from losing weight to recovering from a stroke to families coping with Alzheimer's to dealing with substance abuse.

The important thing about a support group is that the people who are there have something in common. They are all trying to learn new ways of making their lives better and they're there to share their experiences and help each other along. When you're with others who understand, you realize that you're not alone in what you've done or thought. Others besides you have run to the refrigerator at 2:00 A.M. and eaten a half-gallon of ice cream. You have a great deal of empathy for others' struggles and soon learn to tolerate your own much better.

To get the most out of a support group, it's important to attend regularly. There are usually people there who have already reached their goals and have stayed there for a long time. They may have some good suggestions for you but more than that you can see that if others have succeeded, you can, too. You can believe that what you want to achieve is possible.

∞ THOUGHT FOR THE DAY ∞

Try different meetings until you find one that you like. You may feel more comfortable with one group or leader than another even though the goals and information presented are identical.

SEPTEMBER 1

Little Polly Flinders
Sat among the cinders,
Warming her pretty little toes.

NURSERY RHYME

Many people do warm-ups only if they are part of an exercise class. When you're by yourself, you usually don't bother. But you should. Warm-ups get your body ready to work.

It's better to ease gently into exercise. It's not good to stress your heart and lungs with sudden and vigorous exercise after you've been sitting all day. You need to give your body a chance to speed up your metabolism, raise your body temperature, dilate your coronary arteries and get blood and oxygen to your muscles. When you're warmed up, you're less likely to injure yourself.

Warm-ups are easy: Inhale deeply; exhale completely. Bend and stretch, concentrating on the muscles you're about to use. Do some flexibility and range of motion exercises. Walk for five minutes or so before you break into a run. Get those muscles warm. Take your pulse and pay attention to what your body is telling you—some days it will adapt faster than others.

∽ THOUGHT FOR THE DAY ∽

Starting today, begin each exercise period with a few minutes of warm-ups. Use this time to relax your mind and unwind from the stresses of the week. Pay attention to how your body feels. Let it tell you when it is ready to go.

*Things don't change. You change
your way of looking, that's all.*

CARLOS CASTANEDA

Many people find certain social events stressful. To begin with, you may find the socializing duties difficult and uncomfortable. You may also worry about the extra food that is going to be available, a situation in which you often eat to excess. Once you acknowledge the problem to yourself, you can mentally rehearse how you will handle these stresses. You can practice what you're going to say, how you're going to behave and what you're going to eat or not eat.

You can picture yourself walking over to someone you haven't had much contact with for a while. You can practice how you are going to start the conversation. You can see yourself having a social conversation with your boss or someone else who is rather intimidating to you. You can prepare ahead and have in mind a number of things that you can say to keep the conversation going. You can also practice ways to say no to extra food. The more you rehearse conversational snippets, the more at ease you'll be when you finally arrive at the event.

Afterwards you can ask yourself how you did. You can review whether you stuck with your plan. You can decide what worked and what didn't, so the next time you'll know what part of your plan needs more practice or improvement. And you can recognize that your preparation paid off because you could handle the situation better than ever. It may have been a high risk situation before, but now it's a do-able event.

∾ THOUGHT FOR THE DAY ∾

*Any time you feel you have dealt with a stressful event successfully
and got through it without overeating or behaving inappropriately,
remember to reward yourself.*

To follow, without halt, one aim:
There's the secret of success.

ANNA PAVLOVA

You are surrounded by food cues. Much of the time you can ignore them but if you are on a weight-loss program, you become more susceptible than usual. Food suddenly looks better, tastes better, smells better. You become obsessed with the food in the bowl on the table. You want to grab a bite off of someone else's plate. If the person you're eating with has an extra helping, it becomes almost impossible for you to pass it up.

If food cues are a problem for you, especially when you begin a weight-loss program, you might want to consider prepared foods. The idea of prepared foods is to reduce your exposure to food and minimize the amount of time you have to handle food.

Prepared foods needn't be store-bought; you can make them yourself. Make a larger-than-usual stew or casserole; then freeze individual portions. Make a big salad for dinner and take an extra helping for lunch the next day. Prepared foods like these mean that you are making food choices and determining serving portions in advance so it is easier to stick to your food plan. Prepared foods are particularly handy if you want to take your lunch to work and a microwave is available.

Prepared foods are not necessarily a shortcut or even the easy way out. You turn to them when you need to be realistic about risky eating behaviors for you. Of course, it's important that you continue eating the appropriate number of servings from all food groups.

∞ THOUGHT FOR THE DAY ∞

Prepackaged foods are useful to have on hand when you're eating alone or the rest of the family is eating something you would prefer to avoid.

SEPTEMBER 4

Shun the awful shop.

G. K. CHESTERTON

Shopping can be an expensive pastime for some people but it doesn't have to be a time when you lose control. To keep a shopping trip from turning into a shopping spree, here are some things that you can do.

You can remember to HALT if you are Hungry, Angry, Lonely or Tired. When you're filled with negative emotions, you are especially vulnerable. That is when you want to avoid your unpleasant feelings so you buy something you think you want. If you're not careful, you will overshop, overspend and overeat. You should only hit the malls when you're in a good mood and your defenses are up.

Lists are powerful tools. You can make a list at home, writing down only what you need, not what you want. The more specific you are, the better. For example, instead of listing "shirt," you should define exactly what you are looking for—a hunter green, long-sleeved, cotton-knit turtleneck. By shopping only for what is on the list, it will be easier to avoid that terrific yellow sleeveless silk blouse that's 50 percent off. Better yet, call ahead to the store and have the item put on hold. Then you can pick it up and quickly leave.

Leave the credit cards and ATM card at home. Bring cash—only the amount you can afford to spend. Shop with a friend, especially one who is happy to window shop. Stay away from those so-called friends who help you spend your money because they don't have any of their own.

THOUGHT FOR THE DAY

Although sales can provide an opportunity to stock up on basics at inexpensive prices, remember that if it's not on your list and you don't buy it, you're saving 100 percent.

But at my back I always hear
Time's winged chariot hurrying near.
ANDREW MARVELL

You're spinning your wheels. You're working on too many projects at the same time. You're tense and anxious and you're pretty sure your productivity is getting worse instead of better. Here are some tips to use your time more advantageously and help you get back on track.

Start with a game plan that is practical so you can stick to it. Be realistic—you're not going to reinvent the wheel this afternoon; you need the rest of the week. Make a To Do list, then decide what has priority. Even if they're all important, only one can be #1—and you'll be more efficient if you complete it before starting on priority #2. Assume there will be problems. You can probably anticipate what they are likely to be so have an alternative plan ready to go.

Whenever possible, assign others to do the routine tasks. Use your energy for the parts of the job that require more experience and planning. Toward the end of the day, take time to review your priorities and plan for tomorrow. You may need to make some changes in your game plan.

Most important, schedule time every day for exercise and relaxation. To do your best work, you need to be in your best physical and mental shape.

∞ THOUGHT FOR THE DAY ∞

Stay on top of things by keeping your paperwork organized. You don't need a complicated color-coded, cross-indexed system—a few file folders or an accordion file is fine. The idea is to put papers away quickly; then find them again easily.

*Let the most absent-minded of men be plunged in
his deepest reveries.*

HERMAN MELVILLE

Keeping track of what you eat and how much you eat is important when you're on a weight maintenance program. To maintain your weight, you should take in only as many calories as you burn up. However, you sometimes underestimate the amount of food you're eating.

Often you are simply unaware of what you eat. Another reason that you tend to underestimate what you eat is that there is a lot of emotion attached to eating, particularly if you're overweight. When there is a discrepancy between what you really ate and what you think you should have eaten, you unconsciously deny or ignore some of what you have eaten. And last, keeping track of food intake can be a challenge, requiring more discipline than you might think.

There are some clues as to whether food intake is a problem for you. If you don't pay much attention to what you eat, then you should. Chances are you are eating much more than you think you are. Even if you're reluctant to keep a food diary, you'll be doing yourself a favor if you start recording your intake. Last, if you are hostile to the idea of measuring and weighing food, it is probably because you are not willing to face how much you are really eating.

Remember that the process of writing every bite down, the act of weighing and measuring portions is to help you become conscious of what you are doing. Awareness and conscious eating are two important keys to weight loss.

∽ THOUGHT FOR THE DAY ∾

*Ask yourself if you often eat absentmindedly. If so, decide what
will help you become more aware of what and when you eat. Then
incorporate your suggestions into your daily activities for the next
week or two until these new habits become routine.*

Never eat more than you can lift.

MISS PIGGY

A major cause of poor eating is stress. It is a trigger to overeat or eat the wrong foods. Often your eating patterns are stress-induced. Another cause for this kind of eating is dieting. The very thought of dieting can make you feel deprived. But a healthy diet should include a wide variety of foods and plenty of them.

When you're dieting, you sometimes cut back too much on what you are eating. Existing on crackers and tea for a few days is certainly possible but it also sets the stage for an overeating binge, especially when a stressful situation arises. The same is true if you fast. If you haven't eaten anything at all, overeating itself becomes a stress. You overeat, feel bloated and nauseous. And of course you feel guilty about what you've done. You feel that you were bad and wrong. You feel that you misbehaved. You feel hopeless, wondering if you are ever going to be successful. Suddenly your motivation has disappeared and you're right back where you started

Try today to erase the word *diet* from your mind because diets really don't work. What does work is a program of healthy, balanced eating and exercise. A balanced eating plan means you can have plenty of food. You can learn to eat properly and make better food choices than you used to make. You can learn to be satisfied with foods that are good for you. You will begin to look and feel better. You will get stronger and find it easier to exercise. You will feel less stressed. And you will lose weight.

THOUGHT FOR THE DAY

Make sure you have a supply of healthy foods on hand for nibbling. Cut up a variety of crunchy vegetables, put a bowl of fruit on the table and stock the refrigerator with juice, seltzer or diet soda.

One of my problems is that I internalize everything.
I can't express anger; I grow a tumor instead.
WOODY ALLEN

Stresses can be categorized as either chronic or acute. Chronic stress is when you have constant, unrelenting demands made on you. Your job, for example, may have ongoing deadlines that you have to deal with. Or you may be living through a difficult time with a child. Acute stresses are those occasional adrenal jolts, such as the day your car breaks down and you realize it's going to cost a lot of money to have it fixed.

The source of your stress can be either uncontrollable or controllable. Uncontrollable stress is stress that you can do nothing about. A valuable employee takes a job with another company, for example, or a loved one is injured in an automobile accident. Sometimes though you do have some options with the source of stress. In those cases, the stress becomes controllable. If a sales person is rude or gives you poor service, you can always take your business to a competitor.

It's important that you not let the stress take over your life. If you're not careful, you become obsessed—talking about, thinking about, giving all your energy to the stressful problem. When you want to reduce the stress in your life, you can first try to get rid of the source. If that's not possible, it means changing how you react. You may not be able to control the source of the stress but you can control how you react to it. You may have to accept the obvious—that the stressful situation is not going to be resolved itself for a long time. If this is so, then there's no point ranting at the heavens. It's here so you might as well deal with the situation as best you can.

THOUGHT FOR THE DAY

When you're dealing with a lot of stress, remember to give yourself a break. A get-away weekend, an evening at the movies, a walk along the beach will be especially beneficial.

SEPTEMBER 9

*Now, here, you see, it takes all the running you can do,
to keep in the same place.*

LEWIS CARROLL

Treadmills are a good way to make walking or jogging easy
and fun. You use them indoors so you needn't worry about
rain, snow or hot weather. If you like to keep close track of
time, speed and distance, a treadmill is a good choice for you.
If you don't care to know, drape a small towel over the read-
outs and turn on the TV. Measure time by watching your
favorite news program or sitcom.

To begin, turn on the treadmill and set it for the slowest
speed. Once you're moving, adjust the speed to find the pace
that's right for you. As you walk, look straight ahead and keep
your back straight. Walk in a relaxed motion; let your arms
swing if you want.

The railing is for balance. Many users like to touch it with
a finger or rest their hand on it in case their mind wanders. It's
a good idea to hold onto the railing until you're comfortable
with the speed. If you have to hold on to keep from being
thrown off the belt, reduce the speed. If you're bumping into
the controls in the front of the treadmill, speed it up.

∞ THOUGHT FOR THE DAY ∞

*The newer treadmills can be programmed to mimic hills. The incline
of the moving track can be raised or lowered as you walk or jog.*

*Women who set a low value on themselves
make life hard for all women.*

NELLIE McCLUNG

You were no doubt taught to respect the rights of others. But you need to remember that it is equally important to respect your own needs and rights. When necessary, you need to be assertive but not aggressive, in a healthy and appropriate way. Assertive people are honest about what concerns them, what they feel and need. Aggressive people, on the other hand, express their feelings and needs at the expense of others. Aggressive people become bullies. They overpower other people. They insist on winning arguments. They're often rude and sarcastic.

When you spend much time around an aggressive person, you are likely to feel angry or anxious or even guilty. When there are too many aggressive people in your life, you may find yourself coping by overeating. If you have to deal on a regular basis with someone who has an aggressive, even abusive personality, it may help to remind yourself that that person doesn't feel very good about himself or herself either. Even so, you need to learn to speak up for yourself in an appropriately assertive manner.

You should remind yourself that you have opinions and ideas too, and that it's perfectly okay to express them. Sometimes the best solution is to leave, walk away and find another friend. If that's not feasible at the moment, you should work at learning how to set appropriate boundaries; then limit your contact to only what is required by the situation.

THOUGHT FOR THE DAY

*Use body language to your advantage. When you are dealing
with difficult people, be sure you stand tall and with authority.
Look them in the eye. Let your demeanor show that their behavior
is not appreciated.*

SEPTEMBER 11

Cameras, in short, were clocks for seeing.

ROLAND BARTHES

Rona had worked hard to lose weight and dropped three dress sizes. "I didn't want to buy smaller clothes to go along with my weight loss," she says. "My body had changed but I hadn't." When you're heavy, you very often feel very negatively about your body and you don't like the way that you look. When you lose weight, you still tend to think of yourself as being overweight and large. This attitude and self-image makes it very easy for you to regain your weight. You might not even be aware that the weight is coming back on, mostly because you never saw yourself as small. Your mental image is so strong that you let your physical body expand to match it.

One way to get a more accurate self-image is to take some pictures. Ask a friend to take some "before" pictures just as you start losing weight. You may not like to look at them but it helps to know where you started from. You can toss the pictures in your desk drawer where you don't have to look at them all the time. Every time you lose ten or twenty pounds, you can take another set of pictures to get an impression of how far you've progressed. Once you reach your maintenance weight, you can take an "after" picture.

Now is the time to take those first pictures out of hiding. Line them up and congratulate yourself on your good progress and success. Use these pictures to help change the way you see yourself. Hang them on the refrigerator or tape them to your bathroom mirror. Pictures don't lie so let them be a daily reminder of how much you have changed. Use them to reinforce and strengthen your new mental image.

∞ THOUGHT FOR THE DAY ∞

When you look in a mirror, often you look only at your face. Take time to study the rest of your body. The only way you can be realistic about who you are and what you look like is to take a good long look.

The property of power is to protect.
BLAISE PASCAL

When you're carrying around extra pounds, you are often also carrying negative feelings about yourself too. The unhappiness about your weight becomes a general unhappiness. You start to feel powerless about many aspects of your life. You no longer speak up for yourself. Your duties are too hard. You're not strong any more and you want to give up and give in. With attitudes this negative, it's no wonder you find it hard to handle the challenge of losing weight.

When you give yourself messages of powerlessness, it's important that you resist. Negative messages are harmful and will make it difficult for you to achieve your goals. When you hear yourself saying "I can't," you should run to the nearest mirror, look at yourself and say, "I can." You need to constantly remind yourself that negative messages hurt you, slow you down, and spread like a fog through your mind.

You have power within. Sometimes you ignore your power and forget that it is there. Sometimes you give it to another person, letting that person decide what is right for you. Let today be the beginning of reclaiming your own power. Reach down deep inside yourself and grab hold of a small piece of power that is still there. Then tell yourself that you are powerful, you are strong, you can do it.

THOUGHT FOR THE DAY

Take charge of one or more areas of your life—straighten your dresser drawers, work hard at your job, wash and polish your car regularly. Then try to apply this diligence, this power, to other areas of your life.

Unrelieved stress is like having one foot on the gas and the other on the brake at the same time.

TED LORENC, M.D.

Stress causes your adrenal glands to secrete hormones that constrict your blood vessels, stimulate your heart to beat faster and stronger and send less blood to peripheral systems. In short, your body springs into action to give you increased muscle function. But if you don't expend the extra energy, you'll have revved up your engines and slammed on the brakes at the same time. If you do this to your car, you'll damage the engine and wear out the brakes. When you do it to your body, you end up with hypertension or high blood pressure.

High blood pressure can be a result of other causes but don't underestimate the damage that stress can do. You may already be predisposed to high blood pressure because it runs in your family or your diet is too high in fat and sodium. So don't add to the problem by letting stress build up and not do anything to relieve it. Put on your sweats and start working off that extra energy.

∽ THOUGHT FOR THE DAY ∽

If you're trying to cut down on salt, start by throwing away the shaker. Then read low-sodium cookbooks to learn how to spice up old favorites in new salt-free ways.

SEPTEMBER 14

You always pass failure on the way to success.
MICKEY ROONEY

When you are tired, uptight and stressed, it's easy to get into a negative mind set and a negative way of looking at the world. It's a time when you need to be careful lest you start seeing everything around you at its most extreme. For instance, if something doesn't work the first time, you say it will never work at all.

When you're stressed and your world is in chaos, you start trying to control every detail of your life. You become a perfectionist and very rigid in the way you think and talk. You often come to a complete halt if you are unable to complete a task in one sitting or you make an occasional mistake or something is less than perfect. Every setback turns into a major stumbling block because you expect yourself to be perfect. If you make any mistakes, you feel you have failed. And soon you begin wondering why you should try at all since you can't seem to do anything right.

You need to remind yourself that every process, every attempt at something new, has a few false starts and several ups and downs. What's important is not necessarily the experience itself, but what the episode has taught you. If you have learned something, you can repeat the experience and do it a little better. You can see improvement in the way you handle things. You can allow yourself to be imperfect and human.

∞ THOUGHT FOR THE DAY ∞

Be careful about generalizing. Just because something happened once doesn't mean it's going to happen every single time.

SEPTEMBER 15

Sport is one area where no participant is worried about another's race, religion or wealth: and where the only concern is, "Have you come to play?"

HENRY ROXBOROUGH

Joel is an addiction counselor who works with troubled adolescents. He plays basketball several times a week because it gives him the outlet he needs to cope with the stresses of his job. Shooting hoops can be as much fun for one or two players as a team. "If you just show up and start shooting baskets," Joel says, "it won't be long before someone asks you to join their group."

Pick-up games are usually three to five people per team. Whether or not the sides are evenly matched depends on who's playing and how good the other players are. If you are waiting on the sidelines and want to play, call "winners" and you'll get to replace the losers. Joel's favorite basketball games are Horse and Hustle. In Horse, players try to match each other's best shots. Hustle is when you play one on one to 21 points.

What is your favorite sport? Maybe it's time to start looking for some pick-up games. It's not that hard to find a partner for racquet ball, tennis, handball, basketball or soccer. If you want to play, someone else probably wants to play too and that person needs a partner or a team just as much as you do. But you'll never know unless you show up at the courts.

∾ THOUGHT FOR THE DAY ∾

Check with the park district in your community to sign up for a team and play your favorite sport.

SEPTEMBER 16

What it lies in your power to do,
it lies in your power not to do.

ARISTOTLE

As much as you want to reduce the stress in your life, you may not know where to start if you feel as though you have no control. When you feel this way, it may help if you stop to ask yourself exactly what things you feel are out of your control. You need to be as specific as possible. And what you may quickly realize is that you do indeed have some choices. Your choices may be small and limited but they are still choices. If you have to deal with a friend who has been drinking, for example, you can choose not to have a conversation until he or she is sober. You can accept that although you have no control over other people's drinking, you can nonetheless choose not to deal with them when they are drunk.

You may also have to admit that there are occasions where feeling that the situation is out of your control is a bit of an excuse. This is often true when you're trying to stay on a weight loss program. You may feel that when you're at a party, for example, you will have no control over what you eat. The reality may be that you want to overeat. If that is the case, then it may be wiser to choose to socialize around the banquet table. Even if your choice is not the best, it is still a choice and one that is under your control.

Remember that you cannot control situations or other people. But you can always control your response and your reaction to that situation or person. You can choose to ignore the craziness around you. You can choose to make better decisions for yourself and respond in ways that serve your personal needs first.

THOUGHT FOR THE DAY

If you feel that parties are situations where you are likely to lose
control, you should remind yourself that you do have choices.

You must stay the cooling too.

WILLIAM SHAKESPEARE

After a lively exercise session, you feel great—in fact, down-right noble. Your body is warm, your muscles are working, the tension is gone. You've gotten rid of that excess energy that stress has triggered. But just as you warmed up and eased your body into exercise, you need to spend a few minutes at the end and cool down.

When you're exercising, there is significant dilation of your blood vessels. Your heart has been pumping extra blood to your muscles, especially the ones that are exercising—your arms and legs. If you stop moving suddenly, the blood can pool in your feet and legs and your blood pressure can drop precip-itously. You're also most vulnerable to heart arrhythmia at this time so it's important to slow down your metabolism and lower your body temperature.

If you've been running, simply walk for the last five min-utes. Shake out your arms and hands while you're moving. Stretch your muscles to keep them from getting sore later. Do the same flexibility and range of motion stretches that you did to warm up.

Once you've cooled down, congratulate yourself. You're ready to take a shower and return to your day, refreshed in body, mellow in spirit.

∞ THOUGHT FOR THE DAY ∞

As part of your cool-down, get on the floor and work those abdominal muscles. This muscle group recovers faster than any other so you can do crunches daily without harm.

SEPTEMBER 18

No stream meanders, or can possibly meander,
level with its fount.

THOMAS BABINGTON MACAULAY

Learn to handle plateaus, those in-between, leveled-out times that follow an initial rush or flurry of activity. Plateaus in your growth and change are normal. In the beginning of change, there's often a lot of stress, the internal and external pressure to do things differently. After you respond to the stress by making needed and desired changes, the stress lessens, your efforts may become less intense and you hit a plateau. Plateaus are normal. But watch out for complacency. It's one of the dangers you may find at a plateau.

Complacency can set in where stress leaves off. Although you know your situation could be better, you're satisfied with where you are because it's still an improvement over the way things were. Your new routine is helpful, but you're beginning to get tired of it. In the beginning it was new and fresh, but now the novelty has worn off. Perhaps you have lived with stress for so long that you're comfortable with it. And you sometimes even backslide to create those familiar feelings, even though they're unpleasant and negative.

It's okay to level off and enjoy your accomplishments. It's okay to hit plateaus, as long as you don't turn a plateau into a downward slide toward your old patterns and habits. Maintaining the status quo can be its own challenge. And you might want to make that your next goal.

∾ THOUGHT FOR THE DAY ∾

If you're satisfied with where you are right now, enjoy the stability and peace that is yours. Then take a moment and look around. See if there's some advantage to moving on and moving forward anyway.

SEPTEMBER 19

*I'm not afraid of storms,
for I'm learning how to sail my ship.*

LOUISA MAY ALCOTT

How you feel about your weight loss program should be measured by the amount of self-control you feel instead of the numbers on the scale. The scale is only one of several ways to measure your progress. You may have been following your program guidelines very carefully yet the scale disappoints you by showing little or no weight loss. You need to remind yourself that you're in control and did well, so the scale will catch up soon enough.

Let the scale trigger some questions that will help you succeed. If you lost as much weight as you had hoped, think about the things you did right. Ask yourself what behaviors helped the most. If you're disappointed in what the scale showed, ask yourself if your expectations were realistic in the first place. If you gained weight, think seriously about your eating behaviors recently. If you are on a maintenance program, you should be pleased if your weight stayed the same. Review what you're doing that helps keep your weight stable.

Weigh yourself only once a week. If you are afraid that you've gained weight and avoid the scale by not going to a meeting that week, you've given the scale the power to determine your attendance. More important than your weight gain or loss this week is the progress you're making toward achieving your long term goals.

∽ THOUGHT FOR THE DAY ∽

*Remember that weight loss groups are places to make new friends,
learn more about making healthy food choices and learn from others
who have had weight fluctuations over a period of weeks.*

SEPTEMBER 20

Who begins too much accomplishes little.

GERMAN PROVERB

Setting goals for yourself is not as easy as it first sounds. To begin with, each goal that you set for yourself should be a realistic one for you; this means you should be able to reach it. Realistic goals will give you some direction, help you along your path and give you an opportunity to feel successful as you reach each one. It is unrealistic, for example, for a 5'4" adult to set a goal of getting tall. But it might be very realistic to set a goal of learning to accept yourself as you are.

If you have set a realistic goal for yourself, you should be able to outline specific steps that it takes to reach that goal. Each of these steps, of course, can be a goal in itself. It is unrealistic to expect to lose 50 pounds this month. But it is quite realistic to set a goal of losing 50 pounds this year. The specific steps could include what you have to do to lose one pound a week.

Attainable goals need not be large and majestic; small goals are just fine. Jody's goal for exercise was simply to join a health club, then show up five days a week. She knew that as long as she walked through the door, she would exercise. Remember that the more realistic your goals are, the more attainable they will be—and the more success you will achieve.

∾ THOUGHT FOR THE DAY ∾

If you are concerned about your family's choice of foods, a realistic goal might be to introduce one new entree every other week.

A simple child,
That lightly draws its breath.

WILLIAM WORDSWORTH

Breathing is something you do automatically and unconsciously. But how you breathe can offer some reliable clues to your state of mind. Take a moment now to watch your body as you breathe.

Are you breathing from your nose or your mouth? Mouth breathers—assuming there is no nasal obstruction like a cold or broken nose—often take short, fast, shallow breaths due to excitement or nervousness. Try to breathe through your nose. The point is to breathe slowly but in order to slow down your breathing, you'll have to relax and loosen up.

Are you breathing from your chest or from your abdomen? If your chest and shoulders are moving, you're breathing from your chest, probably because you're tense and strained. To learn how to breath from your abdomen, stretch out on the floor. Concentrate on your breathing. Relax your body. Your abdomen should rise with each inhalation and fall with each exhalation. Your chest should barely move.

∾ THOUGHT FOR THE DAY ∾

Pay attention to the rhythm of your breathing when you're relaxed. If there is a pause, it should come after you exhale. Ask a friend to watch a clock and time your breathing. When relaxed, you should breath about 8-12 times per minute.

*If we could give every individual the right amount of
nourishment and exercise, not too little and not too
much, we would have found the safest way to health.*

HIPPOCRATES

Planning your day means taking time each morning (or the
night before) to make some decisions. If you are following a
weight-loss program, you will want to make a meal plan every
day. Your meal choices for the day should include what you're
going to eat, when and where. You should also make similar
choices about exercising. Think about what obligations you
have today; then figure out when and how to exercise.

You should be as specific with your exercise plans as you
are with food. If you are unable to exercise today, then decide
when your next exercise period will be. If you're going to exercise later at the health club or Y, pack your sneakers and shorts
in your workout bag and throw them in the back seat of the car
when you leave the house in the morning. If you're delayed
doing errands or in traffic, you're still prepared to exercise
without having to go home.

Be open to various forms of exercise—try walking, biking,
cross-country skiing, weight machines and other ways of exercising. The more you vary the kind of exercise you do, the
more likely you are to stick with it. If you do the same thing
every day at the same time and place, exercise will soon get
boring. Feel free to change what you do and when you do it. If
you want your body to become stronger and more flexible,
then you must let your mind be flexible as well.

∞ THOUGHT FOR THE DAY ∞

*Enlist a friend and together experience as many different forms of
exercise as you can dream up. Make a game of it and see how much
fun you'll have.*

SEPTEMBER 23

Exercise is nothing short of a miracle.

CHER

When you start exercising, take care to define and set your own goals. Pay attention to the needs of *your* mind and body, not someone else's. Start simple—exercise to feel better, not to compete. Research shows that people who exercise for pleasure stick with their exercise program much longer than those who are training for competition. It doesn't matter if you exercise more or less than someone else. What's important is that you exercise at all. If you must compare, monitor your own progress and compare yourself today with yourself a few weeks or months ago.

Learn to exercise alone as well as with a partner. It's nice to exercise with a friend as long as you don't get too dependent on that person. If your partner is sick or too busy to exercise today, you still can go alone and set your own pace. Partners sometimes sabotage each other too by getting competitive or even subtly giving each other permission to quit altogether.

Trust yourself enough to become your own fitness guru. Give yourself permission to do only those exercises that you enjoy. Allow yourself to ignore the advice of well-intentioned friends who have discovered what is right for them and think the rest of the world should follow suit. Only you know whether in-line skating or country line dancing is the right exercise for you. Trust yourself to know what is best for you. Then start to cheer yourself along your own fitness path.

∾ THOUGHT FOR THE DAY ∾

Exercising alone can be an opportunity to clear your mind.
Concentrate on the feeling in your legs, the sound of your feet slapping
the ground as you move, the sensations in your muscles. When your
workout is finished, you'll feel mentally refreshed.

> *. . . seek out the particular mental or*
> *moral attitude in which . . . he felt himself*
> *most deeply and intensely active and alive.*
>
> WILLIAM JAMES

You've decided to put yourself on a program of healthy eating to lose weight. You know you have plenty of will power and that's a good beginning but you need more. You also need the right attitude. You need to start by honestly assessing why you're out of shape and overweight. You probably have a zillion reasons, the biggest one being that you have too many commitments and not enough time. But you also need to recognize that unless and until you take charge of your time, success and long-term permanent changes will be elusive. The time simply won't be there until you're ready and willing to make some changes. Once you are, you'll find time to do things like take a walk, plan your meals in advance, make a shopping list and exercise.

If you're in the middle of a major upheaval, such as a divorce, a move, or a serious illness, it's probably not a good time to try to lose weight. The danger is that when your life is in an uproar, you turn to food as a crutch to help you over the rough spots. But it's an important time for weight maintenance and moderation. You need to accept the situation as it is; then be reasonable with yourself so you can eat normally and sensibly.

Remember that losing weight is not deprivation, but self-care. It's an opportunity to refocus your energy in a more positive way—on yourself. For example, exercising every day might be a good way to get your mind off your troubles. But if you're not ready, you should allow yourself to be not ready. Then when you are, you'll be successful.

THOUGHT FOR THE DAY

Think what advice you might give to a close friend who is about to start a weight-loss program. Then remember that the friend is you.

Health is not a condition of matter, but of Mind.

MARY BAKER EDDY

Helena is a grade school teacher. On days when her students are more excitable and rambunctious than usual, she keeps herself calm by using the Quieting Reflex, a breathing technique originated by Charles Stoebel. Helena recommends it because "you can use it as much as you need to without anyone realizing what you're doing." Use it in meetings or other situations where you're part of a larger group.

Smile, at least inwardly and quietly say this to yourself: "Alert mind, calm body." Take a slow, deep breath from your abdomen and exhale. Take several more calming breaths and with each exhale let your facial muscles, jaw, tongue and shoulders go loose. With each inhale, imagine a wave of warmth and heaviness flowing over your body from head to toe.

Try this technique the next time you feel tense or anxious. It's a great way to cope when you're in the middle of a stressful situation. Because it only takes a few seconds for each breathing cycle, you can relax and clear your mind at the same time. Then you'll be ready to deal with the crisis at hand.

∾ THOUGHT FOR THE DAY ∾

It helps to think of deep breaths as cleansing breaths. As you breathe, imagine that you are washing away the tensions of the moment, cleansing your spirit, energizing your body and mind.

*Moderation is the silken string running through the
pearl chains of all virtues.*

JOSEPH HALL

When you start a diet, you know you will have to change how you think about food. Here are some ideas to help you find moderation and weight loss success at the same time.

- Start each day with breakfast. Breakfast will keep you from getting ravenous and overeating later. Breakfast eaters have a metabolism three or four percent higher than non-breakfast eaters.

- Be sure to get a least 1,000 milligrams of calcium every day. A couple of glasses of skim milk plus a calcium supplement will do the job.

- Eat beans twice a week. Beans are rich in protein, high in fiber, low in fat and really filling. Add pinto or navy beans to soups and stews, add chickpeas to salads or serve up a side dish of beans or lentils.

- Make pasta the main entree at least three times a week. Too much protein overworks your kidneys and causes you to lose calcium. Try pasta salads or dress up pasta with stir-fried vegetables.

- Choose more whole fruit and less fruit juice. It has more fiber, takes longer to eat and makes you feel fuller. Have fruit every day.

- Eat a carrot and an orange every day. Carrots are loaded with beta-carotene, an important antioxidant and oranges are rich with vitamin C. Other foods with antioxidants are broccoli, cantaloupe, apricots, spinach, sweet potatoes and winter squash. Be sure to include vitamin-rich foods like these in at least two meals every day.

∞ THOUGHT FOR THE DAY ∞

*Remember that fat-free or sugar free foods have calories. It means that
they are substitutes to your food plan, not additions.*

You have to dare to be yourself, however frightening or strange that self may prove to be.

MAY SARTON

You know that some people are more successful than others but you're not always sure why. The reason is simply believing in yourself, believing that you can succeed. And that belief is very often the one thing that determines your success.

People that are negative and pessimistic expect failure. They view every setback as evidence that they are a failure. They don't bother to seek help because they believe that nothing can be done. They see limitations rather than options.

Successful people see setbacks as the chance to learn something, to prepare and have a better strategy for the next time. They are quick to ask for advice. They are flexible and use several approaches to reach their goal, expecting that not every approach will work. When necessary, they change their goals, developing different ones as they gain knowledge and experience in the situation.

Decide today that you can be an optimist. Think through situations, trying to visualize what might happen, then have some alternative plans ready. Look at the obstacles in your path but see them as problems that can be solved. Most important, surround yourself with energetic and upbeat friends.

∾ THOUGHT FOR THE DAY ∾

Remember that achieving your goals takes time and work and energy. Even optimistic people have negative feelings now and then. If you can express your doubts honestly and openly, you'll soon figure out how to regain control and meet the challenges that life brings you.

SEPTEMBER 28

Diligence is the mother of good luck.

BENJAMIN FRANKLIN

One of the most stressful things that can happen to you is to lose your job. Your financial security is suddenly stripped away, along with the daily contacts with friends at work. You feel disconnected and grief-stricken because you defined yourself in terms of your job title. But there are strategies to make it through this difficult period.

It's important to maintain a routine similar to your workday schedule. You should get up early, shower, shave or put on makeup and dress in nice clothes. Looking good will help you feel better about yourself. You should also schedule time out of the house every day. You can read the want ads at the library or have your morning cup of coffee at a local coffee shop. Getting out of the house keeps you in contact with people so you don't feel isolated.

Looking for a job is a full-time job in itself but it may still take six months or more to find something. You should spend no more than four hours a day on the telephone. Being turned down and chasing dead-end leads can discourage even the most optimistic person. You can use the rest of the work day to catch up on professional reading or learn a new skill. A class on computers or public speaking can be worthwhile or try other classes in your job field.

∾ THOUGHT FOR THE DAY ∾

Assign yourself a project every day; then make sure you complete it. It doesn't have to be a big project. Simple ones like cleaning a closet, weeding the garden, vacuuming the car or washing the dog are fine. At the end of the day you can feel good about yourself because you have accomplished something.

SEPTEMBER 29

In your shirt and your socks . . .
crossing Salisbury Plain on a bicycle.

SIR WILLIAM SCHWENCK GILBERT

Bicycling is great exercise, although in many parts of the country you are at the mercy of the weather. If you are happier exercising indoors, consider a stationary bicycle. They're inexpensive and take up very little room so they're popular choices for the family room. As long as you're pedaling, you can watch the news.

Adjust the seat height so that when the pedal is at its lowest point, your knee is slightly bent. Let your feet ride naturally on the pedals. Set the tension knob, or if your machine is computerized, select a program. Start with the lightest tension, or easiest level and gradually increase until you have reached the intensity that is right for you. The idea is to keep your legs moving at a constant speed.

Whether at home or a health club, most people like to watch TV while riding. If you want the sensation of being outdoors, there are video tapes that take you through the woods or along a riverbank path. Some of the newer models are hooked up to a computer and monitor. Select a program and the scenery will move at whatever rate you are pedaling. You can take a ride through a meadow, up and down a mountain path or compete in a race.

∞ THOUGHT FOR THE DAY ∞

It's easy to read while you're pedaling. Prop your book or magazine on the handlebars and time will go by quickly.

SEPTEMBER 30

All the animals except man know that the principal business of life is to enjoy it.

SAMUEL BUTLER

Sometimes you need to find new outlets, new things to do, new interests. Here are some ideas that cost little or no money and can lead to wonderful new hobbies.

Open a garden catalog in the middle of winter and plan a garden for the warm weather. If you're pressed for space, you can choose bright colors and hardy perennials for a window box, an herb planter for the kitchen window or a couple of tomato plants for your balcony.

Go to a travel agent and pick up free information to plan a dream vacation. The library and the travel section of the Sunday paper are good sources of information too. Then start a vacation jar. Every time you pass up a pack of cigarettes or a chocolate milk shake, add to the vacation fund. You'll be surprised how soon you'll be able to afford your dream vacation.

Go to the county courthouse and be a courtroom spectator. Watch divorce cases, lawsuits, traffic cases and more. Real life is much different—and often more interesting—from what you see on television.

Call a local beauty school and let a trainee give you a haircut. Even expensive salons have training classes for their stylists. The cut may take extra time because the stylist trainee is checked at every step but you can save quite a bit of money and have a beautiful cut and a new look to boost your morale.

∾ THOUGHT FOR THE DAY ∾

Exercise is free too. Walk the dog, get on the exercise bike and watch a favorite TV program, go jogging with a friend, join a hiking club or ride your bike along an outdoor path.

Symbols are the imaginative signposts of life.

MARGOT ASQUITH

Most of us have important rituals and formal traditions in our lives. These are the births, funerals, religious confirmations and weddings. These are also the silly stories that are retold when the family gets together, the holiday dinners and religious celebrations with loved ones and friends.

Small traditions are important too. These can be symbols of the many gifts that are in your life, reminders of the things for which you are grateful. It's a good idea to keep small symbols with you, little talismans to remind you of your self worth, your accomplishments and the meaningful events in your life.

Perhaps you keep a sea shell on the counter in your kitchen that you picked up on a vacation trip several years ago. You carry a pretty polished stone and put it in your pocket with your loose change because it feels good in your fingers. You use it as a soothing touch with reality when you're at work talking to a difficult client. A special coin in your wallet commemorates an anniversary or an important milestone in your life. In your wallet, you have pictures of your loved ones and a small card with a favorite saying or a meaningful religious quotation.

Think today about the symbols in your life. They remind you that you do belong in this universe, that there is purpose in your life and that your personal history is valid and meaningful.

THOUGHT FOR THE DAY

Some women wear charm bracelets with each charm having a specific meaning and personal significance. These charms help keep life in perspective because each one is a symbol of something important.

. . . we have a tendency to obscure the forest of simple joys with the trees of problems.

CHRISTIANE COLLANGE

In order to concentrate and keep a perspective on the positive, you need to learn how to relax. You may be aware of stress-busting techniques like meditation or deep breathing but chances are you rarely stop long enough to try them. Yet they do work and they can easily be worked into your busy schedule.

Whenever you find yourself in a comfortable chair, you can do some deep breathing and meditate. If you are stretched out for a moment on the sofa, you can do some muscle relaxation, exercises which involve tensing and relaxing one muscle group at a time, starting at your head and working toward your feet. With some practice, you can become aware of the difference between tense and relaxed muscles.

Exercise is a great way to relax. An easy walk outdoors helps dissipate the tension in your muscles and the fresh air can help clear the cobwebs from your mind, making it easier to concentrate on what you need to do. You can continue to find the balance that sometimes eludes you in the middle of a crisis.

Stressful situations are often quite complex and not easily resolved. It takes some patience to figure out what's happening and what to do about it. You would be wise to assume that res-olution will take a long time. You may also need to accept that the result is not what you originally had in mind. Your expec-tations may well have to change as time goes on and the situa-tion plays itself out.

ை **THOUGHT FOR THE DAY** ை

You should remember that the burden needn't be entirely yours, that others may be able to help. A solid network of friends, family and religious faith will help you stay on track during a stressful time.

*Water is good; it benefits all things
and does not compete with them.*

LAO-TZU

It is important to drink plenty of water, at least 6-8 glasses a day. You're more likely to remember that water is important when you're exercising but you can become dehydrated when you're not exercising too. On a very hot or windy day, your sweat can evaporate so quickly that you're unaware that you need to be drinking water. After a day at the beach or working or playing outdoors, you often feel tired. It's all that fresh air, you think, but it's more likely to be the early signs of dehydration.

When your body overheats, you cool down by sweating. Soon you feel thirsty. This is your body's way of reminding you to drink fluids. If you're exercising heavily, your thirst mechanism may not be accurate. You will need to drink more than you think you need.

Cold water is absorbed most quickly through the stomach. Marathon runners drink at least one small cup of water every 15 minutes during a race to stay hydrated. Various brands of sport drinks claim to replace electrolytes as well as fluids but most people don't need these drinks;they don't sweat enough to lose electrolytes. If you're concerned, however, eat a healthy meal later in the day and you'll be fine.

∞ THOUGHT FOR THE DAY ∞

*Most sport drinks are simply sugar water. The sugar and flavorings
will sit in your stomach before being absorbed. Water is still best for
rehydration — and least expensive as well.*

There is no finer investment for any community than putting milk into babies.

WINSTON CHURCHILL

More and more school-age children are by themselves at home after school and until their parents return from work and these children have more control over what they eat. Many children prepare some of their own meals, especially breakfast. They may pack their own lunch for school and in the afternoon they may fix their own snacks. Working parents sometimes feel guilty about not being home enough so they let the kids eat anything they want. If you do this, you are doing your children a disservice.

The way to best serve your children when it comes to food choices is to be a role model. The foods children ask for often reflect what they are learning from the adults in their lives. If they see you eating nutritious foods, they will be encouraged to make those same choices when you're not there.

Introduce a new food by offering it but let the child turn it down without a fuss. Eventually the child will try the food and learn to accept it. If you make a fuss over their poor eating behaviors, you're liable to reinforce them. The best choice is to ignore these behaviors, especially if they are a bid for attention.

You can let your children make their own choices about food but you should provide a variety of healthy choices for them.

∞ THOUGHT FOR THE DAY ∞

Take advantage of the dinner hour to spend time with your children. You can ask about their day and listen lovingly and patiently to what they have to say.

OCTOBER 5

*Good habits, which bring our lower passions and
appetites under automatic control, leave your natures
free to explore the larger experiences of life.*

RALPH W. SOCKMAN

Everyone goes through stressful periods. At these times, tranquillity seems a long way away but you can find it immediately with exercise. Research shows that exercise releases endorphins, which are mood-elevating hormones. Exercise raises your body temperature and the temperature of your muscle tissues. This warm blood circulating through your body and brain has a stimulating effect. And exercise helps get rid of tension in your muscles so you find it easier to relax.

Every time you exercise, you promote your long-term health and lower the risk of chronic health problems associated with heart disease, high blood pressure and high cholesterol. You burn off body fat, your muscles get stronger, your flexibility improves, your blood lipid profile changes for the better.

If you are trying to lose weight, exercise is vital. As you increase your metabolism rate, you'll burn more calories, even at rest. Because you will burn more calories, your food plan can be less restrictive. The more choices you have, the easier it will be to stay with it. You will hit fewer plateaus and stay on them for shorter periods of time. And most important, exercise helps you keep the weight off.

∾ THOUGHT FOR THE DAY ∾

*Regular exercise also affects your mental state so you feel less
anxious, less depressed, less neurotic. You regain your sense of
well-being. People who exercise feel that they are gaining control of
their lives. They have a sense of accomplishment simply for having
put on those sneakers and walked around the block.*

*Nature is an infinite sphere whose center is everywhere
and whose circumference is nowhere.*

BLAISE PASCAL

To get a better perspective on your own life, it helps to study the natural world you live in. Take a string about 6 or 7 feet long and tie one end to the other to make a circle. Now take this circle of string and put it on the ground. Let the ground inside that circle be the part of the universe that you are going to study very carefully.

Stretch out on the ground with a pencil and paper and draw everything that's in the string circle. Pay attention to what is growing in the circle, what color the soil is. Inhale deeply and try to describe the smell. Count insects and see how many are living in this little universe. Perhaps some are walking back and forth, in and out. Try to describe in words and pictures the many relationships within this universe. If you live in a metro-politan area, you can do the same exercise but pretend instead that you are archaeologists. Take the string circle to a corner of a city lot and study what's inside as though it were a dig. What you find reveals something about your civilization, small clues to a larger world.

You are individually a very small piece of a very large planet. While you live on this earth, you should respect it and appreciate the larger universe that is around you. And you need to understand that no matter what your problems are or how important these problems seem to be, the earth was here before you and it will be here long after you are gone.

∞ THOUGHT FOR THE DAY ∞

Think about your life as if it were a little universe of its own. What is happening in your universe? If visitors from another planet were to visit your universe, what would they find? What would they suggest that might help make your universe a better and happier place to live?

OCTOBER 7

The strongest principle of growth lies in human choice.

GEORGE ELIOT

Researchers have known for a long time that you can handle just about any kind or amount of stress reasonably well if you feel as if you have some measure of control over it. Many of the stresses in your life are clearly out of your control—the weather, the economy, societal changes and the like. But you can exercise some control by realizing that you have choices in how you respond.

Lillian was going to miss a much-anticipated family reunion because of a snowstorm, the worst in her area in a decade. Frustrated at first, she finally realized she could continue to be angry or she could accept the situation and enjoy the beauty of the snowfall. She made a pot of hearty soup, then curled up in front of the fireplace with her husband, soft music, a good mystery and two cats.

Your choices may be limited and mediocre. But you still have choices. No matter what else is happening in your life, you can choose to take care of yourself. And as long as you're doing that, you're in control.

∾ THOUGHT FOR THE DAY ∾

Remember, you can only control yourself. You cannot change or control another person's behaviors but you can control how you respond.

Energy is eternal delight.
WILLAM BLAKE

When you're tired, you avoid exercise, fearful that exercise will take away whatever little bit of energy you have left. But the opposite is true. Exercise energizes you. It makes your heart stronger, speeds up your metabolism, improves your circulation and makes it easier for your body to digest food. Aerobic exercise will improve your respiratory system as well as your heart. By increasing the amount of oxygen that your body can take in, you become more efficient at converting food into energy so you can work longer and faster.

One way to test your oxygen capacity is to ask yourself how you feel after walking up the stairs or carrying groceries in from the car or running to the corner to catch a bus or taxi. If you can do these activities fairly easily without feeling exhausted, then you're getting enough oxygen into your system to carry fuel to your muscles.

If you've been sedentary and know your oxygen capacity needs improvement, it's time to ease into an exercise program. You can start with easy walks, gradually increasing your distance until you can walk three or four miles comfortably. Then you'll be ready to switch to a more strenuous exercise if you choose. You'll know you're in good shape when you can comfortably walk 6 miles, bicycle 12 miles or jog 3 miles.

∞ THOUGHT FOR THE DAY ∞

Swimming is another good exercise for beginners. Underwater treadmills are effective as well. Your buoyancy in the water helps protect your joints but the resistance of the water as you swim or jog works your muscles.

*To cease smoking is the easiest thing I ever did; I ought
to know because I've done it a thousand times.*

MARK TWAIN

Smokers often remark on how having a cigarette calms them
down. What they may not understand is that the tension they
feel before reaching for a cigarette is not caused by stress or
other circumstances in their lives. The tension is caused by
their addiction to nicotine.

Quitting smoking is not easy but it is possible. Think about
quitting in stages. Cut back the number of cigarettes you
smoke each day. Switch to a brand that has less nicotine and
tar. Declare your car to be a nonsmoking area.

You will also need to concentrate on the psychological triggers in your life. For years you may have unconsciously
reached for a cigarette every time the phone rang or coffee was
served. Find substitute behaviors such as sucking on a cinna-
mon stick or sipping water all day. Some smokers give up coffee or alcoholic drinks for a while because the association with
cigarettes is so powerful.

Exercise is an important aid to quitting smoking. If you
start a regular exercise program, you'll be used to moving your
body when you finally do quit. You'll also be quite surprised at
the improvement in endurance once you quit. When you first
quit smoking, you will probably feel deprived and constricted
but exercise helps you do more rather than less. Exercise will
speed up your metabolism, slow down weight gain, reduce
your urge to smoke and make you less irritable.

∾ THOUGHT FOR THE DAY ∾

*The after-dinner cigarette is one of the hardest habits to break. When
you have finished eating, stand up, go for a walk, have an orange, chew
a piece of gum, enjoy a mint or drink a cup of tea away from the table.*

OCTOBER 10

As the arteries grow hard, the heart goes soft.

H.L. MENCKEN

Heart disease is a major killer in this country. Research has identified important risk factors—age, gender, and heredity—that are beyond your control. But there are other risk factors—smoking, high blood pressure, excess weight and cholesterol—that you can modify and a little modification goes a very long way when it comes to heart disease.

If you smoke, your risk of having a heart attack is over twice that of someone who doesn't smoke. More to the point, smokers are more likely to die suddenly than non-smokers. High blood pressure will cause your heart to become larger and weaker. High blood pressure is sometimes called the silent killer because patients seldom feel any symptoms. High blood pressure can also lead to strokes, kidney failure and congestive heart failure. Blood cholesterol level is an indicator of heart disease risk. If your blood cholesterol level goes above 240 milligrams, the risk is double.

You can reduce your risk of heart disease and increase your life expectancy at the same time. You can stop smoking today. You can lower your blood cholesterol by eating a diet that's low in saturated fats and cholesterol. Although there is medication to lower blood pressure, it can often be controlled with a proper diet, restricted salt intake, regular exercise and a sensible weight loss program.

To a large extent, how healthy your heart is, is entirely up to you. Although there is always risk, you can still help yourself to keep the risk as minimal as you can.

∾ THOUGHT FOR THE DAY ∾

Remember that the risk factors for heart disease do more than add up; they multiply. Each factor multiplies the risk of the previous one.

Things are only worth what you make them worth.

MOLIÉRE

Every now and then it is worthwhile to look at yourself and see how you're doing. Think about the stresses in your life and how you are responding to them. Take some time to contemplate the direction you're heading. When you do this, you are really thinking about the priorities you have in your life, the value you give to certain events.

What people or situations have you been giving your time and energy to lately? These are your priorities, whether you chose them or whether they just evolved. Ask yourself what has value to you; then be sure you're making time for what is important to you. Gina was working full time and realized that she wanted to spend more time with her daughter. So every Friday night after she got home from work, it was Girls Night Out. They went out to eat, talk and window shop. They framed posters at a frame-it-yourself store and went to the movies. They painted holiday ornaments, decorated cookies and built a bookcase.

A self-assessment is an opportunity to make changes, an opportunity to grow. And equally important, it's an opportunity to give yourself a pat on the back for the things that you're doing right.

∾ THOUGHT FOR THE DAY ∾

No matter what else is going on in your life, your own health should always be a priority. It's easy to eat nutritious foods. And there's always time somewhere in the day for a brisk walk.

OCTOBER 12

He reaps the bearded grain.

HENRY WADSWORTH LONGFELLOW

It is important to understand the difference between whole grains and refined grains. When grains are refined, the outer covering is separated from the starch inside. The outing covering is then put aside, even though this covering includes many nutrients that you need—iron, thiamin, riboflavin, niacin and some trace minerals including zinc, folate and magnesium. The outer layer is also a good source of fiber.

Most of the breads, rice, and other grain dishes we eat are made from refined grains where only the inner portion is used. You may prefer refined grains because they cook faster. Whole grain brown rice, for example, takes about 45 minutes to cook while instant rice can be ready to serve in five or ten minutes. But what you gain in cooking speed, you lose in fiber. For example, whole wheat bread has almost two grams of fiber per slice but white bread has only .4 grams per slice. A half of cup of brown rice contains nearly two grams of fiber yet refined white rice contains only .2 grams.

Whole grain foods are also low in fat as well as rich in fiber. They fill you up faster, they take longer to chew and keep you feeling full longer. Remember that there are other whole grains beside wheat, rice, corn and oats. Try barley, millet, bulgur and couscous.

∾ THOUGHT FOR THE DAY ∾

Learn to read the labels on foods and look for the word "whole." If the label says wheat flour without the world "whole," then the wheat has been refined.

Crises and deadlocks when they occur have at least this advantage, that they force you to think.

JAWAHARLAL NEHRU

Outside events over which you have no control often disrupt your life. You're laid off or downsized out of your job, a severe storm does property damage, a loved one suffers a serious illness, you're transferred and have to move. Events like these can also be a handy hook to hang all your problems on. Everything was fine, you say, until such and such happened.

In the same way, you also blame your problems on being overweight. If you could just lose weight, you think, your life would be perfect and all your problems would magically disappear. But when you lose the weight, certain issues will still be there. You'll still have to find another job, clean up and repair the storm damage, nurse your loved one back to health, get settled in a new town. It's unrealistic to think that losing a few pounds will solve these problems.

External crises can be very stressful but you need to take care that these situations aren't used to cover up other personal issues. Happiness and self-acceptance have to come from within. You should start loving yourself, approving of yourself just as you are today. Then as external crises come and go, you will be better able to stay centered, secure in the knowledge that these events have nothing to do with who you are as a worthy human being.

∞ THOUGHT FOR THE DAY ∞

Use difficult external events as reasons to practice stress-reducing techniques. There are many to choose from. Just keep trying different ones until you find one that works especially well for you.

A vigorous five-mile walk will do more good for an unhappy but otherwise healthy adult than all the medicine and psychology in the world.

PAUL DUDLEY WHITE

One of the best ways to bolster your immune system is through exercise. Moderate exercise makes your immune system more active and increases the production of the blood cells that you need to fight off infection. Moderate exercise means working out vigorously three or four times a week for about half an hour.

Nutrition is also significant in maintaining a healthy immune system. Zinc, vitamins C and E, selenium and other antioxidants are important. But remember that more is not necessarily better. Too much of one nutrient can act to flush out other nutrients. High doses of vitamins and minerals can also be toxic.

If you exercise regularly, take in only enough calories to meet your energy needs, stop smoking and drinking alcohol, you probably don't need a vitamin pill. However, many doctors recommend a daily multi-vitamin and mineral supplement along with plenty of green leafy vegetables, whole grains, legumes, mushroom, nuts and seeds. Although no one can expect a perfect immune system forever, you can be assured that exercise, proper rest and a well-balanced diet will make the rest of your life healthy. And that, of course, is what living a long life is all about — living it healthfully.

∾ THOUGHT FOR THE DAY ∾

Remember that stress can cause immune system deficiencies. Be sure to practice behaviors that reduce stress, such as meditation or progressive muscle relaxation.

OCTOBER 15

Avoid what is to come.

WILLIAM SHAKESPEARE

Some of the stresses in your life have an easy solution. You can disregard them, overlook them, ignore them. You can stop giving them energy or attention. You can remember that avoidance is a legitimate option. "When I was a teenager," says Keith, "my room was such a disaster that Mom stopped going in because the mess made her nuts. She also stopped doing my laundry. So we were both happy."

If you know someone who is a walking catalog of complaints, it's okay to be busy when that person calls or stops by. You don't have to listen. Laura says, "I never ask Becky how she feels. I already know how she feels. She feels terrible." You don't have to answer every question either. Emily tells about a nosy coworker who began asking about her new job and how much it paid. "I smiled and said I had enough money for a refrigerator and a pair of socks."

Remember today that it is okay to ignore exasperating people and walk away from irksome situations whenever possible. Give yourself permission to avoid situations where your presence makes little or no difference.

∾ THOUGHT FOR THE DAY ∾

A mature person does not run away from responsibilities. If you're accountable, you're expected to stick around and do your part. So you need to save your energy for those times when there are consequences if you don't deliver.

OCTOBER 16

Equipped with microscopy and chemistry.
MICHAEL POLANYI

Many people worry about the additives that are in the foods they eat. Yet without these additives, food would get stale and moldy, ingredients would separate, ice cream would turn to ice, soft candies would get rock hard and salt would clump in the salt shaker. Here are some of the FDA-approved additives that you often see listed on food labels.

Guar gum is a thickening agent used in salad dressings, pudding and ice cream. Modified food starch comes from potatoes or tapioca. It is used to keep foods thick and creamy. It also absorbs moisture so it prevents confectioners' sugar and baking powder from caking. Mono-glycerides and di-glycerides are fats that are used to provide a smoother texture in baked goods. These emulsifiers are considered to be safe because very small amounts are used.

Lecithin is a soybean product used to keep blended ingredients from separating. It also prevents fats from becoming rancid. Some health food sources claim lecithin can lower cholesterol but there is no conclusive proof of this. Carrageenan is a seaweed extract which prevents fats and proteins from separating in foods like ice cream, cocoa and infant formulas.

It is unrealistic to expect that additives and preservatives will be taken out of foods. If this were to happen, the price of every foodstuff would skyrocket. Additives like those mentioned above are very common and, for most people, quite harmless. If you are concerned, there is an answer—fresh foods cooked at home.

∞ THOUGHT FOR THE DAY ∞

Try making your own bread. It's satisfying to knead the bread and watch the dough rise. For extra nutrition, replace some of the flour with soy flour and wheat germ.

Training is everything. The peach was once a bitter almond; cauliflower is nothing but cabbage with a college education.

MARK TWAIN

There are many sources of advice on developing a conditioning routine that is right for your body. You can ask health professionals, fitness specialists and physical education teachers. You can read some books at the library or get in touch with sport groups such as a bicycling club. You can also look at yourself in the mirror, then listen to your body. You know how old you are and what your physical limitations are. You know whether you're overweight or not. If you're honest with yourself, you know what you can handle.

Remember that proper equipment is essential, especially shoes and clothes. You need to take care of your muscles before and after each exercise period; warm-ups, cool-downs and stretches prevent injuries. If you like to play competitive sports like tennis or handball, you should look for opponents who are your equal. If you're playing someone who's quite a bit better, you're much more likely to injure yourself.

You should always pay attention to what your body is telling you. Feeling sore is a message that you need to slow down. If the discomfort doesn't improve fairly quickly, you should be checked out by a health care professional.

∾ THOUGHT FOR THE DAY ∾

Cross-training pays big benefits. When you participate in several sports and activities, you work different muscle groups and are less likely to overuse one part of your body at the expense of another.

OCTOBER 18

Natural forces within us are the true healers of disease.

HIPPOCRATES

Many people take advantage of the spring and summer months to exercise regularly. You get in shape and are comfortable with your routine. However, when winter months arrive, you slow down. You put on heavy clothes, turn up the heat and settle down under the afghan. Your exercise routine isn't as regular and you wonder if you should stop completely every time you catch a cold or come down with the flu.

If the cold has settled in your respiratory system, then you should take it easy and rest for a few days so that you don't overtax your heart and lungs. If you have all the aches and pains of a viral infection, you also need a break to let your body fight off the infection before a secondary bacterial infection sets in. This is a good time to catch up on your reading or rent all those movies you've been wanting to watch.

But you can be run down and still safely maintain your fitness routine, as long as you're reasonable about it. If you're suffering from a head cold and do not have a fever, it's okay to exercise as long as you don't overdo it. That means you shouldn't get overheated or push yourself to your aerobic limit. But you can do mild resistance training and spend extra time on your stretching exercises. Remember that a short session of mild exercise will help you maintain your fitness without doing any harm. It will also improve your outlook.

THOUGHT FOR THE DAY

A long easy walk will keep you in shape without putting undue strain on your body. You should also take care to drink plenty of fluids before and after so you stay hydrated.

OCTOBER 19

Problems, unfortunately, can be addicting.

ELOISE RISTAD

If you're not careful, a stressful situation can take over. You think about it constantly, obsessing with your friends and family. It can permeate every thought and poison every moment. It's your mealtime conversation, your nightly dream.

When this happens, you need to displace some of this energy. Activities that distract you are good because they occupy your mind. If you can free your mind for a while, you can relax and reduce your stress levels. Jack says that when he is stressed, he works on his car. He says puttering around the garage takes his mind off his problems. "It helps to focus on a task. I get very organized—I lay out my tools, I organize my workbench, I take something apart and fiddle with it. By the time I've put it back together and polished it for awhile, I've calmed down."

When you distract yourself with something that is enjoyable, you are simply clearing your mind. You're putting the stress aside temporarily. When you return to the problem, much of the turmoil will be gone. The issues will seem a little clearer And you'll be better able to figure out how to handle the situation.

∞ THOUGHT FOR THE DAY ∞

If you like to bake, be sure to freeze what you make. When the holidays and special occasions roll around, you'll always be ready.

Art is the imposing of a pattern on experience, and our aesthetic enjoyment in recognition of the pattern.

A. N. WHITEHEAD

Elaine decided to give her weight loss program a boost by paying more attention to how she presented the food. "I was anxious to try new dishes that might be healthier," she says, "but my family didn't want to try anything new. But once the meals were dressed up a little, they were excited about new recipes. Once I started dressing up the table and the food, my family was more willing to experiment with new dishes."

Pay attention to the plate that the food is on. If you're using a small plate, portion sizes appear larger. A white plate will make food look more colorful. Green and brown are poor choices for dinnerware because many foods are these colors and tend to get lost visually when on the plate. Royal blue with a gold trim looks elegant and opulent. Floral and border designs add a soft visual interest. Geometric designs are interesting but can look harsh when food is added to the plate. For a more elaborate place setting, put a small plate on top of a larger one.

Take care with how you display the food on the plate. Restaurants often arrange food in a circle, triangle or fan shape. It's also more pleasing to your eye to see food in groups of three, five, or seven. Try three dabs of yogurt in a cold tomato soup or five good-sized croutons on a salad. Be sure to add a centerpiece to your table. Silk flowers require little or no care and make the whole table prettier. You can turn every meal into a special occasion with a little more thought.

∞ THOUGHT FOR THE DAY ∞

When the main dish is accompanied by a high-calorie sauce, put the sauce on the plate first. You'll need very little and since the food is on top, you can see it better. The sauce will coat the food from underneath, so the taste is still there.

The reward of a thing well done, is to have done it.

RALPH WALDO EMERSON

You may be ready to celebrate a success but perhaps you really don't know how. The way you've celebrated in the past may have been inappropriate at best. You would eat too much, drink too much, use the celebration as a stepping stone to a binge. Part of your new lifestyle change is learning how to celebrate appropriately.

One way is to celebrate quietly by yourself. You can write in a diary, privately acknowledging your latest accomplishment. You can give yourself a reward, such as a massage or a manicure. You might decide to go fishing or stay up late and settle in with a bowl of hot-air popcorn and a couple of favorite movies. Learning to enjoy peace and solitude is a celebration too.

You can acknowledge yourself publicly as well and include other people. You can share your successes with close friends and family members or at a support group meeting. You can buy tickets to a special concert that you've been wanting to see. Or you might want to host an afternoon of outdoor games, such as badminton and croquet, to celebrate reaching an important goal. The party itself can be your own quiet proof that you have learned how to have fun in an appropriate way.

∞ THOUGHT FOR THE DAY ∞

Remember to be grateful for what you have today.
You may have more successes than you think.

*No temptation can ever be measured by the
value of its object.*

COLETTE

One reason that you overeat is that you suddenly get a craving. You become obsessed with thoughts of food, often one particular food. These cravings often occur because you haven't eaten that food for a long time so you start to feel deprived. You feel you cannot be satisfied until and unless you have a taste. Not surprisingly, you're more apt to crave foods that can trigger a setback or lapse.

A craving is a true challenge. If it goes on too long, you can open the door to a major setback but this isn't necessary. If you handle these cravings as they arise and if you satisfy these craving appropriately, you can stay on track with minimal risk and with little interference in your program.

When you find yourself craving a certain food, you should acknowledge it. You can then decide to handle it in an appropriate way. You can see if there's a way to include a reasonable portion into your food plan, using the food as extra or optional calories for the day or week. You can also think about an alternative, reminding yourself that pretzels are a better choice than chips and nonfat yogurt with fresh fruit is a better choice than ice cream.

Remember that ignoring cravings will usually intensify them. If your cravings tend to be for the same tastes—salt, sweet, or crunchy, for example—then you need to add more of those tastes to your daily or weekly menus.

∞ THOUGHT FOR THE DAY ∞

Some prepared foods available in supermarkets are designed to satisfy cravings yet still be part of a healthy diet. Just read labels carefully and plan ahead so that you incorporate these tastes into your weekly food plan.

*The results of philanthropy are
always beyond calculation.*

MIRIAM BEARD

You can get so downtrodden by the unavoidable stresses in your life that you begin to feel you have nothing to offer another. You are so overwhelmed by your own needs that you lose sight of others around you. Have you volunteered your time lately? Here are some things that you can do that will help another and remind you that, yes, you do have something to contribute.

Volunteer at the nearest hospital, ask your neighborhood center or community college about teaching literacy to adults, read to children at the library, train to become a lifeguard at the pool, take some first aid courses and become an EMT. Wash clothes one night a month at a shelter for the homeless, rent a wheelchair and take a senior citizen to the mall for an afternoon of shopping. Coach a soccer team, sing in the chorus at your place of worship, join a hobby club and write a column for the newsletter.

Remember that volunteering your time is a good way to support a favorite charity. You'll get more satisfaction and pleasure than if you had merely donated money.

∞ THOUGHT FOR THE DAY ∞

*If you want to bring about changes in your community, be a volunteer
worker for a politician who is running for a local office.*

Families are about love overcoming emotional torture.
MATT GROENING

Unfortunately, no matter how much you would like their help and support, there are people who simply cannot or will not support your efforts to make changes in your life. Sometimes your changes become alarming to others. Your success makes them feel uncomfortable because you're demonstrating an ability to change that they cannot manage. You realize that someone you truly care about is unhappy with what you're doing to improve yourself and may even be undermining your efforts. If you're around a person who sabotages you often and regularly, there are some things you can do.

You can start by acknowledging the problem. Admit that someone you care about really isn't helping you. You are probably already aware of what that person should do. But more importantly, you need to think about the changes you must make about that other person. For example, if someone else does most of the cooking, it's unrealistic to expect that their cooking will change just for you. But you could ask for something extra, like a great big salad for everyone to share.

You don't want to hurt your loved ones feelings but you do need to be clear and assertive. Try and enlist them in your meal planning. If they can participate in it and feel that they're making some decisions with you, it may help. The important thing is to be patient and tactful. And remember to say thank you often. Try to reinforce good behavior instead of focusing on their sabotage.

THOUGHT FOR THE DAY

Remember that the family chef may feel that preparing and serving food is an act of love. When a member of the family goes on a weight loss program, the chef may feel rejected.

OCTOBER 25

I get by with a little help from my friends.
JOHN LENNON AND PAUL McCARTNEY

Have you reached a point in your life when you realize that you must make a change? You realize that your behavior is hurting yourself and others. You understand you should make healthier meal choices. These are big changes that will take time, practice and effort, so it will help if you can feel that you have support from those around you. Family and friends, however, aren't mind readers and they won't know what you need at any given moment unless you tell them.

You may find it difficult to accept and admit that you need help occasionally. But asking for support isn't enough. You have to be specific. Some of you like to talk at length about what you're doing; others prefer not to discuss it. Some like pep talks; others would rather quietly go it alone.

You need to be selective when you ask for help, understanding that not everyone can give you the support you want. Friends who are struggling with the same issues may not have much energy left over to help you. They may have their hands full taking care of themselves. They also may be envious if you're a little more successful or have had a head start.

It's also important how you ask for help. You can state your needs clearly without being demanding. If you become resentful whenever you think someone passed up a chance to be supportive, you are being unfair. You need to be reasonable and realistic in your expectations. If you ask too much, you may end up with nothing. After all, the problem ultimately belongs to you and so does the solution.

∾ THOUGHT FOR THE DAY ∾

Remember that others may have different goals from you. Your program may be right for you but you should allow others to follow a different one. The choice is theirs, not yours.

OCTOBER 26

Eat breakfast like a king, lunch like a prince,
and dinner like a pauper.

ADELLE DAVIS

Sometimes it seems that you're bombarded with food cues and triggers. You're tempted to eat inappropriately or eat the wrong foods. But there are some ways that you can minimize these situations.

First of all, you don't have to buy foods that trigger the urge to eat. When you're grocery shopping, you should avoid those aisles that feature ice cream, crackers, chips, candy or whatever your most dangerous food is. If these items are not in your house, they won't set off a binge. Next, all foods should be kept out of sight. You can store food in a pantry or in a cabinet that you don't use all the time—anywhere except in view on the counter top. You should also make sure that there is no food on your desk at work. You don't need sneaky candy bars calling your name from your lower desk drawer. You may also want to ask coworkers and family members not to eat certain trigger foods in front of you. Most people will respect your wishes, as long as you don't make them feel that your diet is their responsibility.

When eating at home, serve food from the stove rather than serving family-style at the table. It is easier to measure portions at the stove or counter, and once seated, you give yourself a chance to think before you get back up to put that second or third helping on your plate. When you're in a restaurant, it is wise to ask the waiter to take the bread basket or other munchies off the table. If your dining partners want to munch, you can at least push the chips to the opposite side of the table.

THOUGHT FOR THE DAY

Designate certain areas off-limits for food. For example, declare the
car, desk and bedroom food-free zones.

Those who think they have not time for bodily exercise will sooner or later have to find time for illness.

EDWARD STANLEY, EARL OF DERBY

Aerobic exercise does a lot for your body. Your metabolism, the way your body produces energy to function, will increase and become more efficient. There will be fewer fat deposits in your body so you will find it easier to reach and maintain a healthy weight. You will have higher blood levels of high-density lipoproteins (HDL) which help control cholesterol. Your heart will be stronger and pump more blood with fewer beats. You'll have a decreased risk of coronary heart disease.

Exercise is considered aerobic when you raise your heart rate to a "target zone" and maintain it for at least 20 minutes. To find your target zone, subtract your age from 220, then multiply the difference by 75 percent. If you're 35, for example, your target zone is 220 - 35 x .75 or 139 beats per minute. You're probably in your target zone if you're flushed or sweating slightly and can still carry on a conversation. If you're gasping for breath, slow down; you're exercising too hard.

Walk or jog for five minutes; then take your pulse. Slow down or speed up, as needed, and continue taking your pulse every few minutes until you are in your target zone. Pay attention to how you feel so you can steadily maintain your exercise at this level for twenty minutes or more. As your heart and respiratory systems get in better shape, you'll have to increase the intensity a bit to stay in your target zone.

THOUGHT FOR THE DAY

Another way to find your target zone is to rate yourself on a scale of 1 (barely moving) to 10 (maximum effort). If you feel you're exercising at level 6 or 7, you're in your target zone.

OCTOBER 28

Beware of all enterprises that require new clothes.

HENRY DAVID THOREAU

If you have a closet full of clothes, you need to assess how many of them you need. If you take a good look, chances are most of the hangers are filled with clothes that you wear rarely, if at all. If this is the case, maybe it's time to clean out your closet.

The whole process will probably be easier if you enlist the help of a trusted friend. You should start by trying on every single article of clothing you own. Your friend gets to sit back, relax and act as judge. Let the friend decide whether each piece is a keeper or not. If anything hasn't been worn for a year or more, is out of style, falling apart, no longer fits or was a shopping mistake, it goes into a basket. (Make sure you have a deal with your friend that her closet is next!)

Now take what's left and sort it into outfits. The leftover pieces that don't go with anything also go in the basket. Hang up the pieces of each outfit together—on one hanger, if possible. Add accessories to the hanger too. When you get dressed each morning, reach for a hanger and everything you need will be together.

Last, get rid of the clothes in the basket. Have a garage sale, sell them at a consignment shop or donate them to a shelter. Your closet will be clean and someone else may find a treasure.

∾ THOUGHT FOR THE DAY ∾

If you feel like you're getting rid of most of your clothes, you probably are. Just remember that you're keeping what you love, what looks good, what you enjoy wearing.

OCTOBER 29

*Where the guests at a gathering are well-acquainted,
they eat twenty percent more than they otherwise would.*

ED (E. W.) HOWE

If you're overweight, there are times when you wish you could avoid food altogether. You feel so out of control that you dislike eating, shopping or anything that has to do with food. You just can't seem to cope with food in an appropriate way. Too often you eat mindlessly, paying no attention to what you're putting into your mouth. You're in a hurry and eat on the run, in the car, at your desk, in front of the television. Although your physical hunger is quelled, the eating experience is not satisfying. You don't allow yourself to enjoy the taste, the texture, the smell of what you are eating. You feel deprived.

You need to become aware of what you're eating. You can start your day by laying out an eating plan. You can decide when you're going to eat and whether it will be a meal or a snack. You can plan these eating times around your schedule for that day. When you sit down for a meal or snack, it will be helpful if you take a few deep breaths to relax and slow down so that you can enjoy your food. You can minimize distractions by turning off the television, shutting your book, folding up the newspaper. Your goal is to remain conscious of what you're eating. Then eating can be a pleasurable and satisfying experience. And when it is, you will once again feel in control.

∞ THOUGHT FOR THE DAY ∞

*If you're eating with other people, you can use your mealtime
for socializing and relaxing conversation. Work, business or family
matters can wait until the meal is over. Rather than overeat, sip
water or seltzer or nibble at a large salad instead of the basket of
crackers and rolls.*

*Change is the constant, the signal
for rebirth, the egg of the phoenix.*
CHRISTINA BALDWIN

In order to lose weight and to keep it off, you are going to have to make some changes in your life. This doesn't mean drastic changes. You can still eat in restaurants and go to parties. But you will have to modify some of your behavior. You will have to change some old eating habits and replace those habits with better ways of thinking about food.

Your environment—where you live, where you work, how you play—has cues that trigger you to eat. Triggers can be situations. You run into an ex-lover, you change jobs, you attend a family reunion. Certain foods can be triggers too. One taste of ice cream and you're standing in front of the freezer eating out of the box.

As you make changes, you need to become more aware of how your environment affects you. You can identify the kinds of eating patterns that you have. Then you can work to replace inappropriate patterns with appropriate eating behaviors. You can do your best to decrease the trigger foods and trigger situations that are around you. You can plan for those situations or events that revolve around food. You can track your progress and get your body moving. And soon you'll be leaner, healthier and happier.

∽ THOUGHT FOR THE DAY ∽

*Think about situations in your past that were triggers for
inappropriate eating. Decide today what you will do if those
situations pop up again.*

A ruffled mind makes a restless pillow.

CHARLOTTE BRONTË

You know that aerobic exercise is good for your body. What is easy to forget is that this same exercise is also good for your mind. When you're angry, stressed or otherwise upset, your body tells the world. Your hands are clenched, there's a scowl on your face, your muscles are tight.

Exercise, however, brings about a change. The tension in your muscles starts to dissipate fairly quickly and soon you're feeling looser and breathing more deeply. And before you know it, the emotion that is making you tense begins to melt away too.

Exercise is a wonderful outlet for the stress and negative emotions that have to be dealt with from time to time. When you're exercising your body, you are also giving your mind a period of mental relaxation, a chance to detach for a while. Exercise puts you in a better frame of mind and it shows — you're happier, brighter, more positive.

∾ THOUGHT FOR THE DAY ∾

Use exercise today to help keep your stress in check. You don't have to wear yourself out. Just keep going until those cobwebs in the corners of your mind get smaller or even disappear. A little less anxiety and tension is nice for a while.

NOVEMBER 1

For fast-acting relief, try slowing down.
LILY TOMLIN

There are times when you feel there is too much stress in your life. Although you can't rid yourself of stress completely, there are some things you can do to reduce it somewhat.

One of the most useful techniques is to take time each morning to review your schedule. Taking a few minutes to organize your day will help give you a feeling of order, a feeling of control. Making a list helps you set priorities so you can be sure to get the most important things done first. You may not be thrilled with what you have to do but at least you'll have made a decision as to when and how much time you're going to devote to each task.

You can also learn to delegate responsibility. Perhaps another member of your family could stop at the store on the way home from work. If dirty clothes are piling up, you can use a drop-off laundry or let others in the family do their own laundry.

You can experiment with different routines. It may help to do your grocery shopping at night so that you have more time to sleep in on the weekend. You may want to do chores on your days off that relax you, such as gardening or painting, and try to accomplish other errands on the way to and from work.

∞ THOUGHT FOR THE DAY ∞

Physical activity is a great stress reducer because it helps dissipate the tension that has built up in your muscles. It also gives you a mental break at the same time.

Women are not inherently passive or peaceful. We're not inherently anything but human.

ROBIN MORGAN

We all know people who are submissive to the point of turning into victims. They allow others to violate their space. They find it difficult to say what they want. They ignore their own needs and give up their rights to someone else; they may even deny that they have any rights.

If you tend to be too submissive in your everyday life, there are some techniques that will help you become more assertive. First of all, you may need to recognize that it's okay to speak up for what you need. It's okay to express your feelings; they are valid simply because you feel them. It's okay to say no and it's okay to negotiate. Remind yourself that compromise is fine as long as the other person is giving way too. When only one person is backing down, that person is probably being submissive.

Learning to be assertive may take some practice. But the more you learn to ask for what you need, the easier it will become. Remember that to ask for something you need or to take time for yourself does not mean you are selfish or demanding. Asking for something shows that you respect your own needs.

∾ THOUGHT FOR THE DAY ∾

Use role-playing to practice being appropriately assertive. Think of a situation in which you were too submissive. Either alone or with a trusted friend, act out the situation again but this time practice being more assertive. Keep practicing until you can be assertive in a real situation.

NOVEMBER 3

Even I don't wake up looking like Cindy Crawford.

CINDY CRAWFORD

You are bombarded with messages about body image. Advertisements in magazines, actors on television, the attitude of society in general, all tell you that they are normal and you are not. No matter how much weight you lose, no matter how hard you work to get in shape, you think you should be thinner, taller, stronger. You no longer have any sense of what "normal" looks like. You only know that you're not it. But it's time to look in the mirror again.

It's time to accept your body as it is right now. No matter what's happened to you with age and weight, there is bound to be some part of your body that you can appreciate. You may have beautiful hands, lovely feet or long legs.

You can do a lot to improve your image. Remind yourself that there is never any reason to be dirty. If your shirt has a stain on it, take it off and put on a clean shirt. If the stains are permanent, throw it away and buy a new one; shirts can be inexpensive. There is no reason to be sloppy either. Tuck in your clean shirt, neaten your sleeves and make sure your collar is turned nicely. Add shoulder pads if you are overweight or round shouldered, as this will help square off your shape and give you a better look. Put a belt around your waist. Shine your shoes. A touch of mascara and blush will make a big difference too. Press your pants if need be. Even jeans look better if they're pressed with a crease in them.

❧ THOUGHT FOR THE DAY ❧

Looking clean and neat will go a long way towards helping you accept your body. The more you can learn to like your body, the more you will like yourself. Feeling positive about your body empowers you and gives you a better sense of your own worth.

NOVEMBER 4

It is common sense to take a method and try it.
If it fails, admit it frankly and try another.
But above all, try something.

FRANKLIN DELANO ROOSEVELT

Sometimes the stress in your life gets you down. You seem to
have a chronic cold. You feel blue and down in the dumps.
Nothing works, you say. You become dubious of any solution,
pessimistic about all suggestions. Rather than try something
new, it's easier to say "No, that won't work." A doctor special-
izing in internal medicine says that dealing with patients in this
frame of mind is stressful for him. "If the patient is very pessimistic or negative, I know that I probably won't be able to do
much to help."

Perhaps it's time to look within yourself for the answer.
Perhaps it's time to try again. There is help available, there are
solutions, but only if you want them, only if you're willing to
open your mind and hearts. If you're waiting for a person or
situation to change, you may have to wait forever. But if you're
willing to work on how you react, your life can take a new
turn.

Make an honest effort today to look at the stresses in your
life with an open mind. Can you make one phone call and solve
the problem? Of course not. But that phone call can be a start.
You can ask a professional for advice. You can listen to a
trusted friend or co-worker. You can join a support group, read
a book, watch a video on the subject. You can make a commitment to wanting improvement.

∾ THOUGHT FOR THE DAY ∾

If a friend or loved one is feeling down, it is still okay for you to feel
up. You can commiserate without joining in.

To be a man is precisely, to be responsible.

ANTOINE DE SAINT-EXUPÉRY

As parents and guardians of your children, you teach them to own the consequences of their behavior. You don't allow your youngsters to make excuses. You insist that they learn how to take responsibility for themselves and their decisions. Yet as adults, many people use excuses inappropriately. You avoid responsibility and try to justify rather dumb actions. You're too busy to take care of yourself, you say. You look for reasons to do things that you know you shouldn't. It's a special occasion, you say, that only comes once a year.

Some of your excuses involve putting the blame on others. Your mother made you taste this cake or you had to attend your son's baseball game. Your boss made you work late or your children keep eating snacks in front of you. You allow outside factors to be responsible for how you feel and what you do.

Remember that you are responsible for your own actions. You own the consequences. It's time to stop making excuses and start being honest with yourself and responsible for your actions. When you take responsibility for your behavior, you give yourself power.

∾ THOUGHT FOR THE DAY ∾

If a member of your family is difficult to wake up in the morning, stop trying. Buy them their own alarm clock and let them be responsible for themselves.

NOVEMBER 6

Coffee should be black as Hell, strong as death, and sweet as love.

TURKISH PROVERB

Most coffee drinkers know that if they drink too much coffee—more than four or five cups a day—they will get the coffee jangles. They get jittery, have trouble going to sleep, sometimes develop heart palpitations and even some anxiety. Caffeine is a powerful stimulant and in small doses, it can be useful. It wakes you up, improves your appetite, helps you concentrate and can even improve your physical reaction time. In large doses, however, you can get overstimulated—your heart rate increases and your blood pressure goes up.

Caffeine is also a drug and is somewhat addictive. Research indicates that if you're healthy and aren't overly sensitive to the effects of caffeine, you can enjoy it in moderation. Children, however, should avoid caffeine as they are likely to be more sensitive to the side effects than adults are. Women who are pregnant or have hormonal difficulties such as hot flashes, fibrocystic breast disease or PMS should avoid caffeine too. Coffee, even decaffeinated coffee, increases the production of stomach acids; people with ulcers, nausea or any other stomach related disorders should avoid caffeine products. The effects of caffeine can last four to six hours so evening coffee can cause sleeping problems.

To cut down on caffeine consumption, drink more juices, caffeine-free colas, herbal teas and water. Remember that moderation is the key. When caffeine is consumed in moderate amounts, it's not the villain that it's sometimes made out to be.

∾ THOUGHT FOR THE DAY ∾

To minimize caffeine withdrawal symptoms, cut back one cup or glass per day each week until you are consuming no caffeine. Instant coffee drinkers can mix regular and decaffeinated coffees, gradually increasing the decaf.

When the mind is thinking, it is talking to itself.

PLATO

The way you perceive something usually determines how you are going to respond to it. If you see the glass as half empty, you're going to respond negatively. If you see the glass as half full, you're going to respond positively.

Although you may prefer to think that outside events or other people trigger your feelings, the truth is you're responsible for your own perceptions; how you perceive things is the result of how you think. Your attitudes and beliefs are reflected in the messages you give yourself. When you say "I can't" or "so-and-so won't let me" or "it will never work," you are giving yourself only two options—all or nothing, and very often nothing.

You need to make an effort to listen to your own self-talk. If it is negative most of the time, then you need to work on changing it. You need to practice being positive. You need to learn how to say "yes I can" or "this time it will work" or "I will give myself permission." No matter how negative your early years might have been, you can remember that being an adult has its advantages. And the biggest one is that you can use your experience to help yourself think and talk more positively today. You can pat yourself on the back. And you can give yourself permission to be whatever it is you want to be.

∽ THOUGHT FOR THE DAY ∽

Keep a tally of the statements you make about yourself and whether they are positive or negative. If most are negative, make an effort to restate everything in more positive terms.

Daylong this tomcat lies stretched flat.

TED HUGHES

To appreciate how good it feels to stretch your muscles, watch a cat. It awakens from yet another nap, then stretches slowly, deliberately, luxuriously. It knows that a good stretch takes a few minutes. It will arch its back, push out one paw, then the other, slowly continuing the stretch one body part at a time. The cat is getting its muscles and body warmed up and ready for action.

The purpose of stretching your body is to reduce the tightness in your muscles and prevent cramps. If you improve your coordination and range of motion, you'll move more freely and suffer fewer injuries. Stretching is good for you, regardless of your physical condition. You just have to adapt the stretch to your own body—your general health, muscular tension and flexibility. Although your flexibility will improve as your muscles loosen up, there is no need to push. In fact, if you push too hard, you'll injure yourself. Let the flexibility come on its own.

The secret to stretching is to do it often and in a gentle manner. Remember that stretching is not a competitive sport. It should relax you and help ease the tension in your muscles. Stretch whenever you feel stiff, such as when you first awaken, when you've been standing or sitting still for a while or when you just want to feel good.

∽ THOUGHT FOR THE DAY ∽

Be gentle with yourself, especially in the beginning. You only need to hold the stretch for 20 - 30 seconds to get the benefits.

People who cannot feel punish those who do.

MAY SARTON

Some people use their feelings as a way of getting attention. They make the rest of the world hostage to their emotional fits. Personal interactions become exaggerated and full of perceived affronts and insults. Every situation is an excuse for an emotional free-for-all. They involve others, roping them in by threatening an emotional hoohah. "If I don't get my way, I'll get angry and have a temper tantrum." "If life doesn't go my way, I'll overeat, overdo, overindulge." People who use their emotions as a weapon forget that their feelings are valid only for themselves and that the rest of the world isn't responsible for coming to their rescue.

There are better ways to get attention than by being hostile and threatening. It is better to get attention because of your positive behavior rather than be resented and feared because of your negative behavior. When you ask others to rescue you, you need to be aware that they probably resent your constant emotional traumas. They want you to take care of yourself. The more you can take care of yourself, the more control you will feel and the less satisfaction you will get from noisy and intense bouts of emotion.

Remember that whatever you feel is valid for you. What's not valid is expecting someone else to change those feelings for you. If you practice expressing your feelings in a more moderate way, you'll find that other people will be more willing to come to you and offer assistance. In the end, however, the only person that can comfort and help is alone.

∽ **THOUGHT FOR THE DAY** ∽

If you get what you want by being an emotional bully, you're ultimately pushing people away. You may get what you ask for but you'll be enjoying it alone.

NOVEMBER 10

So you see the imagination needs moodling—long, inefficient, happy idling, dawdling and puttering.

BRENDA UELAND

When you want to make a change in your life or want to reduce the stress that you're living with, it is sometimes hard to imagine, much less believe, that you can do it. You picture in your mind a situation that has happened before but it is difficult for you to put a new picture in its place, one where you can see yourself using different and effective techniques. One useful technique that has worked for many people is affirmations. These are positive statements about yourself and your ability to take charge of any situation you are in.

Start by making a list of positive statements about the situation that you want to change. *I will go to this party without overeating at the banquet table. I say no. I ask for what I want.* Write these affirmations on a piece of paper and hold them in your hand. Look at yourself in the mirror as you say them out loud. Memorize them. Say them ten times a day. Say them over and over until you believe in what you're saying. Now visualize yourself in the old situation but using new behavior. Visualize yourself at the party talking to people, having a good time but standing far away from the banquet table. Hear yourself saying no in a firm tone of voice. Picture yourself going to your boss and asking for an overdue raise or asking your partner for a romantic evening together without in-laws or children.

The more you picture these new behaviors in your mind, the more you affirm to yourself that you can do it.

∾ THOUGHT FOR THE DAY ∾

Affirmations that others have found useful are: I love my body and I want it to be healthy. I am an attractive person and deserve respect. I no longer need to invest emotional energy in people who take advantage of me.

What makes life dreary is the want of motive.

GEORGE ELIOT

Learn to motivate yourself with positive reasons. If you can figure out the benefits in a situation, you can use these outcomes to motivate yourself. Learning to ask the question "What's in this for me?" is not as selfish as it sounds.

Motivating yourself negatively—with fear, for example—is an uncomfortable way to live. And, it doesn't necessarily work for very long. If your doctor tells you if you don't do A, then B will happen, you may be afraid and make the change to alleviate your fear. But once the initial scare has passed and that motivation has subsided, you may revert to your old ways. Or, you may become so frightened by the fear of B that you become immobilized and stay exactly where you are. Sometimes you feel bitter and resentful about being forced into changing against your will so you childishly rebel against the suggestion and continue in a downward cycle.

A better way to motivate yourself is with positive rewards and outcomes. If you eat better and exercise more, there's something in it for you. You're going to feel better. You're going to enjoy looking at yourself in the mirror. Your body will work better. You'll have more energy and vitality, more zest for life and more life to live. When you have a positive motivation for change, you start a positive upward cycle. You make the change for a positive reason. You feel better and you want to continue because it feels good. Instead of simply decreasing fear, you increase your happiness and pleasure. Change becomes fun.

∞ THOUGHT FOR THE DAY ∞

Having fun with change is contagious.
The more you motivate yourself positively, the more
your example will motivate and inspire those around you.

NOVEMBER 12

Keep the faculty of effort alive in you by a little gratuitous exercise every day.

WILLIAM JAMES

It's common to feel like you're chasing your tail and getting nowhere. You exercise regularly but feel like you're on a plateau. You're losing your will, wondering if all this sweat is worth it. You need a new way to keep yourself going and urge your body on.

Try keeping an exercise journal to record what you're doing. Most people keep track of the basics—today's distance and time, mileage for the week or month and some personal best records. One of the benefits of recordkeeping is that you can reward yourself periodically—a new CD for every 50 miles walked, for example. But you can record anything you want—how you felt before and after a particular workout, the temperature outdoors, whether or not the sun was shining, what you wore, where you went.

When you exercise regularly, there's no guarantee that today's workout will be easier than yesterday's. But over a longer period of time, such as month to month, you will be able to see that your fitness has improved. You'll be going farther and moving faster. And most important, you'll be looking and feeling better.

∽ THOUGHT FOR THE DAY ∽

Use your journal to plan longer workouts along new routes. Try to go in one big circle so you can avoid the temptation of finishing early. If you have to retrace your steps, it's too tempting to forego that last repeat.

NOVEMBER 13

It's very important to define success for yourself.

CATHLEEN BLACK

When you are on a weight loss program, you tend to measure your success entirely by the scale. If you've lost weight, you're successful; if you maintained or even gained a little bit, you consider yourself unsuccessful. There are other ways to measure success, however. Regardless of what kind of program you are on, you will be more realistic and accurate about your success if you measure your behavior. These changes are as important as the number of pounds you lose.

If your eating habits are changing, you are doing great. If you feel better and look healthier, this is a good sign too. Another important measure of your success is when people comment on your positive appearance. Watching your body fit into smaller size clothing is probably everyone's favorite measure of success. The amount of exercise you do is another valid measure. As you get in shape, your workout sessions are undoubtedly getting longer or more intense. You're walking a longer distance in the same amount of time.

In the long run, losing weight depends on your behavior so your behavior should really be the major focus of how you evaluate yourself. Consider yourself successful if you're learning to manage stressful situations without turning to food. You're successful if your lifestyle is changing from a sedentary lifestyle to one that includes more physical activity. If the scale disappoints you this week, focus on the behavioral successes that you have already achieved, for these are the successes that will keep you thin.

∽ THOUGHT FOR THE DAY ∽

Be kind to yourself when you have a setback.
This will teach you where the pitfalls are so you can
learn how to handle them better the next time. Learning
what doesn't work is just as valid as learning what does.

Too many people let others stand in their way and don't go back for one more try.

ROSABETH MOSS KANTER

One of the ways you help yourself is to set goals. But you need to make sure that your goals are relevant to you—your needs, your abilities, your lifestyle. Sometimes you find yourself attracted to someone else's goals, forgetting that their lives are different from your own and the direction that is right for them is liable to be wrong or unworkable for you. Brian used to strive for the same running goals as his wife but was never able to achieve them. "Finally I set goals that suited what I could do," he says. "I had to remind myself that she had been the high school track star, not me. The exercise program that worked for her was simply too intense for me."

When you assess your personal goals, you should also consider the changes that occur in your lives from year to year. You get married and divorced and remarried; your babies turn into teenagers; you change jobs; you move across town, across the country. You need to remind yourself that what was relevant to your situation yesterday might not be so timely or practical today.

Honor who you are today when you set goals for yourself. Make them relevant to your needs and desires, not someone else's. Your neighbor may have aspirations to be a gourmet chef but you may be happier planting a glorious flower garden.

∞ THOUGHT FOR THE DAY ∞

One way to find relevant goals is to make a list of things that you would like to achieve in the next year or so. Then set goals that will help you reach the most important thing on your list.

The motion of a muscle — this way or that.
WILLIAM WORDSWORTH

One of the goals of getting in shape is to make your muscles stronger. While losing weight, it is important to do some resistance training so you'll burn fat instead of losing muscle. Resistance training has many important benefits. As you become stronger, daily activities like carrying a bag of groceries will become easier. Resistance training also puts stress on your bones. This kind of positive stress will help maintain, if not increase, bone density. This is an important benefit for both men and women who are concerned about bone loss and osteoporosis.

Circuit training is a popular form of resistance training at health clubs and gyms. Machines designed to work specific muscle groups are set up in a circuit so members can go from one machine to the next and exercise all major muscle groups. These machines are good because they control your range of motion and make the correct muscle groups do the work. Circuit training is quite safe, though you should check with a fitness specialist to help you use the machines correctly.

There are all-in-one machines designed for home use that use rubber pulleys or have a tension setting of some sort to increase the resistance weights. They may look similar to club machines but there are some significant disadvantages. For one thing, they are expensive. Many of these are poorly designed as well so it is tricky to change the setup from one sequence to the next. Last, unless you hire a personal trainer, there is no one to check that you are using the equipment properly.

THOUGHT FOR THE DAY

Remember that resistance training will simply give you a more toned look. You don't have to worry about large increases in muscle mass; this requires hormones that women generally lack.

Is it enough to know that one creature likes what you do and the way you do it and that that creature is your cat?

NAOMI THORNTON

One of the easiest ways to relax and let go of the day's tensions is to sit in a chair with a purring cat on your lap. When Randy found Mugsey on the streets of Philadelphia, he was going through a difficult period in his life. "I was divorced, broke and depressed. But Mugsey was glad to see me anyway."

Research confirms what many pet owners have been saying all along—that pets can help you live longer and reduce your risk of stress-related diseases. When you're stroking a pet, your blood pressure decreases and your heart rate slows. You relax, enjoying the feel of their fur and the warmth of their bodies. Pets are loyal companions too. They don't judge you or criticize you. They let you be who you are.

Cats can be wonderful pets. They are fairly self-sufficient and easily adjust to being indoors all the time. Because they typically sleep 12 or more hours a day, they are happy to sit on your lap any time. They're warm, furry and generally fastidious and clean. They're good listeners too. "Mugsey knew all my secrets," Randy says, "and never told."

∽ THOUGHT FOR THE DAY ∽

Install a shelf above your desk or workbench for kitty to sleep on and you'll have company whenever you're there. And kitty will be out of harm's way.

*It isn't so much what's on the table
that matters as what's on the chairs.*

W. S. GILBERT

Some people find it difficult to dine at a restaurant or someone else's home if they are trying to make wise meal choices. But you can eat out and still feel in control at the table. It really is possible to have a guilt-free meal as part of an afternoon or evening of fun.

If you're eating at a restaurant, first decide what you want to eat; then choose a restaurant that can meet your food needs. If you're not sure about the menu, call early when you're figuring out your meal plan for the day. You'll feel in control if you've included your restaurant meal in that day's food plan.

When ordering from a menu, simple is best. If everyone else in your party is having an appetizer, order a cup of broth-based soup or ask for your salad to be served when the other appetizers arrive. For an entree, broiled fish or poultry is always delicious with vegetables of the day. Look for grilled, broiled, steamed, poached, stir fried or roasted rather than breaded, batter dipped or fried. For dessert, fresh fruit and coffee will be satisfying and filling.

Remind yourself to concentrate on the social part of your evening instead of the meal. You'll have more fun if you give your friends the same attention you have been known to give to your plate.

∾ THOUGHT FOR THE DAY ∾

*If you eat out or eat away from home, you may need to redefine
what makes a meal. It's perfectly okay to have your largest meal in
the middle of the day. Allow yourself to have a sandwich for breakfast
or cereal and milk or juice and toast for your evening meal.*

NOVEMBER 18

Our plans miscarry because they have no aim.

SENECA

Shopping for food becomes more difficult when you're stressed. When you hit the grocery store, you're rushed, disorganized, already tired and hungry. It's not surprising that you buy too much, buy impulse items and then overeat when you get home. Because you're in a hurry, you don't plan ahead. If you're the grocery shopper for the family, here are some tips to help improve your food shopping skills.

First, think about the week ahead. Ask yourself how many meals you really expect to prepare and eat at home. Check your calendar to see if Leslie's soccer team has an away game or if this is the week of Luke's overnight field trip. Ask family members what foods they would like to be eating this week. With a little planning, you can prevent overbuying, overspending and minimize those extra trips to the grocery store. Second, keep a running shopping list on your refrigerator or cabinet door. Encourage everyone in the house to add to the shopping list. If you are on a weight loss program, list the foods that you want to be eating this week.

Last, learn to read price labels on grocery store shelves. These labels show the price per ounce or pound so that you can compare brands and sizes to get the best buy for the money. Pay attention to nutrition labels too. Remember that your goal is to get the best nutritional value as well as the best buy for your money.

∾ THOUGHT FOR THE DAY ∾

Remember to take your shopping list to the grocery store. You want to enter the store with some direction and focus rather than aimlessly wandering up and down every aisle. Aimless wandering leads to impulse buying.

NOVEMBER 19

Lie in the sun with the child in
your flesh shining like a jewel.

MERIDEL LE SUEUR

Physicians often encourage pregnant women to exercise as long as the mothers-to-be adhere to special exercise guidelines for pregnant women. In general, you should lower the intensity of your exercise and perhaps exercise for a little shorter period of time than you do when not pregnant. Warm-ups and cool-downs are especially important. Be sure to start and end your exercise sessions gradually, then stretch out gently. If your pregnancy is into its fourth month or more, you should not do any exercises lying on your back. In general, low impact activities like walking, swimming and cycling are best as these activities help avoid jerky, bouncy or jarring movements.

Be careful not to get overheated. During the summer, outdoor exercise should be done during the cooler parts of the day, like early morning or late afternoon. Exercising in an air-conditioned health club is fine as long as you don't use saunas, steam baths, hot tubs or Jacuzzis. Massage during pregnancy can be very beneficial, but make sure your massage therapist has special training in prenatal massage.

Be sure to check with your physician so that you know how to monitor your heart rate. You will want to stay within the heart rate range that your physician feels is best for you and your baby. Remember that moderate, low-impact exercise during pregnancy will make you feel better and, best of all, will get you in shape for an easier delivery.

THOUGHT FOR THE DAY

Be sure to drink plenty of water before, during and after exercise
to prevent dehydration.

The body says what words cannot.
MARTHA GRAHAM

When you want to become fit and stronger, put your body into training. Try to improve your conditioning with the combination of stress plus recovery. When you exercise, you're pushing your body, putting it under stress, damaging it very slightly. Because your body is predisposed to improve, it will heal itself and in the process become stronger. However, if you put too much stress on your body, if you damage it too much, you'll injure yourself. It takes patience because to train right is to train slowly.

If you're training hard, but not seeing any results, then you're training too hard. You're not resting enough between sessions to allow your body to heal and grow stronger. If you're catching more colds and seem to be more vulnerable to the flu, you're training too hard; excessive training will depress your immune system. If your resting heart rate is going up, you're training too hard; an elevated heart rate is a sign you need more recovery time between sessions. You might also need to make each exercise session less intense.

If you're training properly, your blood will carry more oxygen to your muscles and organs and will remove waste products more efficiently. You'll start to look and feel better so your mood should improve too. If you're irritable, you're probably overdoing it. Proper training will help you sleep better. Exercise works off excess muscle tension and helps lower your resting heart rate so it's easier to relax and get more rest.

∞ THOUGHT FOR THE DAY ∞

If you're doing resistance training, work the larger muscles first. Start with thighs, abdominals and chest, then move on to back and shoulders. End your workout with triceps and biceps, as these are the smaller muscles.

I am also five three and in the neighborhood of one thirty. It is a neighborhood I would like to get out of.

FLANNERY O'CONNOR

If you have been carrying around excess weight, you know that you need to drop some pounds but if you have a lot of pounds to lose, it may seem like an impossible task. Furthermore, you worry that unless you lose a lot of weight, it won't make any difference. Well, there's a nice surprise for you.

Experts and research have shown that as soon as you start to lose excess pounds, your health will show an improvement. In fact, losing as little as 10 percent of your excess weight can have a positive effect on lowering your cholesterol levels and blood pressure. That means if you have 40 pounds to lose, once you've lost four, you will be making an improvement in your health. If you have 200 pounds to lose, you'll be in significantly better health as soon as you drop the first twenty. Many times, the first step in improving your weight is to decide not to gain any more. When you choose to stay where you are, you can be pleased that at least you have stopped the problem from getting worse.

Decide today what is a realistic goal for you. Do you want to reduce your weight by 10 percent, 10 pounds or do you simply want to stop gaining? Remember that any loss of body fat is beneficial to your health. Today, do what is right for your body; do what is right for you.

∾ THOUGHT FOR THE DAY ∾

People who exercise regularly lose weight faster and find it easier to stick to a program of healthy eating.

Procrastination is the art of keeping up with yesterday.
DONALD ROBERT PERRY MARQUIS

When you're stressed, tasks at hand often overwhelm you. They seem too big, too much to do, too impossible. Here are some ways that Stephanie Winston suggests to help you get going.

- Make a list of the pros and cons. The pros usually win, especially when your cons are versions of "I hate this project" or "I just don't want to."
- Set a reasonable deadline for yourself. If you have a big project, break it up into small parts so you know what you have to do every day.
- Learn to delegate. When you're working on a team, you're more likely to be committed to getting the work done on time because your work is needed by other members of the team. Team members can also check each other's work. When other people contribute by doing one part of the job, they are learning something and the job gets done sooner. If it is feasible, hire outside help from an agency, such as cleaning services or temporary secretarial services.
- Let go of trying to be perfect. The idea is to finish, not be faultless. It takes energy to procrastinate. It might be more efficient to get to work and finish the job.

∞ THOUGHT FOR THE DAY ∞

If you're still having trouble getting started, put your work in front of you. Stare at it, picturing in your mind what you have to do to get started. Visualize yourself doing each step. Then think how good you will feel when the work is finally completed.

If all the world were paper,
And all the sea were ink,
And all the trees were bread and cheese,
What should we do for drink?

ANONYMOUS

Do you ever feel that you're drowning in a paper sea? One way to get a handle on the paper clutter is to deal with it as soon as it comes through the front door. Kenneth was on an extended business trip. He called his son every night and asked him what had arrived in that day's mail. "I had him throw away advertising circulars, requests for contributions, unwanted catalogs and other third class mail on the spot," he says. "The stack of papers waiting for me was small and I knew everything in it was important and needed my attention."

Jesse has a system for bills. He has a small folder with four pockets labeled week one, week two, week three, week four. When bills come in, he checks the due date and files it in the appropriate week. Another family uses the in-box system. Every member on the family has a special in-box where the mail is sorted every day. At least once a week family members are expected to sort through their own in-box and deal with the paper in it.

If the pile of papers on your desk is nearly as tall as you are, start at the top. As you sift through, throw away as much as you can; then sort and group the rest. Concentrate on the pile until you can see your desk top again. You'll be surprised what you can do in 15 or 20 minutes.

∾ THOUGHT FOR THE DAY ∾

If you have grade school or elementary age children, display their art work and school papers on the refrigerator for a while; then put them aside until the end of the school year. During the summer let your children sort through their papers for that year. Put the ones that are most important to them in a scrap book.

The first fall of snow is not only an event, it is a magical event. You go to bed in one kind of world and wake up in another quite different, and if this is not enchantment, then where is it to be found?

J.B. PRIESTLEY

A winter sport that has long been popular in Europe is cross-country skiing. Unlike other snow sports, you don't need deep snow or mountainous slopes. A thin cover of snow on any kind of terrain is enough although a flat or gently rolling terrain is preferred.

Cross-country skis are longer and skinnier than downhill skis and are clamped onto the ski boot at the toe. Ski poles are used to propel the skier along the path and for balance. The movement is similar to walking, in that the skier's foot flexes and the heel moves up and down as the skis glide along the path. Any clothes will do as long as the skier is warm and has freedom of movement. Because cross-country skiing generates a lot of body heat—it's one of the most aerobic, calorie-burning workouts you can do—most skiers prefer layers that can be peeled off as they get warm. Cross-country skiing can be as easy as your abilities allow. The easiest way to learn the basic ski and turn movements is to take a class. Most stores offer instruction and rent equipment at a nominal price.

Cross-country skiing will give you a new sense of the outdoors. After a snowfall, the land is softer, more rounded. The light glitters as it reflects off the pure white snow, making the air seem even clearer, cleaner, crisper. Put on your skis and become a part of this virgin landscape. Learn to enjoy the outdoors all year long.

THOUGHT FOR THE DAY

You can also work out on a cross-country ski machine at your local health club or Y. The machines will give you a good workout but being outside on a trail is more fun.

People need joy quite as much as clothing.
Some of them need it far more.

Margaret Collier Graham

It helps to stay in control when you do some advance planning. You schedule meetings and projects at work, for example, and you organize household errands and social activities for the weekend. You feel more productive when you make the effort to get organized and then stick with your plan. But sometimes you have to throw your plans out the window.

If there's a medical emergency, you willingly drop everything and rush to the hospital to meet your loved ones in the emergency room. But you should be just as willing to toss aside your plans on occasions that are spontaneous and joyous as well. If a loved one has exciting news, be willing to share the excitement of the moment. The project you're working on will be there an hour from now but the spontaneous expression of joy on your loved one's face may not.

It's easy to lose sight of what is important. You get caught up in deadlines, homework, spring cleaning, a TV program, business deals—projects you refuse to put aside. But ask yourself how important this project will be in five years. At that time, are you going to say to yourself, "Thank heavens I cleaned the garage instead of sharing an afternoon with a best friend"? You are always grateful for joyous times that you spend with friends and loved ones. Your regret is that there weren't more of those moments. Make sure you have them in your life today.

THOUGHT FOR THE DAY

Call a friend and go out for coffee so you can catch up on each other's lives.

NOVEMBER 26

The car has become the carapace, the protective and
aggressive shell, of urban and suburban man.

MARSHALL MCLUHAN

Few things are as aggravating as having your car refuse to
start on a cold winter morning when the wind is blowing and
the snow is ankle deep. With a little preparation, however, you
can get your car ready for winter.

Keep your gas tank full. That means you should head for a
gas station when the gauge is at the halfway mark. If your car
is parked outside when it's cold and windy, park so the engine
is away from the wind. To keep your battery from getting too
cold, it may help to hang a 75 watt light bulb under the hood
and leave it on overnight. If you live in a very cold northern climate, it might be worthwhile to install a battery heater. Always
select an antifreeze that will protect you to at least 25 degrees
below zero, or lower, depending on where you live. Although
the outside temperature may not drop that low, the wind chill
factor will make it colder than the thermometer shows.

Check your tires regularly to make sure they are inflated
properly. As the temperature goes down, tires will deflate one
pound of pressure for every 10 degrees of temperature drop.
When spring arrives, check again. Your tires can overinflate
when the weather gets warm and hot.

∾ THOUGHT FOR THE DAY ∾

A defroster for your door lock won't work unless
you can get to it. Instead of the glove compartment,
keep one in your house, another in your briefcase or purse.

NOVEMBER 27

Be free, all worthy spirits, And stretch yourselves, for greatness and for height.

GEORGE CHAPMAN

To get the maximum benefit from your exercise, it's a good idea to stretch both before and afterward. But it's also important to stretch correctly or you could do some damage. If you're just trying to stay strong and flexible, it only takes about five minutes to stretch the major muscle groups.

Before a workout, hold a stretching position without moving. Slowly and *gently* stretch into the position that you want and hold it for 30 seconds. Take care not to bounce. Be sure to breath deeply and slowly while you hold the stretch. While you are stretching, you will feel tension in your muscles; hold the stretch until you feel the tension release. If the stretched muscle begins to shake, it is being overstretched, so ease up. Pain is also a signal that you have stretched too far. If you are stretching before exercise, be very gentle with yourself. Your body and muscles are cold and this is an easy time to cause injury. After a workout, you'll make the most gains in increasing your flexibility because your body and muscles are warm and ready to be stretched.

Remember that increasing your flexibility takes time so work at it at least three times a week. Simply concentrate on stretching the muscle groups that you're about to use or just did use. With a little persistence you'll soon be feeling less stiff and more limber.

∞ THOUGHT FOR THE DAY ∞

If you're coming back from a recent injury, ask your doctor to recommend easy exercises to increase your range of motion. Exercising in a warm-water therapy pool will also help increase flexibility.

No man ever looks at the world with pristine eyes. He sees it edited by a definite set of customs and institutions and ways of thinking.

RUTH BENEDICT

Experts in the field of stress are careful to point out the difference between stressors and stress. Stressors are the occurrences in everyone's daily life. These are for the most part neutral. It's how you react to them that defines stress. For example, if it's raining on a Saturday, it is simply raining. There's nothing inherently positive or negative about rain. Whether or not the rain is stressful depends on your reaction. If your baseball game has been called off due to weather, you may be upset and stressed. But if the wet weather means you can now read a book instead of mowing the grass, your reaction to the rain may be relief and delight.

Whenever you feel that something is stressful, you should take time to think about it. Ask yourself why you are finding this particular event to be upsetting and unsettling. Think about the meaning that this episode has for you. Then see if you can give it a new meaning, one that is not stressful for you. For example, if you are getting ready to leave for vacation, you might feel put upon that no one is helping or stressed that you have to do it all yourself. Or, you can focus on the excitement of getting to go away and feel good that you're so organized in advance.

∽ THOUGHT FOR THE DAY ∽

Start keeping a list of events that are stressful and see how many of them can be turned into a more neutral happening simply by putting a new name on the experience. This is harder than it seems because it is always easier to jump to the familiar. But it's worth the effort. You'll soon realize that many of the events that you find upsetting can be turned around and what's left is worthy of your adrenaline and energy.

NOVEMBER 29

There is no love sincerer than the love of food.

GEORGE BERNARD SHAW

Is snacking always bad? Not necessarily. Just have nutritional snacks on hand and use these nutritional snacks as part of your meal plan for the day. Some people use their snacks to get in extra fiber or dairy products. Rosalie recommends yogurt topped with cereal or peanut butter on an apple or banana. She often adds cottage cheese to a plate of cut-up vegetables and fruit. Hot-air popcorn or light microwave popcorn are good choices to add fiber. Dried fruit and nuts or low-fat cheese and crackers are good choices for extra fiber too.

Take a deep breath and get rid of hard-to-control snacks. You don't need bags of peanuts stashed in your desk drawer, potato chips lurking in the pantry or a bag of candy hiding in the glove compartment of your car. Replace these with healthier snacks like hot-air popcorn and dried fruit.

Make a specific plan for snacks—decide what your snack will be, when you can have it and how much is allowed. Make yourself pay attention to portions too. If you're realistic and avoid snacks that are trigger foods for you, you'll find it easy to stick to your plan.

∽ THOUGHT FOR THE DAY ∽

If you're often unaware of when you're snacking, keep a food diary. Writing down every handful of peanuts keeps you honest by making you aware of what you're doing.

NOVEMBER 30

Whisky drowns some troubles and floats a lot more.
ROBERT C. EDWARDS

It's common to have trouble coping at one time or another. You're stressed and unsure what is the best or right thing to do. You're at a loss as to how to handle the situation or person. You're fearful that the problem will get worse. If you're not careful, you might turn to a substance to quell the stress and satisfy an emotional hunger. The substance may cover up your unpleasant feelings or temporarily disconnect you from your problems but you will never feel satisfied because you have ignored your emotional needs. What you're hungering for, what you're looking for is something that a food or a substance will not satisfy.

You need to take care of and nourish your minds and emotions as well as your body. You can take a break by taking a walk or listening to some music or sitting down with a good book and having a cup of tea. You can express your emotions by seeking some privacy and crying or talking out loud, purging yourself of the overwhelming sadness or anger that is weighing you down. You can ask a friend to comfort you by listening quietly to what you have to say. You can look for professional guidance and try to find new strategies for dealing with a difficult situation.

When you try out new strategies, you are helping yourself by trying to bring about changes in your response or in the situation that is giving you problems. You will be happier and more satisfied when you learn to deal with your feelings without turning to another substance to separate your emotional needs from your physical needs.

THOUGHT FOR THE DAY

If you're not sure what it is you need, make a list of things you wish for or want. Add to the list for a week or longer until certain patterns and needs become clear.

One never notices what has been done; one can only see what remains to be done . . .

MARIE CURIE

It's always good to think ahead but sometimes it pays to look backward. When Justine first quit smoking, she found it difficult, if not impossible, to think about not smoking for the rest of her life. But she could look back at the day she decided to quit. "I started concentrating on how many days had passed since my last cigarette," she says. "I hated to repeat those first two days so I hung in for one more day. Then I had a three-day investment that I just couldn't bear to throw away. I just kept looking backward for the next six months until I was over the hump."

Decide right now to take a walk every day this year. If that seems impossible, then decide to get off the couch and walk just this once. Then tomorrow look back at how noble you felt when you returned. And head out the door for Walk #2. Every day look backward and focus on the investment you've made toward your year. As the number of daily walks add up, be proud of your efforts. Be proud of your efforts and keep in mind how you walked in the rain in order to keep your record going. Pin a gold star on your jacket for every pair of sneakers or walking shoes that you wear out this year.

Let yourself look backward occasionally. It helps when you can look back at something you have done, when you feel good about a decision you have made in the past. Looking backward reminds you that starting was hard but keeping a good thing going is pretty easy.

THOUGHT FOR THE DAY

Have a contest with a co-worker. Agree on an exercise program and see who can stick with it the longer. The loser buys a new sweater for the winner.

℘   ℘

Knotted with love
the quilts sing on.
TERESA PALMA ACOSTA

A recent study commissioned by an association representing the sewing industry discovered what millions of women have long known—that sewing relieves stress. The study showed that while test groups of women were sewing, their blood pressure and heart rate dropped. This occurred among novices as well as experienced seamstresses.

Cindy says that she likes to feel fabric. "Material can be smooth, nubby, rugged or as light as gossamer. Look around a fabric store. Everyone is touching the fabric." Desiree, a quilter, enjoys working with color. "Color is glorious. As long as I'm awash in a sea of color, I'm happy." Many people have favorite pursuits that offer benefits similar to sewing. Build a model boat or plane to experience tactile pleasure—the lightness of balsa, the perfect details molded into each plastic piece. Then finish it with paint and trim to suit your eye.

Perhaps the most satisfying part of any hobby is that you are creating something. It is enormously satisfying to make something from scratch, whether it is a cake, a pair of shorts or a gazebo. It is special simply because you made it yourself.

∾ **THOUGHT FOR THE DAY** ∾

Remember that what's important is the
process of creating, not the end result.

DECEMBER 3

Less is more.
ROBERT BROWNING

Your life is frantic, frazzled, fast. You struggle through a maze of details and duties. You buy, accumulate and collect things, all of which require care and upkeep and soon you have so much stuff, you've lost sight of what's really important in your life. The solution is to simplify.

An essential part of simplifying is learning to cut corners, eliminating the things that are not essential to the task at hand. If you're writing a report, for example, it might be nice to print it out on purple paper with a blue border. What's important, however, is that the information in the report is accurate and up to date. So delegate the final presentation to someone else or print it out and be done.

Another part of simplifying is letting go of unnecessary extras. Think about your car, for example, and where it's driven and by whom most of the time. It's nice to have a big car with all of the amenities but a smaller car with fewer options will get you to the grocery store and train station every day just as easily and more cheaply. A luxury car is great on long trips but perhaps you are more likely to fly to faraway destinations anyway.

A simple party is just as much fun to give and certainly less stressful than an elaborate one. The camaraderie and warm wishes of good friends are more important than the centerpiece on the table.

When you simplify your life, you'll start to enjoy it more. So replace the chaos with some peacefulness. Simplify.

∾ THOUGHT FOR THE DAY ∾

Think about your plans for today or this week. Ask yourself how many unnecessary duties you have. Chances are you can say no to most of these and the result will be more time for yourself.

DECEMBER 4

Good Lady,
Make yourself mirth with your particular fancy,
And leave me out on't.

WILLIAM SHAKESPEARE

Some people find meditation difficult. But there are other ways to give yourself a mental break. An easy one is simply to daydream. The idea is similar to meditation but instead of focusing on one sound or your breathing, you imagine yourself in a place that you would like to be. Dave often daydreams about flying a small airplane. He feels the shape of the propeller, smells the gas, hears the sound of the engine starting, sees the ground below. He imagines a trip in as much detail as he can.

Daydream today about a favorite outing, a quiet peaceful place you like to visit. If you like to fish, then daydream about your fishing trip in great detail. Picture yourself stepping into a small rowboat, feel it rock, listen to the sound of the water lapping against the pier. Smell the bucket of bait, feel yourself row to the middle of the lake. Imagine yourself casting a line and reeling in a fish.

Let your daydreams take you where you want to go. Plant a garden, walk along a beach or listen to a concert of your favorite music. You can take a break and use your daydreams to put you in a more tranquil mood.

∞ THOUGHT FOR THE DAY ∞

Daydreams can also help you get to sleep. Tonight when you turn off the light, imagine where you want your dreams to take you.

DECEMBER 5

*Our life is frittered away by detail . . .
simplify, simplify.*

HENRY DAVID THOREAU

You sometimes confuse your needs with your desires. Think for a moment about what your needs really are. Needs are things that are basic to your well-being—food, water, clothes, a warm and safe place to live, a job. In today's mobile, high-tech world, you probably also need a telephone and a car or access to public transportation. You have emotional needs too—the need for friendship, a sense of well-being, serenity.

Once these basics are met, you start to chase desires. The problem is when you get them confused. For example, you need to dress appropriately for your job. Yet a new outfit doesn't seem to satisfy you. And you already have a closet full of perfectly good clothes that are still in style. Maybe what you really need is a job that you like.

Make a list of what you want; then look at it a second time. Ask yourself if you might be substituting material things for emotional needs. You want fancy jewels but what you really need is a relationship built on trust. You want a trip to Nepal but you really need tranquillity in your daily life. You want to party but you really need good friends. Remember that satisfying the desire may not satisfy the need. Make sure you know the difference.

∽ THOUGHT FOR THE DAY ∾

When you concentrate on fulfilling your needs, you'll find that you can simplify your life a great deal. Once your needs are met, you can stop chasing and start living.

DECEMBER 6

There is more to life than just increasing its speed.
MAHATMA GANDHI

Kyle used to start every day the same way—jumping out of bed and into a cold shower, throwing on his clothes, and running out the door with a mug of coffee to drink in the car. Until he had a mild heart attack. Now he begins each day more gently. He sets his clock radio so that he awakens to music instead of an alarm. He drinks his coffee and has a bowl of cereal while still in his pajamas. He takes a warm shower, gets dressed and walks to the car. "I only get up 20 minutes earlier," he says. "but it sets the tone for the day—I'm just more relaxed and in a better mood all around."

If your job includes a lot of sitting, get on your feet every now and then. Stand up when you're on the phone and give your back and neck a rest at the same time. Gaze out the window for a few minutes. Get the kinks out of your neck by pressing ear to shoulder on each side, then tilt your head up and down for an easy stretch. Make some changes in what you see. Put up a new poster, change to a different coffee mug, bring in new pictures of your family.

At the end of the day, eat dinner with your family "on" and the TV off. Use this time to keep family relationships strong by sharing and listening. You can get more out of life by making just a few small changes. You tend to underestimate the effect of just a few seemingly small changes. But if you make them, you can slow down enough to enjoy life more.

∞ THOUGHT FOR THE DAY ∞

If you live alone, make meals pleasant by setting the table for yourself, sitting down and enjoying your meal. Use soft music instead of the TV if you like background noise. Invite a friend over occasionally when you're in the mood for company.

The only reason I would take up jogging is so that I could hear heavy breathing again.

ERMA BOMBECK

If you haven't exercised for a while, you may experience some aches and pains. If you think there is a serious problem, you should see your doctor right away but most problems can be solved by you.

Start by making sure you are dressed appropriately for exercise. Your clothes should fit comfortably and allow plenty of movement. Loose-fitting garments like a t-shirt, shorts and sweat suit are good for just about any exercise.

Make sure that you're wearing the right shoes. Walking and running sneakers are designed to give your foot support to move in a forward and backward direction. Sneakers designed for racquet sports like tennis are designed for side to side movement and give very little support for forward and backward movement. Other sneakers are designed strictly for casual wear and don't provide adequate support for any exercise.

Pay attention to your body posture too. Hold your head up high so that you have a long neck and a straight back. Pull in your tummy and squeeze your buttocks without overarching your back. Keep your knees and elbows slightly bent, never locked.

Keep your exercise within your own personal comfort zone. If you work out on a regular basis, you'll find that very quickly you will be able to increase the frequency, intensity and duration of your exercise. Trust your body—it wants to get more mobile and it will.

∞ THOUGHT FOR THE DAY ∞

Some exercisers have problems with chafing at their inner thighs, armpits or feet and toes. It may help to put petroleum jelly or cornstarch between the parts that rub together.

It is seldom in life that one knows that a coming event is to be of crucial importance.

ANYA SETON

We all have days when we're so behind in your errands and obligations that it seems catching up is hopeless. You feel out of control, stressed, overwhelmed, not knowing where to begin. You can start with a few little strategies that will make a big difference.

Make sure that you're always prepared with the things you need every day. If you do office work at home, you'll need desk supplies like staples, stamps, paper clips and stationery. If you commute to work, buy bus or subway tokens before you use the last one. If your car is your primary mode of transportation, keep an eye on the gas tank and fill it up when the gauge is approaching the quarter-tank level. That way you'll always be able to get where you need to go, especially when there's a last-minute crisis and you're running late.

At home, set up an emergency shelf and make sure it's stocked. Keep a first-aid kit on hand with iodine, bandages, Ipecac and aspirin or other pain reliever. If there's a power failure, you'll need candles, matches and a flashlight with fresh batteries. Canned or boxed foods are important too. You can fix a few emergency meals with tuna fish, macaroni and cheese, soup, powdered milk, coffee and cereal.

Take a few minutes this week to get prepared for an emergency. Remember that some emergencies—like running out of gas—needn't happen at all.

THOUGHT FOR THE DAY

If your children are in elementary school, keep a box of cake mix, icing and cupcake liners on hand for those last minute I-forgot-to-tell-you parties at school.

DECEMBER 9

When a dog is drowning, everyone offers him drink.

GEORGE HERBERT

Many people treat their pets better than they treat themselves. Perhaps you buy specially-formulated food for the animals in your house yet fill your own body with sugar and fat. You make sure that your dog gets outside for some exercise every day yet you are likely to remain on the couch. You would never offer tobacco to your cat yet you merrily puff away on cigarettes for years. You provide fresh water for your goldfish yet gulp down beer and alcohol to whet your own thirst.

Think about how you've been treating yourself recently. Make sure you offer yourself the same care and compassion as you give your pets. Start with good foods prepared well so that you're getting the proper nutrition throughout the day. Be sure to drink plenty of fluids; your body needs six to eight glasses of water every day. Daily exercise is important to keep yourself limber and in shape.

You set boundaries for your pets with fences and leashes. You may need some limits too, in how you spend your time, in the things you do and with other people who exasperate you.

THOUGHT FOR THE DAY

Take a lesson from your pet and curl up for a brief nap as often as you need. Let yourself be your own pet today.

DECEMBER 10

I live temperately, drink no wine, and use daily the exercise of the dumbbell.

BENJAMIN FRANKLIN

Most athletes do resistance training in order to improve their performance. They want to strengthen specific muscles for their sport as well as improve their overall conditioning. You can start at any age as long as the weight is appropriate for your conditioning—whether it's 1 pound weights or 100 pound weights. Resistance training can improve your muscular endurance and overall strength. If you keep at it and watch your caloric intake, you'll soon notice a decrease in body fat too.

When you train with weights, you stress your muscles to make them stronger. The stress breaks down your muscle a tiny bit, but if given a chance to rest, it will repair itself and become stronger. Of course, if the stress is too intense, you can do serious injury to the muscle. If you're using a moderate weight for your body, you should be able to lift it about 10 times. The tenth lift should be hard, but not painful. Do not increase the weight until you can do two or three repetitions (reps) of 10 easily.

If you have access to weight machines, give them a try. They're easy and fun to use and make it easy to isolate specific muscle groups. You change weights by moving a pin. Free weights are inexpensive and take up little space so you can use them at home. They are perhaps better for all around conditioning as they will improve your balance and coordination along with strength.

∞ THOUGHT FOR THE DAY ∞

If you want to increase your strength, use relatively high resistance and low repetitions. For greater endurance, work with relatively low resistance but a higher number of reps.

DECEMBER 11

I want there to be no peasant in my realm so poor that he will not have a chicken in his pot every Sunday.

HENRI IV [HENRY OF NAVARRE]

Sometimes you get into such a rut with the same old recipes that you are out of ideas. You think if you see another piece of chicken, you'll grow feathers. But look again. Chicken is popular for good reason. It is a meat that can have many flavors and there are many wonderful ways to prepare it and still end up with an entrée that is low in fat and nutritious.

A traditional way to fix chicken is to roast it. Rub the skin with oil, sprinkle on the tarragon, and bake it in the oven. Or, try marinating boneless skinless chicken in low-fat yogurt that has been flavored with paprika, cumin or coriander; then bake until done. For a guilt-free "fried" food, dip skinless pieces of chicken in egg white and flavored bread crumbs and then bake. If you want to leave the skin on, brush it with a balsamic vinegar and brown sugar glaze to give it a dark color and rich taste (just remove it before eating). Or, marinate boneless chunks of chicken. Add some chile peppers, gingerroot and scallions to your marinade to give it some spicy punch; then skewer the meat with red pepper and onions and you'll have delicious chicken kabobs ready for the broiler or grill.

∞ THOUGHT FOR THE DAY ∞

Chickens store fat right under the skin. Remove the skin before cooking and you will have removed most of the fat.

*Light is the first of painters. There is no object so foul
that intense light will not make it beautiful.*

RALPH WALDO EMERSON

Sometimes the world is heavy. You walk bent over, stooped,
burdened by the problems of your life. And the dark, gray skies
of winter can make your problems seem more intense. When
this happens, you sometimes need to work at finding light.

If there are no clouds, wrap up against the wind; then go
outside and sit in the sun. If it's a cloudy day, turn on every
light inside and sit under the brightest bulb you have. Start to
think about summer. Hide your winter coat in the back of the
closet and pull out a lightweight jacket. Turn up the heat for a
while and put on some summer clothes—shorts, sandals and a
t-shirt. Get out some crayons and construction paper and make
some bright flowers and a big shining sun for the front of your
refrigerator. Spread a sheet on the floor and have a summer
picnic. Make some cold chicken sandwiches, hard-boiled eggs,
some carrot and celery sticks and a glass of lemonade.

Now close your eyes and imagine how lightweight you are.
Picture yourself as light as the steam that escapes from a
teakettle. Stand up and hold yourself as though you were a
cloud hovering over a mountain peak. Open your hands and
stretch out your arms, letting the burdens of the day softly fall
off your shoulders. And when you go to sleep tonight, allow
yourself to float like a feather into tomorrow.

∞ **THOUGHT FOR THE DAY** ∞

*Use color to maintain a sunny outlook. Wear colors that are bright
and cheery. If you wear a drab uniform, wear neon-colored undies.
The world won't know but you will.*

DECEMBER 13

A penny saved is a penny earned.

BENJAMIN FRANKLIN

If you are suffering from a cash crunch, making ends meet can be difficult. At times like these, saving money for a rainy day seems impossible. But there are some ways to save money that are easy and fairly painless.

To start, you need to know where your money is going. Nickels and dimes add up so keep track of every cent for a week or more. Then look for at least one daily or weekly expense that isn't really necessary. Figure out what it's costing you for a year and you might find it easier to eliminate it. For example, if you are spending 80 cents a day on coffee or soda from the vending machine, that figures out to $4 each week or more than $200 every year. Saving that amount may make it easier to bring a thermos from home instead.

Then get those credit cards paid off. The interest you're paying every month is money that could be in your pocket instead of in the credit card company's. Put your credit cards away and start to write checks. If there isn't enough money in your checking account, delay the purchase until you can afford to pay for it in full. Don't carry extra cash either. It's harder to make impulse purchases if you have to write a check for everything.

Next, eat at home instead of eating out. Fast food meals are expensive as well as high in fat. To make meal preparation easier during the work week, cook on the weekend and freeze individual portions that can be reheated in a microwave. If you commute in your car or otherwise drive a lot, pack a cooler with sugar-free soda and picnic meals instead of stopping for a greasy hamburger on the road.

THOUGHT FOR THE DAY

Plan ahead if you're planning to purchase a big ticket item this year. Appliances, carpeting, cars and the like usually go on sale once or twice a year. Look for price reductions in discount stores.

DECEMBER 14

*The truest expression of a people
is in its dances and its music.*

AGNES DE MILLE

Dancing is wonderful exercise. It improves your posture, balance and flexibility and makes your body stronger. But dancing also frees your spirit and helps you let go of your inhibitions. If you take a dance class, you'll be surprised at how much better you look, feel and move in only a month or two. These classes are comparable in cost to exercise classes. You'll need a leotard or loose fitting clothes and perhaps specialized dance shoes.

Ballet classes will improve your flexibility and posture and also tone and define your legs and hips. In advanced ballet, you can burn as many as 600 calories in a one-hour class. Flamenco dance will give you an excellent leg and upper body workout and the fiery music and rhythm of the castanets will help you dance off the tension of the day. Belly dancing concentrates on isolating your rib cage, shoulders and hips, and will trim your waist at the same time. Modern dance usually involves more reaching and stretching than other dance forms; dancers are often barefoot and dance to a drum beat. Ballroom dancing with a partner looks easier than other dances but it requires coordination, control and concentration. If you want to learn the club moves, try hip hop or line dancing. Square dancing, clog dancing and tap are fun to learn too.

To learn any of these dance forms, call your local dance studio. They can refer you to other teachers if they don't teach the particular form you want to learn. Sign up for lessons and you'll be signing up for entertainment, escape and a great workout.

∾ THOUGHT FOR THE DAY ∾

*One of the best things about dance is the musical
accompaniment and contagious rhythm. Use the music
to bridge a connection between your mind and body.*

DECEMBER 15

Envy and wrath shorten the life.

ECCLESIASTES 30:24

When you are stressed, the last place you should be is behind the wheel of a car because you're likely to take your stress out on the other people on the highway. Instead of being a defensive driver, you turn into an aggressive one. You pull up too close to the person in front of you because they're moving too slowly. You honk, flash your headlights, slam on the brakes, step on the accelerator and make rude hand signs. When you're driving like this, it's time to get off the road. It's time to realize that it's not the other driver that's the problem. It's you.

Make sure you understand your car and how it behaves in traffic. Be aware of how much time it takes to merge into highway traffic or safely change lanes. Know for sure how much room you need to come to a full stop. When you see a yellow light, don't speed up; stop and wait for the next green light. Don't block intersections, don't honk at everything, don't tailgate. Take a deep breath when a hostile driver is nearby; then get out of the way.

Take time today to examine your own attitude when driving. Perhaps it's time for you to substitute respect for aggression. Be courteous and respectful to other drivers. Let the other driver pass if he wants; be content to follow at a reasonable distance. Smile and wave instead of shaking your fist. If you do your part, perhaps the next driver will too.

∽ THOUGHT FOR THE DAY ∽

Make sure that you really do know the rules of the road. The last time you read the state laws for drivers was probably when you were a teenager getting ready to take your driver's test. Next time you are at Motor Vehicles, pick up another copy and read it. It is better than you remember.

DECEMBER 16

Tir'd eyelids upon tir'd eyes.

ALFRED, LORD TENNYSON

Chronic Fatigue Syndrome (CFS) has been maligned as a complaint by overworked professionals who are really just tired hypochondriacs but CFS is very real. It is a debilitating fatigue that goes on for many months or years. It tends to mimic mononucleosis and flu symptoms including fatigue, swollen lymph glands, fever, chills, muscle and joint aches. The difference is that the symptoms persist for six months or more, followed by listlessness and depression.

Research done by the Centers for Disease Control and Prevention shows that it is a disease, most likely caused by a virus, and that it is an immune system dysfunction. The good news is that CFS is not a fatal, progressive disease and it is not contagious. It can, however, last several years, is more common among women and its victims often have allergies.

To be diagnosed with CFS, you must have had at least eight of the following symptoms continuously for the past six months: chills or low grade fever; sore throat; tender lymph nodes; muscle pain and weakness; extreme fatigue; headaches; joint pain with no swelling; neurological problems, including confusion, memory loss, and visual disturbances; sleep disorders; and the sudden onset of any of these symptoms. You should also have experienced a debilitating fatigue at the same time.

Proper medical treatment includes anti-depressants, non-steroid anti-inflammatory agents and histamines for allergy symptoms, along with plenty of rest and a good diet.

∽ THOUGHT FOR THE DAY ∽

If you suspect you have CFS, see a reputable medical doctor who specializes in this syndrome. You should also join a support group or seek counseling to help you deal with the psychological side effects of this disease.

DECEMBER 17

We have to do with the past only as we can make it useful to the present and the future.

FREDERICK DOUGLASS

At one time or another, each of us has faced difficulties, tragedy, defeat and loss. But sometimes these circumstances are so overwhelming that you can't let go of them. You hang on to them, clutching these events to your chest as though they were a lifeline, letting them define who you are and how you think and act from that moment of misfortune onward.

Perhaps you are angry about your past and for good reason. Your past experiences may well have been quite difficult, even harsh and abusive. Or you may be burdened by a great loss, feeling a void too overwhelming to face, much less accept. If you are not careful, however, you will let your anger and grief drain you of energy, energy you need for finding happiness today.

As painful as these experiences are, you can still learn from them. You can realize that in spite of the misfortunes of your past, you still have choices. You can let go of the past. You can practice forgiveness. You can learn how to take better care of yourself so that tomorrow is better.

Start by taking an honest look at your own attitude. Remember that you have the power to take charge of your life. You can begin concentrating on the present and the future. You can decide to move forward and make some changes.

Today is today. Let it be a fresh start for peace within yourself.

THOUGHT FOR THE DAY

If you don't know where to begin, start by writing down the events in your life that still disturb and upset you. Then write down the lesson that each of these events brings. Be sure to include the changes that you made—or need to make—in order to make your life better today.

DECEMBER 18

As I was going up the stair
I met a man who wasn't there.
He wasn't there again today.
I wish, I wish he'd stay away.

HUGHES MEARNS

Do you go out of your way to avoid climbing steps? Do you head for the elevator or escalator instead, telling yourself you're too tired, too stressed or too late to use the stairs? Yet after work, you head for the stair climbing machines at the health club because you know it's an excellent cardiovascular workout.

Steppers are easy to use. Just get on, set the timer, adjust the speed and start climbing. The most common mistake that people make is leaning forward and resting their arms on the handrails. Be sure that you are standing up and holding your back straight. Use the handrails for balance, not resting. When you lean over, you work your gluteal muscles more and make them bigger. If you stand up straight, you'll tone your legs and buttocks without making them bulky. You'll also burn more calories if you stand up straight. Because leaning burns 10 percent to 20 percent fewer calories, you'll actually be using fewer calories than the readout indicates.

Relatively inexpensive step machines are now available for home use. It might be a nice change from the stationary bike for a while. Like the bike, you can put it in front of the TV or prop up a book or magazine and read while you're working out. Remember that you needn't step faster or deeper to get a good workout. You only have to stand up straight.

THOUGHT FOR THE DAY

To be sure you're using the correct form, watch yourself in a mirror. And every time you work out, pay attention to your body to keep old habits from coming back.

DECEMBER 19

Phylicia dreaded going to work. Her company was downsizing and the stress was taking a toll on everyone. "For three days before a business trip, my boss was just impossible. Nothing was right; everything was wrong. And I found myself thinking that way too." To keep life in perspective, Phylicia took time one evening to make a list of things that she was grateful for. "I had twelve things on my list—stuff like my car was working, my children were healthy, a close friend lived nearby." Then she posted it on her front door and read it aloud every morning.

It's easy to lose track of the good things in your life when you're stressed. You are so focused on what is going wrong that you forget what is going right. You forget to be thankful for what you already have, things that make life easier, even possible. You have antibiotics to cure infections that would otherwise be fatal. You have telephones so you can be in contact with anyone in the world. You have easy access to transportation—cars, busses, trains and airplanes can take you anywhere you want to go. You have books to read, television to watch, daily newspapers to keep you informed. You have fresh fruits and vegetables in your grocery stores year around.

Take time today to think about the things in your life that are good; then make your own gratitude list. Be sure to include the things that you already have and probably take for granted, things like a second car or the extra television in your bedroom or the neighbor who fed your cat and picked up your mail when you went away for a few days last year.

∞ THOUGHT FOR THE DAY ∞

Do something today that another person will appreciate. But do it quietly, even anonymously. Open a door, say thank you, return a lost item to its owner without asking for a reward.

Be free, all worthy spirits,
And stretch yourselves, for greatness and for height.
GEORGE CHAPMAN

A common response to stress is tension in sore muscles. A good way to dissipate this kind of tension is with stretching exercises. Here are some easy ones for your neck, arms, back and legs:

Try a head and neck roll, especially if you spend a lot of time at your desk or in front of a computer. Drop your head to one side, trying to touch your shoulder with your ear. Then very slowly roll your head across your chest toward the other shoulder. Never let your head roll or drop backwards. The rolling motion should be from shoulder to shoulder across the front of your body.

To stretch your arms, raise them over your head, palms up, fingers together. Push and hold your arms straight up for 15 seconds. Repeat until you feel less tension in your arms and shoulders.

To ease your aching back, lie on the floor with your knees bent, then push the small of your back toward the floor and hold. You will be tilting your pelvis to straighten your back. Although the stretch is a small and subtle movement, it is very effective if you do it several times a day.

Finish up with a leg stretch. Crouch on the floor like a sprinter waiting for the starting gun. Then slowly straighten one leg out behind you and gently lower your torso toward the floor. Hold this position; then repeat with the other leg.

Stretches like these are an important aspect of keeping stress under control. They work best if you do them gently two or three times throughout the day.

∞ **THOUGHT FOR THE DAY** ∞

Exercise benefits your mental attitude as well as your
body. Every time you exercise, you are making a commitment
to taking care of yourself, to finding a balance.

DECEMBER 21

A good cook is a certain slow poisoner, if you are not temperate.

VOLTAIRE

One way to think about choosing foods is to think in terms of the amount of fat and fiber that you're eating every day. This is a useful technique if your eating schedule varies from day to day or if you need flexibility and like to have a lot of choices. Just be sure that you read food labels carefully and write down all the fat and fiber grams as you consume them during the day.

You should have at least 15 grams of fat every day, with a maximum of 35 grams. Because many foods have small amounts of fat included, be sure to take into account the portion size as well. One half of an English muffin, for example, typically has one gram of fat so a whole one would have two grams.

Women should eat at least 20 grams of fiber every day; men should eat 25. The maximum is 60 grams of fiber in any one day. It is best to get your fiber from foods instead of supplements. High-fiber foods contain vitamins and minerals that supplements don't. The easiest way to get enough fiber is to eat five or more servings of fruits and vegetables per day. Fruits and vegetables have lots of fiber, almost no fat and many of the essential vitamin and minerals that you need.

Foods that are low in fat and high in fiber are complex carbohydrates such as whole grain breads, rice, barley, cornmeal and dried peas. Starchy vegetables like potatoes, corn and pasta are also good sources. These foods will help fill you up. Protein is important too. Good sources of protein besides meat are dried beans, legumes, poultry and fish.

∞ THOUGHT FOR THE DAY ∞

Stay away from refined sugar and alcoholic beverages. Sugar, rich foods and alcohol are high in calories and have little or no nutritional value. And they can be habit forming.

DECEMBER 22

*I always felt that the great high
privilege, relief and comfort of friendship was
that one had to explain nothing.*

KATHERINE MANSFIELD

It's normal to fall into the If Only trap. If only X happened,
you would be perfectly happy forever. If only I would win the
lottery, if only I would lose 30 pounds, if only I had a new
dress, new hairdo, new house, new car, new job... There are
many things that will give you a temporary lift but in the long
run what you need are friends.

Long-lasting satisfaction with yourself and your life comes
when you have loving, intimate relationships with others.
Intimacy means sharing, listening and supporting each other
with an open mind and heart. "My best friend lives next door,"
says Jenna. "We have watched our children grow up together.
We've held each other's hand through the bad times and celebrated the good times. But mostly we've had fun just sharing
those routine everyday moments with one another."

No matter how much stress you have to endure and work
through, it would be worse if you had to go it alone. A financial windfall would be nice and certainly it would make your
creditors happy. But if you have good friends that you can
count on and trust, friends that you are willing to go the extra
mile for, you have already won the lottery.

THOUGHT FOR THE DAY

*Plan a fun afternoon or evening out with your
friends. Get together and see a movie, go roller-skating
or meet in the park for a potluck picnic.*

I never felt used for my body.

ARNOLD SCHWARZENEGGER

If you are just starting to do resistance training with free weights or dumbbells, make sure you are doing the movements correctly. If you are out of shape, you may be better off doing the exercises without any weights at all until you regain some flexibility and strength. If your range of motion is limited, you probably should try to bring it closer to normal limits before adding weights.

Resistance training is usually done in sets of repetitions (reps). If you are just starting this kind of training, do each set only once. Do as many repetitions that feel comfortable, up to 20. The last few repetitions of each of these exercises should be difficult. If you can do two sets of 20 and feel like you can keep going, then increase the weight to the next smallest increment. Once you increase the weight, it may be several days or even weeks before you are comfortable with two sets of 20 reps again. Just continue your training until you're ready to increase the weight again.

Remember that lifting weights, even light ones, puts stress on your muscles. But they recover quickly, becoming stronger than before. The major muscle groups in your upper and lower body need at least one day, preferably two, to recover completely.

∾ THOUGHT FOR THE DAY ∾

Pay attention to your breathing when doing resistance training. To give your muscles the oxygen they need, exhale or contract the muscle when you lift. Inhale or extend the muscle when you relax.

DECEMBER 24

*I don't care to belong to any club
that will accept me as a member.*

GROUCHO MARX

If you're thinking about joining a health club, make sure you join one that will meet your needs. You should assess yourself and what you like. If you prefer to exercise alone, you want to be sure there are enough stationary bikes, stair steppers, treadmills, free weights, rowing machines and the like available during busy hours. If you enjoy working out with others, check to see that there are a wide variety of classes offered.

Consider the location and the time of day you like to work out. People who work long hours may want to utilize their lunch hour for exercise and will need a health club close to work. Others may prefer a club that is within a few miles of their house or apartment.

Be sure to ask for a tour of the facility so you can get a sense of the club's membership. Look around at the time of day that you would normally be exercising. Make sure there are people in your age group that appear to be at approximately your level of conditioning. Take a good look at the equipment to see if it is being properly maintained. Check the locker room. The showers should be clean and stocked with shampoo, conditioner, body lotion and towels.

Although health clubs can be costly, there are ways to save some money. Check with Human Resources to see if your company is affiliated with a local health club. Wait for a special offer at the club you wish to join. Short-term introductory memberships can be a good bargain. If you know a member, ask if you can try out the club as their guest a few times.

∾ THOUGHT FOR THE DAY ∾

*Remember to ask about the instructors. Find out what training they
have and whether they are CPR certified.*

*There may come a time when the lion and the lamb will
lie down together, but I am still betting on the lion.*

JOSH BILLINGS

Many women worry about osteoporosis, a decrease in bone
density which can result in fractures. Any fracture is serious
but a fracture of the hip or spine is especially troublesome. A
first step to counteract this problem is to get 1500 milligrams
of calcium daily. In many cases, hormone replacement therapy
is also recommended. One of the best ways is also one of the
oldest—build stronger muscles with exercise, especially
strength training.

Research shows that women in particular will benefit from
strengthening the muscles in their hips, knees, back and
abdomen. As their muscle mass increases, so does bone density. Researchers have also discovered that people with
stronger muscles have better balance; this is important because
it helps prevent falls that can cause fractures. Women who do
strength training exercise also find that they become more
physically active as they become stronger. The more fit they
become, the more energy they have.

Remember that strength training won't necessarily build
large bulky muscles. Although muscle mass does weigh more
than fat tissue, it will take many months of intensive training
for you to see an increase in weight due to increased muscle
mass. An added bonus is that you can eat more calories without putting on more fat.

∞ THOUGHT FOR THE DAY ∞

*Buy two small five-pound or ten-pound free weights and do arm
exercises while watching the evening news. You'll be surprised how
quickly you can tone up your biceps and triceps.*

DECEMBER 26

No one is injured save by himself.

ERASMUS

Minor muscle injuries can be more stressful that you think. They may start off as fairly minor but without proper care, you can be laid up for several weeks, unable to exercise.

When you first strain your back or sprain an ankle, you should remember the RICE formula—Rest, Ice, Compression and Elevation; the most important of these is ice. Fill a plastic bag with ice cubes and then use an elastic bandage to hold the ice on your injury. Do this every three hours for 20 minutes for the first two days. Rest your body and elevate the injury if possible. Aspirin or ibuprofen can relieve the pain and reduce inflammation.

When the swelling disappears, use heat if the injury still bothers you. Use a warm moist towel or a heating pad three times a day for 30 minutes. Heat is especially soothing if your injury is from overuse. After three to five days, if you can move without pain and support your weight on the injury, you're ready for some easy stretches and light exercise. Trust what your injury is telling you—when it stops talking, it's healed.

∾ THOUGHT FOR THE DAY ∾

While you're healing, keep your muscles toned by using some of the gentle stretching and strengthening exercises of yoga.

*I can understand that memory must be selective, else it
would choke on the glut of experience. What I cannot
understand is why it selects what it does.*

VIRGILIA PETERSON

Misplacing your car keys or forgetting where you put your
favorite baseball hat aren't signs of senility, merely reminders
that you need to work on improving your short-term memory.
Try these tips to help you remember those pesky details.

Sometimes you forget because you weren't focused on what
you were doing. Make yourself pay attention. Talk out loud: "I
am putting my keys on the kitchen counter next to the toaster."
Then take a mental picture of your action. Make a list. The act
of writing helps you pay attention and makes the information
more permanent in your mind, so keep a calendar on your
refrigerator, a notebook in your pocket or purse. If you're
reading, pause every now and then and review the important
points in what you just read. Relating the information to yourself will help you remember it. Concentrate on your senses—
how does something look, smell, sound or feel. Sensory
impressions can be long-lasting; that's why a certain song
reminds you of your first date with your significant other or
the smell of white paste brings back memories of grade school.

When you meet new people, look at them directly and try
to use their names aloud in conversation. Pay attention to their
features and what they are wearing. Use acronyms or rhymes
to remember details. For example, HOMES stands for the
great lakes—Huron, Ontario, Michigan, Erie, and Superior.
You probably remember how many days are in each month by
recalling the rhyme that begins "Thirty days hath September."

∾ THOUGHT FOR THE DAY ∾

*Stimulate your brain by exercising your mind. Card games, crossword
puzzles, learning a foreign language and playing a musical instrument
are good ways to stay intellectually active and mentally sharp.*

√ *The best career advice given to the young is "Find out what you like doing best and get someone to pay you for doing it."*

KATHARINE WHITEHORN

Women who have been homemakers for some years may have some hesitation about returning to the job market again. If you are about to go back to work after taking time off to raise a family, here are some suggestions that others have found useful.

Begin by making a list of the skills and experience you have now. You're older, more mature and have more life experience and new skills since you last worked. You may require flexible hours or a more casual atmosphere. If you need to update your skills, take some community college courses.

A good way to ease back into an office environment is to do temporary work. You can experiment with working again without making a permanent commitment. You can find out about companies by working there as a temp; you will also be sent to firms that you might not have considered before. When you are looking for a job, be sure to network with people as well as read the newspaper. Some experts estimate that classified ads only list about 20 percent of all jobs; the rest are filled through networking. Tell everyone you know that you're looking for work; then follow up on each suggestion and lead. Have your résumé ready—typed, proofread copies ready to send. When you interview, remember that first impressions count. You need not buy new clothes but you should be neat, clean and dressed conservatively.

THOUGHT FOR THE DAY

You might also want to consider starting a small business from your home. Consider such services as word processing, income tax preparation, maid service, day care, yard work, gardening or personal shopping.

It is quality rather than quantity that matters.
SENECA

If your self-worth is at a low ebb, you may feel that quality is an indulgence that you have not earned. You tell yourself that after you've been on an exercise program and lost weight, you'll buy better clothes, prepare better meals, treat yourself to a good haircut. But if you're going to feel better about yourself in the future, you should start treating yourself with care right now.

Work on ways to put more quality into your life, realizing that the issue is not money, but attitude. Look for samples of expensive perfumes. Put gourmet food into your weight loss plan. Dress to make yourself sparkle—wear bright colors, fun costume jewelry and beautiful makeup. Let meals be a celebration; use your best linens, china and crystal to set the table. Linger over a well-prepared meal so you can leave the table with a feeling of enjoyment and satisfaction. Take time to get excited about something other than food. Open yourself up to art, music, literature or whatever your passion is.

Recognize that when you treat yourself as someone special, others will see that specialness too. You have many important attributes—your intelligence, your honesty, your ability to get along with others, your smile—that make you attractive yet have nothing to do with your weight. But the cycle of affirming yourself as worthy has to start with you.

∾ THOUGHT FOR THE DAY ∾

Quality can be less expensive than quantity. For example, rather than binge on a bag of cheap chocolate candy, treat yourself to one succulent chocolate truffle.

DECEMBER 30

No act of kindness, no matter how small, is ever wasted.

AESOP

It's common to have days when we're drowning in stress, surrounded by negativity. Those are the days when a small gesture from another person makes a big difference. Think about that rainy evening when you were exhausted and someone let you move ahead in line because you had fewer items in your grocery cart. Remember how important that small gesture was to you at the time. And recall how a stranger's smile once brightened an otherwise dreary day. Gestures like these should be passed along to others.

Take today to put something positive into someone else's life and reduce their stress a notch or two. Compliment a beautiful tie or a new hairdo. Pay attention to what other people are doing that pleases you and remark on it. Say how much you appreciate the good job they're doing. There are non-verbal gestures too. Smile, open a door, hold the elevator, let someone in a hurry go first. Offer your seat on the bus to someone who looks tired.

Give verbal praise. Tell a friend that you enjoy his or her company. Tell your children that they are the best. Tell your spouse that you love him or her. Touch your loved ones. Hug them, pat them on the back, put your arm around their shoulder, squeeze their hand.

These gestures are small and may even seem too easy to be important. But it's the small positive things that you do for others which can make a big difference in their day. And your day will improve too because nice feelings multiply when they are shared.

∾ THOUGHT FOR THE DAY ∾

Remember to appreciate what comes your way. Say thank you often. Saying thank you aloud is a reminder that there are pleasant people in the world and their good deeds are worthy of notice.

*The silent upbraiding of the eye is the very poetry of
reproach; it speaks at once to the imagination.*

CLARA L. BALFOUR

Make sure your body language is saying something positive
about you. When you're slouched with rounded shoulders and
head bowed, you look depressed and probably feel that way as
well. But if you're standing tall and looking someone in the eye,
you will appear confident and secure. Although much of your
body language is unconscious, learn to become more aware of
your own and use it to your advantage.

Try to be at the same height and position as the person you
are speaking with. If one is standing and the other is seated,
the person standing will seem to be more intimidating and will
have more power and control of the conversation. When
you shake someone's hand, shake it firmly as a sign of self-
confidence. Use eye contact effectively: look the other person
in the eye but don't stare. When you break eye contact, move
your eyes down instead of up so you don't appear to be rolling
your eyes in annoyance. When you're meeting someone for the
first time, a slight tilt of your head will make you look friendly
and cooperative.

Pay attention to the amount of personal space your friends
and coworkers need when they are carrying on a conversation.
People having an intimate conversation will stand closer
together than they normally do. If you're standing too close,
you will be invading the other's space and he or she may
unconsciously take a step backward; if you're too far away, you
may appear uninterested or the other person may move closer
to you.

⁐ THOUGHT FOR THE DAY ⁐

*Remember that a genuine smile will always relieve tension and put
others at ease and you will be perceived as a warm and open person.*

INDEX BY TOPIC

A

B

C

D

E

F

G

H

M

N

O

P

Q

R

S

T